THE END OF TIME

THE ◆ END ◆ OF ◆ TIME

Religion, Ritual, and the Forging of the Soul

RICHARD K. FENN

The Pilgrim Press
Cleveland, Ohio

The Pilgrim Press, Cleveland, Ohio 44115
Copublished with the Society for Promoting Christian Knowledge,
London, England

Printed in Great Britain on acid-free paper

02 01 00 99 98 97   5 4 3 2 1

ISBN 0-8298-1206-7

CONTENTS

ACKNOWLEDGEMENTS

For the Rt. Revd Robert L. DeWitt

Usually the editors of a manuscript such as this are mentioned toward the end of the acknowledgements, but they properly belong here at the beginning. Alex Wright has been particularly persistent and supportive in seeing this work through earlier stages and in giving me ample opportunity for revision. Catherine Mann has likewise been reassuring and creative in her suggestions for the text, and I thank them both for seeing this work through to completion.

I wish to thank David Martin for an early suggestion, fifteen years ago, that I pay attention to the agonies surrounding liturgical revision in the Anglican Communion. His sense that something fundamental was at stake not only in the decisions but in the passions evoked by liturgical change has kept me from settling too soon for an 'answer'.

I wish also to thank a Bishop of the Episcopal Church, Robert L. DeWitt, for his demonstration of the intimate connection between the passion of the street and of the liturgy. He shepherded the city of Philadelphia and the Episcopal Church through a very difficult valley indeed. It is to him that I dedicate this book.

INTRODUCTION

Time is the matrix of social life: witness the use of calendars and schedules to order activities from planting to killing. Conversely, social life becomes a temporal matrix in which individuals, groups and communities live, move and have their being with the assurance that they will be known and remembered: their lives being part of a social order that transcends time. Indeed, it is a source of terror to individuals when they become unsure of their society's capacity to avert disaster, to achieve purification, and to manage the succession of generations, or to restore an idealized past in order to guarantee its future. At the very least, this book is about the ways in which societies and individuals come to terms with the passage and the tyranny of time.

For both societies and individuals, however, time can become a disappointment, a threat or a tyrant; it is always running out. Societies must maintain themselves over generations in the face of all sorts of dangers to their continued existence. Some of these dangers are external: enemies and diseases that break down the boundaries of a social order. Societies therefore require the capacity to foresee and to avert imminent dangers. Other dangers are internal: sedition and disaffection from within that can turn the generations against each other and destroy families or other institutions crucial to the continuity of social life. It is therefore necessary for societies to renew their lease on life, as it were. Some societies, for instance, renew themselves by casting out alien and destructive influences, by purifying themselves of past grief and grievance, and by restoring the community to a measure of harmony and wholeness. Societies also need to create a new chapter or season in the life of individuals and groups: to ensure, for instance, that individuals pass from one stage in life to the next, so that one generation indeed may succeed another. Any society unable to manage the succession of generations will indeed run out of time. At such moments people may become very anxious indeed. This book explores in some detail what might be called 'temporal panic': the conviction that time is running out on the social order and on the self.

We live toward the end of a century which has seen the collapse of entire social systems through war or through internal decay. Time has run out not only on nations and empires but on peoples consumed by genocide carried out by their fellow citizens. When fear that time is running out on one's own people or nation becomes widespread, it may also become epidemic, as it did, for instance, in Europe between the two world wars. Under these conditions fascism developed a profound appeal to several European peoples and nations. Indeed, fascism has destroyed some nations in order to save them.

Although it is beyond the scope of this book to study fascism as a modern political system or to survey the conditions under which it has arisen in various countries in Europe or in Latin America, I will argue that fascist *tendencies* are not only widespread in modern societies but that they are endemic to many social systems. Indeed, I will try to show that they are an inevitable by-product of the attempt to bind the individual to a social order that claims to transcend time; they are chronic. It is important to distinguish fascist tendencies from fascism as a well-developed social system. Such tendencies, I will argue, can be found in a wide range of societies. Moreover, fascist tendencies become intensified under certain conditions, and it is one purpose of this book to investigate the nature and range of those conditions. For instance, we will be examining anthropologists' reports of hill tribes in Bolivia and New Guinea as well as analyses of fundamentalists and of millenarian movements in the United States of America. Panic over running out of time comes to the surface of social life, I will argue, whenever a community, a people or a nation finds its survival, integrity, wholeness or continuity threatened by internal or external influences. While it is not always the case that this panic produces social movements that one could call fascist, I will argue that fascist movements arise from and exploit anxiety and panic over running out of time.

Societies tend to store up time so that they will not be surprised or threatened by unforeseen opportunities and dangers but able to respond, as it were, in a timely fashion. Thus they have wealth and grain, armies and loyalties in reserve. Societies also need to bring each new generation into line with former generations so that basic beliefs and institutions can be perpetuated; thus they have rituals that call for sacrifice, and techniques for schooling the young in the ways of the old. Societies need to rid themselves of unwanted influences and to lay to rest outstanding grievances; thus they have ways of putting current troubles in the past and of declaring themselves to be in a new year or era freed from the burdens of the past.

Although it is often the case that sociologists will discuss these societal ways of constructing time as aspects of religion, as opposed to magic, I will argue that magical tendencies are exhibited whenever a society or an individual seeks to buy time or renew it, to create or even restore time through proclamations or personal gestures, through rituals or through social movements. Charisma, as sociologists often put it, is magical, whether it is collective or personal, institutionalized or the inspiration and authority behind a popular movement.

Individuals often construe time in various ways that may not coincide and may even conflict with the times constructed by the social order. Individuals have their own dreams of accomplishment and satisfaction, and the times of which they dream may be far in the future or quite imminent. Dreams of forestalling dreaded events and impending disasters, like dreams of seizing opportunities, require relatively swift action. They may be projected on to a distant and ambiguous future, like the millennium, or, again like the millennium, be foreseen in the very near future indeed. The past can be as troubling to the individual as the present and future, however, and the ways that individuals construe the past may continue to be disruptive for societies that seek to monopolize the social construction of time. Rituals, I will argue, have been the first line of defence against such a conflict between the collective and personal sense of time.

To relieve and control the potential conflict between the way that individuals and societies construe and construct time has been the function of ritual in many societies. I will therefore focus on ritual as a primary locus for observing strains in the social construction of time. For rituals to work, of course, requires that societies possess a legitimate monopoly on the way that time is experienced, understood and projected. Rituals in modern societies, although they may still be for some communities and groups a first line of defence against conflict between personal and social time, are more like a Maginot Line than a Chinese wall: permeable and of dubious value when push comes to shove. Fascist movements have developed their own rituals for expressing and controlling temporal anxieties and panic. Indeed, I will argue that fascist rites have been more important as the ordinary rituals of a society have failed to reconcile personal with collective time.

Fascism as a religious movement is an important, if somewhat neglected, topic in the sociology of religion. That neglect is strange, since it is difficult to address secularization or fundamentalism without commenting on the relationship of the two to fascism, especially in Western societies. However, the study of ritual is one area in which the traditional concerns of the sociology of religion can be seen clearly to converge on the conventional topics of the sociology of politics and of political science.

I will argue that not only the failure of societal rituals, but also their success, can be extremely problematic both for social systems and for individuals. Indeed, when they succeed, rituals not only express and control fascist tendencies but also place individuals under severe social pressures that can produce strong countermeasures of psychological defence. Conversely, I will argue that when they fail, rituals release fascist tendencies into social movements that may have a lasting and often disastrous effect on the society as a whole. It is therefore dangerous for any society to run out of time. When time becomes of the essence of social life, the call for sacrifice can be answered on the streets, in the fields and in secret locations rather than in the sanctuary.

In a civilization that takes time very seriously, as does the West, the foundation is laid for fears that one will not have something to show for the time that has been spent or for one's lifetime. An ethic of responsibility that makes time the measure of commitment calls for sacrifices. These sacrifices, moreover, may be called for by institutions and organizations that have a vested interest in absorbing as much of the individual's free time as possible. Certainly time in the West has become a commodity, the price of which has been going up for decades, as corporations and communities compete with each other for a larger share of the individual's time. Under these conditions, calls for sacrifice become mundane rather than extraordinary.

The purpose of sacrifice is to let a new day dawn, full of promise and security. No one knows this better than fundamentalist Christians, who have long prophesied that untold suffering will precede the millennium. For many Christians, indeed, Israel's return to the Middle East as a nation-state is a harbinger not only of better days but of the catastrophic tribulations that God has promised to bring on his own people as chastisement for their sins and as prelude to their conversion prior to the Second Coming.[1] Time is increasingly short for the Jews, according to these Christian prophets, because it is getting shorter for Christians themselves. As Boyer puts it:

> Premillennialism is a complex system. It is *not* merely a theological mask for Jew hatred. Yet important structural components of this ideology encourage an obsessive preoccupation with the Jews as a people eternally set apart, about whom sweeping generalizations can be made with the sanction of biblical authority. Premillennialism also incorporates a view of Jewish history that, while not condoning anti-Semitic outbreaks, sees them as foreordained and inevitable.[2]

Boyer goes on to point out that Hitler, too, saw himself as an actor carrying out a small piece of God's planned punishment and redemption of Israel.

This book thus develops a very particular paradox. On the one hand, to counteract the tyranny of time that is forever running out, individuals and nations claim a measure of eternity for their own place in history. On the other hand, such claims to special graces are always subject to the test of time. For those who seek to transcend time, the passage of time is therefore filled with significance and danger. For instance, to be, like Israel, God's most favoured nation is to be slated for the hostility of Satan and the wrath of God. Time for Israel is foretold, foreordained and yet always running out. Time exercises a sort of lordship over Israel; everything has been foreordained and foretold. 'Israel in this scheme is, as we have seen, "the only nation on earth to have its history written in advance".'[3] Israel therefore serves as a convenient image or even as a double for any social system or people that feels either the tyranny or the terror of time. Israel is a double for any community that lays claim to a special grace or dispensation and is therefore especially unsure of its ability to stand the test of time. Thus Israel serves the traditional functions of the double, as Rank described it: as an ideal, yet also as a rival and finally as a sign of one's own mortality.[4] In every community or people that sees in Israel a model for its own eternal place in history, the passage of time represents a continuous threat and exercises a peculiar form of tyranny.

It is therefore not surprising that fascism developed a strong anti-Semitic programme. Israel is, after all, the very double of the nation as fascism sees it: the vehicle for personal salvation and the object of moral commitment and sacrifice. As Sternhell reminds us, of course, it is hard to speak of fascism without gross oversimplification, because it was a complex movement full of contradictions.[5] Nationalist on the one hand, it saw the nation as the historical community in whose death and resurrection were written the fate of the soul. On the other hand it was an international movement among the larger nations of Europe, and some fascists saw the movement as extending to Japan and China as well. Although fascism despised much of modernity, especially the fragmentation of the nation into warring classes and the degeneracy caused by the unflagging pursuit of individual interests, according to Sternhell fascism did love the truly modern and boldly embraced a future distinguished from the past.[6] Anti-materialist to its core, fascism nonetheless celebrated the human body and dignified athletics as a spiritual discipline. Running through these contradictions, however, is the constant attempt to redeem the times by restoring a time of primitive vigour and harmony.

Thus fascism is more than an ideology seeking to conceal its contradictions; it is a religious movement whose rituals could visibly embrace contradictions in order to encompass and transcend them. Indeed, as Sternhell makes clear, fascism lived in and through its ceremonies and rituals.[7] It was a political drama of the salvation of the soul through the rebirth of the nation.[8] No wonder it could not bear the thought of Israel, whose permanence as a historical community of salvation represented both an ideal and also a threat to the historical success of fascism. Thus considered, fascism is a religious movement with a strong basis in ritual and ceremony.

Fascist *tendencies*, however, can be found in various societies under quite specific historical conditions. As a tendency, fascism is not simply an ideology, a reaction to modernity, or a strategy for reviving the nation-state. Rather, I will argue, fascist tendencies make the community in whatever form, e.g. tribe, ethnic group, or nation, the vehicle for the transcendence of time. A people seeking a new lease on life may dream of a fresh start, purified of whatever is sullying its virtue or sapping its strength. The society may therefore seek to relieve itself of certain burdens or impurities in order to be refreshed for a new season. To remove aliens, cut welfare and lower taxes are the outward and visible signs of fascist tendencies in American society: a point to which I will return in the concluding section of this book.

More intractable forms of pollution or degeneracy call for the restoration of a time of relative innocence or vitality. For such a people, the dreamed-of time is a past long gone: a time of original rather than merely relative innocence and strength. To realize this dream of restoration therefore requires a time span in the future commensurate with the time lost since the age of original strength and innocence: a millennial *Reich* or kingdom.

Ritual and the Renewal of Time

The more a society is distinct from its environment, the more that society needs time. As Luhmann puts it, 'A system must carry out processes that are relatively independent of the environment, *and for that it needs time*.'[9] To put it the other way, a society runs out of time when it cannot adequately differentiate itself from its environment. As Luhmann points out, modern societies are particularly hard put to it by the media, as anyone knows who has seen foreign policy shift with each new television broadcast of starvation or massacre. In modern societies,

Luhmann argues, everything is an environment to everything else. That is, every part of a modern society must take into account the presence, the interests, and possible reactions of every other part. Time runs out on a social system when its boundaries become permeable to outside influences. The more complex the environment, and the more it impinges on a society in a variety of ways, the more that society must be able to buy time; otherwise it will indeed perish.

Let me suggest an example. The once-sacred 'doctor–patient relationship' is now part of a system that includes liability lawyers, insurance companies, health management organizations, and efficiency experts. Often the mass media invade the privacy of medical consultations, as research findings are publicized and new products are advertised with slogans like 'My doctor said . . .'; illnesses are discussed on talk shows, and health policy debated in public forums that focus on the patients' rights to choose a doctor or be reimbursed for the treatment of particular maladies. Under these conditions doctors have far less time to use their own discretion, to deliberate over possible courses of treatment, to temporize in particular situations, or to experiment with certain procedures, let alone to keep up with the rising tide of medical publications and information.

The conventional wisdom is that modern societies are highly differentiated, and there is some truth in that as far as formal structures are concerned. The American Medical Association is separate from the American Bar Association, for instance, but in their interaction with each other the members of these two organizations are uncomfortably close: so much so that they encounter each other within the protection afforded by the rituals of the courtroom. Indeed, it is difficult to know when a doctor orders certain procedures out of what is called 'defensive medicine', i.e. with an eye to a possible lawsuit for negligence. The 'environment' of medical practice has become not only much larger but more difficult to distinguish from the practice of medicine itself. In the concluding chapter I will have more to say about the collapse of categories in modern societies. That collapse foreshadows a widespread feeling that the system itself is running out of time and may result in calls for draconian, even fascist remedies.

The more that a society's environment impinges on it, the more the members of that society are likely to feel that the social order itself is running out of time. An impending disaster or the possibility of war may make death seem like a clear and present danger; the call may then go out for sacrifices. Less imminent, but more immanent dangers may make a society feel that the enemy, so to speak, is within: a fifth column, unwanted immigrants, foreign ideas, unsocialized youth, unbridled sexuality, and other forms of both social and natural pollution. Under these conditions there may be increased demand for attempts to purify a society of contaminating influences, people, ideas and objects. New controls on drugs, immigration and other 'outside influences', along with stringent measures to discipline criminals, socialize the young, reform education, and enhance patriotism may signal a nation's fear that its environment is not safely outside the walls but has entered within its gates. When measures to defend or purify a society fail, the public becomes nostalgic for a period in which the nation was young, its leaders were authoritative, and its people were more energetic and virtuous. Such nostalgia may create demands for a return to native pieties, e.g. 'to put God back into the public schools' or save the family homestead. These demands, if they are not satisfied by the appropriate ceremonies, may result in a demand for fascist solutions. Such demands are becoming increasingly vocal in the United States, as conservative religious groups gain a purchase on party politics.

There are various ways in which individuals and societies face the scarcity of time, but only some are located in the 'real' world of adaptation to complex and often threatening environments. Realistically speaking, both individuals and societies need time in order to respond to their environments and to shape them according to their wishes. Their wishes, however, may often have a large component of fantasy mixed in with realistic apprehension and expectation: for instance, the belief that a society is the recipient of special graces or of divine inspiration. Such a belief, however, requires that the same society stand the test of time: a test that may be more or less imminent or violent. To believe that one's society or one's soul can transcend time thus provides only a temporary respite from temporal panic; time still will tell whether or not that belief will be vindicated. Some individuals and peoples therefore long for such a vindication in time sooner rather than later. Some anxiety or even panic over the passage of time is thus grounded in reality, and some is grounded in perennial human longings and aspirations that seek to transcend time and are inevitably therefore impatient with its mundane passage.

Ritual combines both the realistic and the unrealistic apprehension of time in significant, and occasionally potent, symbolic gestures. On the one hand, ritual seeks to avert danger, groom the young for adulthood, lay to rest old grievances, or restore old virtues to a social system. To adapt to its environment, indeed, a society must ward off danger, manage the succession of generations, settle old quarrels, and renew and transmit its basic virtues. On the other hand, however, the invocation of supernatural sources of protection, authority and inspiration ensures that time will test and perhaps disappoint the nation thus endowed. The desire to transcend time once and for all reflects the fear, to borrow the words of a familiar hymn, that the stream of time will indeed bear all a society's sons and daughters away. One function of ritual is precisely to obscure the distinction between reality and myth in the social construction of time.

Ritual and the Defence of the Soul

There is another distinction that rituals tend to obscure: the distinction between social obligation and individual initiative. There is a good reason for this obscurity, of course. Societies tend to put their members under varying degrees of social pressure: some societies more, some less. Societies relying heavily on ritual are among those which exert the heaviest moral pressures on their members. Those pressures, I will argue, can be quite dangerous to the individual's own psychic strength; the soul can be crushed under the weight of demand and expectation. Indeed, as I will argue later, the magical aspects of ritual not only impress the social order on the psyche but also provide rudimentary defences for the psyche against being overwhelmed by social pressures. Accusations of witchcraft, for instance, are a typical case of a ritual which asserts the primacy of the society's moral order while at the same time allowing individuals to use its rites to relieve themselves of the weight of social disapproval.

While there are relatively few accusations of witchcraft in contemporary American society, there are widespread allegations of evil. In his study of fundamentalists, for instance, Charles Strozier notes that they are virtuosos in discerning evil in and under the signs of the times.[10] In accusing others, for instance, of being the unwitting accomplices of Antichrist, these fundamentalists may be seeking to ward off social pressures that are overwhelming them with feelings of helplessness and guilt. Strozier is quite clear that the moral climate of many fundamentalist communities is 'suffocating' and may indeed crush the inner self: a point I will take up again in discussing Susan Rose's study of conservative Christian schools.[11] One sign of a soul or inner self that is being crushed, I will argue, is that time seems to the victim to be terribly short.

Certainly these fundamentalists see the passage of time as a perennial threat. Not only is the dreaded day of accounting always imminent; the fundamentalists themselves live under excruciating and self-imposed time pressures of their own. Strozier reports that they feel that the end is nearer than even they themselves realize; as one put it, '. . .I am gripped with a sense that it is not as much time as we think.'[12] Others feel that the best that they can do is to temporize: to buy a little time by acts of charity, devotion or penitence. Mixed with these apprehensions, which stem from their beliefs, are more realistic complaints that the pace of life itself is drastically increasing.[13]

Strozier, who is reluctant to interpret others' religion as pathological, does not explicitly make the point, but it is clear that many fundamentalists are caught up in a temporal struggle of their own making. To be sure, there are some who have known the sort of violence and oppression that are endemic in an oppressed or victimized nation; they can speak authentically of the Book of Revelation without dramatizing themselves or merely projecting their own inner turbulence on the world.[14] They feel a scarcity of time against which they must defend themselves with all the panoply of faith. Imposing on themselves serious burdens of guilt and social responsibility, however, they also suffocate themselves in a climate of their own making. Their prophecies are self-fulfilling, because time does indeed seem to run out on a self that is being deprived of vital nutrients.

The world, its major issues and events, thus become a theatre in which the soul can act out its own dramas of loss and redemption. It was not long ago that Americans were quite visibly engaged in spiritual contests to determine the fate of their souls. In the New England colonies, some individuals were accusing others of defaming their characters, but the spiritual stakes were far higher than mere reputation. In some cases these charges were brought by persons accused of being witches. Such charges had in fact endangered not merely their reputation but their lives, and counter-suits for defamation of character were a way of averting possible disaster. In one case, the trial of Ann Hibben, the charges were brought by a carpenter whose reputation was at stake; Ann Hibben had accused him of inflating the prices he had charged her for his work. Ann Hibben lost the trial, was excommunicated, and a few years later convicted of being a witch. She was executed in 1656.[15] It is clear that in such trials, individuals are bringing to bear serious social pressures on others in order to defend themselves from similar pressures that threaten quite literally to crush their souls. The alternative to such litigation is often a spiritual death that leads to the death of the body as well as of the soul.

This book is essentially about social dramas in which the soul is conceived and forged, transformed and rescued, purified and restored. The dramas are social, since they are integral to the way in which groups or communities, even whole societies, defend themselves from the real or symbolic threat of death. They are also intensely personal, since they help to create the internal structures of the self. What moderns have come to call in psychoanalytic terminology the ego ideal and the super-ego were impressed on the soul in these dramatic encounters between social duty and personal desire, between paralysing fear and the promise of social favour.

Is the modern self that emerged from these spiritual dramas quite different from the one that we would find in a truly 'primitive' society or perhaps even in the Graeco-Roman world of antiquity? In the modern world, so goes one argument, the self is surrounded and buttressed by the legal and social institution of the Individual.[16] It is in antiquity or in relatively simpler social systems that we can still observe the underdeveloped ego that was profoundly vulnerable to social suggestion and prone to hysterical displays of fear and desire. Perhaps so; nonetheless, the psychoanalytic account of how even the modern ego develops assumes a long period in which the ego is relatively empty and lives off emotional capital that it begs, borrows or steals from those in its immediate emotional vicinity. Those borrowings, I will argue, make all souls, even modern ones, particularly susceptible to social pressures and vulnerable to negative suggestions.

In this book I will be discussing some of the ways in which rituals have been employed to create, defend, and eventually to channel and to control the innermost self of individuals. For lack of a better term I will be calling that innermost self the soul.[17] In the face of excruciating social pressures, and when overwhelmed from within by passions that defy control, individuals can indeed temporarily, perhaps even permanently, lose their inner selves. At some fundamental level the person is effaced or even destroyed.

To those convinced that the besetting sin of Western societies, and perhaps particularly of the United States, is a rampant individualism, it may seem irrelevant to focus on the ways that the soul can be crushed. Conventional diagnoses of what bedevils Americans suggest that varieties of narcissism and individualism, of undisciplined and inflated egos, are responsible for the widening tears in the social fabric.[18] A closer look at the psychoanalytic account of narcissism, of course, would remind one that such an ego is underdeveloped rather than genuinely strong. Such an ego, I would go on to add, is particularly vulnerable to social pressures and to the hostility of others. Its own inchoate rage is often mirrored in a bureaucratized social system whose cruelty is palpable although impersonal. O'Keefe has suggested that thousands of deaths in American society are in fact due to such cruelty.[19] On the one hand, individuals are subject to extraordinarily high levels of 'daily verbal aggression': levels which would easily prove lethal to individuals in more 'primitive' societies that lack support for the autonomous ego and the individual. On the other hand, they are increasingly laid off from work, forced to retire early, or moved into nursing homes against their will. These are experiences which can make a person feel helpless and unwanted: emotions known to be related to sickening and premature death.

It is therefore a mistake to underestimate the extent to which societies and individuals mirror to each other unreasonable demands and suppressed hatreds. For instance, in his account of witchcraft accusations in the seventeenth-century American colonies, Demos focuses on the case of a sixteen-year-old indentured servant: a young woman who was apparently possessed by Satan.[20] In fact, the possession was extraordinarily theatrical, and many members of the community were called upon to witness her demonstrations of diabolical rage. Demos describes how the young woman in question coped with passions that, '... driven underground ... survived in archaic form to present her developing ego with a constant threat of disruptive intrusion'.[21] Indeed, at moments she apparently lost touch with her inner self and was either consumed by rage or frozen in apathetic and stunted emotional expression. What is most striking about his analysis, in my view, is that the entire community was engaged in this drama of the soul.

According to Demos, during several months the community not only witnessed the young woman's torments but interrogated and challenged her demon.[22] At times it was the young woman who appeared to be consumed with a malignant and greedy spirit; at other times it was she who charged those around her, especially the clergy, with being possessed by the spirit of greed. Indeed, there was a process in which the community and the agonized young woman seemed to mirror those parts of each other that both parties were at some pains to ignore or deny. The community placed extraordinary pressures on the young woman to account for the spirit that was possessing her. In return she countered by accusing two women of the community of witchcraft. As I will argue especially in Chapter 1, such accusations are a primitive defence of the soul against the often crushing weight of social expectation. In Demos's account these accusations, and many others like them throughout the New England colonies, suggest that the soul of many an individual was on the verge of collapse in the face of passions that could not be readily acknowledged, let alone satisfied, and in the face also of hostile and unreceptive communities that demanded their own satisfactions from the beleaguered individual. These are the same conditions which have been shown to be conducive to the release of fascist tendencies into the body politic.[23]

In these dramatic spiritual contests between society and the individual, there was a certain symmetry in the charges and counter-charges. The young woman allegedly possessed by a demon, in Demos's account, accused the clergy and local women of being the personifications of greed, of carrying on a masquerade in which the face of virtue conceals an inner rapacity. Conversely, the community divined that the young woman herself was possessed of a rapacious spirit that could destroy them all if it were allowed to triumph in the soul even of one such young woman. The community's denial of its own greed mirrors the refusal of the one possessed to acknowledge that it is her own passions that are proving disruptive. She represents the hideous possibility that could afflict them all if their rituals, their community prayers and petitions, exhortations and sacrifices, should fail to avert the danger.

Rituals are staged in this hall of mirrors in which individuals project their own fears and aspirations on to their societies, only to find themselves framed by their own reflections. Societies in turn project on to individuals their own myths and fantasies, only to find that the individual will simultaneously resist, resent and obey the call to self-sacrifice. Rituals thus provide a theatre of unhappy compromise between the self and the social order. However, if ritual were to fail, more stringent measures would be required to purify the community of its internal pollution; rites of self-sacrifice are replaced by executions or assassinations. The possibility that ritual can fail to ward off danger to the society thus underlies the demand for sacrifices that prove the transcendence of the social order over evil and death.

Coming to Terms with Magic, Charisma and Ritual

I would agree with Walter Burkert, who impresses on us three points: that ritual, when it becomes religious, refers to the supernatural; that religious ritual impresses itself on the individual, who is thus 'imprinted' with the forms of his or her community; and that religious ritual is extremely conservative, i.e. persistent over time.[24] It is no accident, I would suggest, that precisely these characteristics are attributed by other scholars to the most individualistic of all forms of action and authority: i.e. charisma. Charismatic authority itself claims supernatural inspiration, makes lasting impressions on others who surrender to the authority of the charismatic leader, and is extremely conservative in that it seeks to consolidate its gains from one group of followers, or from one generation, to the next. Ritual, like charisma, is designed to leave a permanent mark on the soul: a self-realization impervious to the passage of time.

However, charisma is also a source of innovation and instability and may be conducive to panic or frenzy if individuals claim for themselves authority and inspiration that require no certification by the social order other than the belief and commitment of the charismatic's own entourage. There are rituals, therefore, that embody social protest and rebellion, and these may embody and perpetuate fascist tendencies long before these tendencies take the form of social movements. It is well worth knowing what ceremonies are taking place in the streets or in secret as well as on the stated times and occasions of ritual that seeks to impress the social order itself on the soul of the individual.

Weber used the term 'charisma' interchangeably with 'magic' in order to describe actions based on belief in the actor's access to supernatural powers. As O'Keefe reminds us, however, Weber did not distinguish charisma from magic, which he discussed frequently throughout his work on the sociology of religion. 'Charisma', then, is simply another word for magic; 'that is the key for including all charismatic sects and movements in a study of magic'.[25] Magic, then, like charisma, refers to 'certain striking qualities of human action, speech, and thought'.[26] This usage of the term 'magic' enables us to place the discussion of charisma in a far wider context. In using the term 'magic' in this way Weber also intended to criticize modern societies. His views on the 'disenchantment' of the modern world and its loss of spiritual vitality in a welter of technical and official functions are widely known. In this study, then, magic will be used to interpret ritual as a means by which the institution of the individual was developed: an individual marked by both submission to and rebellion against the very social pressures that gave it birth. I will be arguing that from this particular crucible emerged a self for whom time was of the essence.

Ritual is a two-faced god, as it were. In rites of initiation individuals found their own charisma first borrowed by priests and chiefs, and then given back to them in the form of duties and rights. In this process individuals became alienated from the ownership and control of the means of producing and perpetuating themselves through ritual. Indeed, the ownership and control of the ritualized means for producing the individual became increasingly concentrated in the court or the kraal of the king, to whom the chiefs must give their allegiance, and it also became centralized in the temple. In a later context, for instance, I will be discussing the importance of the gate or archway in ritual. Over one gate in Rome was the figure of the god Janus: presiding, as it were, over the goings-out and comings-in, the passages and the passing, of individuals in their symbolic encounters with death.

On the one hand, therefore, rituals, like other forms of magic, appear at first to give the individual a way of expressing, defining and establishing the very existence of the self in the eyes of others and in the face of a potentially threatening environment. Nonetheless, ritualized magic, like charisma, appears to come to the individual from outside; it is like a special grace. To own and control that source of power is therefore difficult and requires careful discipline, not only because magic is capable of strong effects, both positive and negative, but because individuals and social institutions inevitably seek to concentrate and monopolize it in their own hands. Thus individuals seek the disciplines needed to acquire magic: the right words, substances, times, and places.

Magic, however, is exceedingly difficult to concentrate, let alone to monopolize. As every temple cult and state religion has discovered, individuals and groups seem to be able to generate their own sources of magic and to oppose the monopoly of the political and cultural centre with their own sources of inspiration and authority. It is in this dialectical tension between the central institutions of a society and popular forms of magical control that the institution of the individual with its own rights and duties has been forged in Western societies.

Like charisma, magic is also everywhere and anywhere: pervasive in its scope although very concrete and particular in its manifestations. That is, a society can seem to be somewhat magical to the individual, precisely because, like magic, it is pervasive, ubiquitous, and yet concentrated here and there in particular institutions. Individuals also use magic, then, as a way of appropriating what is modelled for the individual by the larger society. In so doing they fail to recognize that magic is merely an individual potency that has been expropriated by an élite for its own manipulative or coercive purposes. The dialectic of which I speak is clearly in the eye of the sociological observer rather than in the mind of the individual actor.

Ritual and the Dialectic of Claims to Priority and Precedence

In terms of their individual lifetimes, of course, individuals are always preceded by society and brought into being, as it were, by parents and other social institutions to whom they owe their existence. These institutions do not seem to the child as mere repositories of individual potencies but clearly take precedence and seem to have a priority of their own. It is only an adult insight that societies and institutions are the complex result of individual actions and interactions in the past. Moreover, societies are apparently prior to the individual not only in the temporal order but in status and power. A society's claim to priority is manifest particularly in religion. Indeed, religious rituals in certain societies may exhibit the properties of externality and coerciveness: note the religious 'options' for self-expression that certain churches present in contemporary societies like the United States, where religion is often advertised as a means of 'finding oneself'.

Granted that societies seek to expropriate from individuals the means of an individual's own self-definition and self-assertion, the process of expropriation is nonetheless dialectical. As O'Keefe put it: 'magic is the expropriation of religious collective representations for individual or subgroup purposes'.[27] Thus magic, as religion expropriated for personal use, enables the individual to prevent 'collapse' and the subgroup to avoid 'extinction'. Ritual thus embodies what O'Keefe calls 'the endless dialectic between magic and religion that is part of social change in advanced societies and civilizations'.[28]

Indeed, O'Keefe's major contribution to a sociological study of religion, I believe, is his proposition that magic defends the self and the individual from social pressures and against the threat of psychic extinction. Social pressures can in fact threaten the individual with the death of the inner self. Whether they do or do not threaten the psychic life of the individual depends not only on the intensity of the pressures but on the vulnerability of the particular self to those pressures. The self is particularly vulnerable which lacks any emotional distance from those who are the source of the pressure. Most vulnerable are those who lack any rights, relationships, roles or other sources of social power for defence against these pressures.

The poor, the outcast, those who are subordinate or of low status: these are the individuals who have the most difficulty in breaking the spell cast by social duty or rejection. That is why, as we shall see, they experience their own time as being not only unbearable but mercifully short. The end is coming, so many of them believe, when they will be the witnesses rather than the victims of massive tribulation. When the resentments of the desperate take the form of social movements proclaiming that the end is in sight and that a new social order is therefore imminent, fascist tendencies have a way of getting out of control.

The individual who most needs relief from the moral pressures of society is also likely to be one who is least able to claim priority for his or her own sources of inspiration and authority. Magic, however, enables the beleaguered individual to undertake action unfettered by tradition or by the rational and customary calculation of means and ends, interests and advantages, causes and effects. Only by imitating and co-opting popular magic for its own purposes does a society succeed in making certain magical acts obligatory for both the community and the individual, i.e. a 'religious duty'. Action that originated as magical, when it becomes part of civic ritual, then buys time not only for the individual but for the community. The wish for a magical potency that can guarantee the self is thus preserved and yet subverted by religion. However, even in civic rituals individuals can once again feel that magical powers are at their disposal. These rites momentarily permit a return to the magical universe of childhood and infancy, whose unconscious wishes and fears can persist far into adulthood.

When rituals fail to satisfy the demand for re-entry into that magical kingdom, however, the individual oppressed by the moral weight of the social order will be especially vulnerable to the appeal of charismatic leaders. It is as if the charismatic leader has 'the keys of the kingdom' and can once again perform acts that not only will enable the community to remove or eliminate its enemies but also will assure the self of its existence and capacity to act even in the face of powerful social institutions and of death itself. Ritual is most effective in softening the antisocial effects of such magical acts of self-constitution when its rites effectively imitate the unconscious and provide customary and traditional emblems for magical thinking. A society that is vital thus enables individuals to experience their own passages and crises in terms of the society's particular temporal order; conversely, such a society also requires that individuals feel its critical moments with the same intensity as they would their own. To dramatize this interplay between individual and societal time, I am arguing, is the primary function of ritual.

Ritual and the Advent of Death

In this book I will be trying to demonstrate the truth of this proposition about ritual by showing what happens not only when rituals succeed but when they fail. My interest in this project began in the course of writing an earlier study on the crisis of succession in Israel after the death of King Herod the Great.[29] For instance, there are numerous accounts in Josephus of occasions on which the festivals in Jerusalem at that time, and for many years afterward, were interrupted by violence. On one occasion a Roman soldier bared his genitals. First, the crowd of pilgrims responded with violence; one report by Josephus mentioned that they stoned the Roman soldiers.[30] Second, they responded with panic as reinforcements were brought to the Temple; many thousands died in a stampede through the narrow passageways leading from one of the courts. On another occasion a report of pilgrims being killed as they passed from Galilee through Samaria on their way to Jerusalem prompted many pilgrims, already in Jerusalem, to leave en masse for battle with the Samaritans.[31] Here I mention these events simply to show that the possibility of panic and indiscriminate violence is always just below the surface of collective celebrations. Nonetheless, the ritual framework holds, on many, if not most, occasions. Thus the Passover, for instance, provided a means for establishing collective presence – and the rudiments of spiritual self-possession – in the face of the approach of death: death in the form of an enemy such as Rome or in its inevitable, 'natural' aspect as the fate shared by all.

Ritual requires, however, that the threat of death be made external to the community: quite literally that death pass over the community and be visited upon the alien or the enemy. That victory over time is won, as it were, by removing death from the precincts of the community; it is the 'Egyptian' on whose sons death is to be visited. What should happen, therefore, if it were the members of one's own community that presented the threat of death?

Precisely such conditions did obtain in Jerusalem prior to the outbreak of the civil war in 66 CE. As Josephus (*Ant.* XX, 160ff.) tells the story, Judaea, while under the procuratorship of Felix, had been suffering from 'brigands and impostors'. These had dominated the countryside, but at Felix's invitation some of them had come to the city of Jerusalem. (Felix had sought to use them to kill a troublesome high priest, Jonathan.) Josephus goes on:

> Certain of these brigands went up to the city as if they intended to worship God. With daggers concealed under

> their clothes, they mingled with the people about Jonathan and assassinated him. As the murder remained unpunished, from that time forth the brigands with perfect impunity used to go to the city during the festivals and, with their weapons similarly concealed, mingle with the crowds. In this way they slew some because they were private enemies, and others because they were paid to do so by someone else. They committed these murders not only in other parts of the city but even in some cases in the temple; for there too they made bold to slaughter their victims, for they did not regard even this as a desecration. This is the reason why, in my opinion, even God Himself, for loathing of their impiety, turned away from our city and, because He deemed the temple to be no longer a clean dwelling place for Him, brought the Romans upon us and purification by fire upon the city, while he inflicted slavery upon us together with our wives and children; for he wished to chasten us by these calamities.[32]

Thus it would have become impossible to distinguish friend from enemy: those on the side of life from those on the side of death. So far from placing death beyond the gates of the household of faith, death was now on the inside of those same gates. The blood smeared on the portals, so to speak, would be human rather than that of sacrificial animals; conversely, animal spirits would be released, and indiscriminate killing and panic would take over, as indeed they did during the civil war itself. The purification which rituals failed to accomplish was achieved in the fires of war.

It is necessary, first of all, for ritual to hold death at bay: to keep it outside the sacred precincts of the community. On the other hand, to enable an individual to accomplish certain critical passages in and through time it is necessary to confront death, as it were, head on. Indeed, I will be pointing out how such a symbolic confrontation with death, in the form, for instance, of a death's head, has been an integral part of ritual in antiquity, and remains so in many liturgies of the Christian Church.

Ritual thus intensifies time not only by making death pass over the community to a place outside its gates, but by making the individual pass safely through the gates of death. Death is known as a presence in the community by its absence, and in its absence by its symbolic presence. To accomplish this feat it is necessary for ritual so to intensify the time that all times, past, present, and future, inhere in the critical moment of the rite itself.

I am suggesting that rituals in antiquity provided a defence against death not only by placing it outside the society's borders but also by creating a symbolic confrontation with death itself. To survive the encounter with death, however, requires extraordinary, even supernatural, power; only priests are allowed into the inner sanctum of the Temple, for instance, and even priests, if they are not properly prepared, may not survive the encounter. No one looks upon the face of God and survives, unless it be one endowed with the extraordinary charisma of a Moses.

From a purely sociological perspective, I would argue, ritual is a device for making all the members of society, both the living and the dead, present to each other regardless of the passage of time. That sense of synchronic presence can only be accomplished, however, if ritual captures all the various ways of experiencing and ordering time that are current in a particular community. This means that rituals must capture the ways that individuals construe time as well as the way that societies construct it in official histories, calendars and schedules. Time as it comes toward an individual or community, and time as one enters into it; time as a test of individual or corporate claims to transcendence, as well as momentary experiences of transcendence over time; time as running out on a community, and time as the matrix of all social life; time as an inexorable passage into the terrors of death, and time as something that one can renew and create: all these must be captured within ritual if a community is effectively to subsume personal experiences of time and the individual's attempt to gain a measure of mastery and control over time itself.

If ritual works well, all the members of a society will be present with each other. Those who have gone before and are now in the past will also be found in the future, so that one can both anticipate the future as a return to the past and, by remembering those who have died, anticipate one's own posterity. The rigorous passage of time will not disrupt the tissues of the society but will pass overhead, as it were, with its destruction visited on the members of another society who must lament the loss of their own future. Ritual, when it is effective, enables individuals to stand the test of time: to confront the unbearable prospect of death without panic and without being petrified. Those who thus withstand the test of time and have taken their part in the proper sequences of life will thus be coeval with one another.

This book therefore belongs along the border between sociology and psychoanalysis. On one side of that border, the unconscious mind can be found as it makes its own constructions and performs its own ceremonies. On the other side, one can investigate the ways in which social practices cramp the movements of the mind and channel it in certain directions. There are gates through which the mind must pass on to well-defined social territory. At these gates, however, emissaries from social institutions can inform the mind of its rights and duties, its possibilities and the dangers that it should anticipate. One might imagine the psyche as containing tables where negotiation takes place between representatives of the unconscious mind and the representatives of the social order. There also are cells where certain impulses are carefully guarded: watchtowers from which surveillance is kept not only in the day but even during the night-time activity of dreaming. The border between the unconscious mind and social reality is a place in which outbursts or even explosions may disrupt the smooth flow of negotiations, and it is a place where the outcome of those negotiations depends as much on what is not said but only imagined as on what is actually transacted. Tendencies toward fascism begin, but do not end, in the unconscious.

If this metaphor for the ambiguous territory that is explored by psychoanalysis and sociology seems a bit too military, consider this passage from Peter Gay's essay, *Freud for Historians*:

> The human mind appears [to psychoanalysis – RKF] much like a modern military dictatorship: inordinately suspicious, addicted to secrecy, insatiable in its demands, armed to the teeth, and not very intelligent. It employs battalions of

> censors to prevent domestic news from leaking out, and of border patrols to prevent hostile ideas from reaching, and possibly subverting, its people. Yet often neither the censors nor the patrols have the wit, or the agility, to carry their assignments through. At night especially, but also at unguarded moments during the day, messages, disguised as dreams, slips of the tongue, or neurotic symptoms get out; and perceptions, dressed in innocuous garb, get in. Both, however, pay a price for their intrepid penetration of the energetically defended frontiers: they are gravely distorted, treacherously translated, sometimes crippled beyond cure.[33]

This is a picture of the mind as proto-fascist: guarded against subversion from within, or penetration from without, and crushing the very souls that it claims to protect. The super-ego, Freud noted, was like the state, and in many ways the super-ego was in fact the outpost of society within the self. The individual's own compromises with reality, then, in many ways mirror the society's own techniques for survival.

Of course, there is always more resistance to social pressures on the psyche. The poor typically have been more likely than the comfortable and the rich to wish or to fear that the end of a system is at hand. As we will note in discussing the work of Norman Cohn, the poor during the Middle Ages were eager to believe that a particularly charismatic or forceful character was a harbinger of the end: perhaps the Messiah, in whose presence the future actually begins. The targets of these movements were nobles and princes, the rich, and the clergy: all of whom preferred to believe that the system of which they were the primary beneficiaries had more time at its disposal. On occasion, however, even the Church had to embody elements of millenarianism in its own leadership and practices in order to win back the poor. Certainly officials engaged the millenarian expectations of the poor in movements for expansion, conquest and settlement: the crusades being a prime example.

To summarize: societies begin to run out of time for many reasons: not only when disaster is imminent or when influences, once thought to be due to outsiders, clearly threaten to disintegrate a society from within, but also from internal sources of disruption or dismay. Every society will run out of time if it cannot transform young people into adults and single people into married ones. The older generations must find successors, and families must be formed to bear children. That is why we will find ritual that seems to specialize in transforming individuals from one stage in life or condition to another: even from being a living member of the community to an ancestor.

All these rituals, if they are successful, will score victories over the inexorable passage of time. Some enable a society to stand the test of time and confront disaster. Others manufacture time in the form of new seasons and years unburdened by what can then be newly designated as the past. Still other rituals create seasons in the life of the individual which extend the life of the social system for yet another generation. Other rituals, we will find, restore a timeless past in which the departed return and mingle with the living. These rituals, I will argue, exhibit not only the longing for a timeless social order but the illusion of magical control. When the genie of magical control over time escapes from the bottle of liturgy, so to speak, longings for the transcendence of time escape the confines of ritual and invade the social system through movements that exhibit a variety of fascist tendencies.

· 1 ·

RITUAL AND THE MAKING OF TIME: A TYPOLOGY

Societies are always running out of time for one reason or another. The environment impinges in many ways, and every time a society's boundaries with its environment are threatened or breached, the society in question must respond more or less quickly. A social order may be threatened or distressed because of the advent of outside forces or the intrusion of alien influences. Enemies appear on the horizon or outside the city gates. Unwanted immigrants, the sick, the poor, and the promiscuous bring pollution within the city; the corrupt values of the cultural centre erode traditional ways of life on the periphery, and the young leave the farm for the metropolis.

Not all the dangers to a social order are external, of course. From the viewpoint of the social order, any individual may be as alien and threatening as the natural environment. Indeed, spirits and ghosts often inhabit the psyche; and they may live in the bush while troubling the community. As I will point out in this chapter, individuals have ways of interacting that often ignore or violate social patterns and constraints; they make friends or enemies, find lovers and partners, go on journeys and enter into exchanges with others in ways that defy or transcend social convention. Individuals may also experience their own passions or the presence of others in ways that evoke nature rather than society; they lose control or become possessed in ways that make them acutely aware of the danger of losing themselves. Thus, a society begins to find time increasingly scarce as interaction tends to escape from the net of social control.

As individuals escape social constraints on their relationships, they experience themselves in new ways. The young spurn their legacies or seek wisdom from alien sages. The solitary find unfamiliar spiritual companions. The innovative send coded messages through electronic mail to confidantes on the other side of the globe. Under these conditions it is difficult for a society to contain individuals' sense of themselves within familiar or conventional categories. These internal gaps in the social order make it difficult for a society to be a matrix of time.

Rituals provide a temporal matrix by manufacturing moments that endure, renewed seasons, new chapters in the life of the individual, or even new epochs based on the recovery of the past. Rituals accomplish their feats by defining the temporal horizon for both the individual and the larger society. Thus some rituals may avert a terrible danger by calling a people to war or readying an army for battle. Other rituals may cast out the old bread or sweep away the past year's sacrifices in order to make room for a new year. Still other rituals may enable the young to become adult, the single to leave their former families and join new ones, or enable the departed to take up new positions among those who have gone before. There are other rituals that summon the past into the present and make up for lost time; thus the departed return to help the living to plant the fields or cope with missionaries and colonizers.

However, rituals also embody and express a bundle of contradictions. They take what is internal to a society, e.g. human nature, and make it seem external, i.e. as due to animal or ghostly spirits or alien influences. Other rites correspondingly take what is external to a society, e.g. the dead, and make them participants with the living in the process of social regeneration. The same rites may take the future and put it in the past, even while they take the past and put it in the future. In rites of protest, individuals may rebel against the social order, only to embody a new order as repressive as the one that is being superseded or overthrown. Rites of initiation that seek to impress the social order on the character of the individual may suffocate the self or produce resistance in the form of magical or millennial protest. In seeking to place unwanted influences outside a society or to keep them there, rituals open themselves up to contradiction from social forces that they cannot control.

One contradiction seems to characterize most rituals. That is, in seeking to transcend the flow of ordinary time, rituals open themselves up to the erosion of time. Rituals can buy time for a society by enabling the young to wear masks and bear spears, but the transforming effect even of these highly charged performances may wear off in time: sooner rather than later if the initiates were not wholly persuaded of their own transformation. Churches that have relied on ordinations to impose a new social character on the clergy have long known that the effects of that particular rite wear off in time. As the power of ordination or other rites of initiation begins to erode, time begins to run out on the churches themselves.

A Typology of Ritual

It may help to summarize these introductory comments in a diagram. In Figure 1, the horizontal axis represents the degree to which communities or societies are differentiated from their environments (from a high degree of such differentiation on the left to the lowest possible degree, on the right). Societies that

Figure 1

The degree of internal integration	The degree to which a social system is differentiated from nature and from other societies: High	Low
High	Cell 1	Cell 2
Low	Cell 3	Cell 4

Primary function of ritual:
Cell 1 .... Transformation
Cell 2 .... Aversion
Cell 3 .... Purification
Cell 4 .... Restoration

have strong boundaries (cells 1 and 3) are less likely to be invaded by enemies or polluted by other outside influences. Of the two, societies typified by cell 3 are the more likely to be subverted from within by children who refuse to become adults, by individuals who refuse marriage or reject its constraints, and by departed spirits that refuse to join the community of ancestors and remain to trouble the living. That is because the latter societies are typically less well replicated either in social interaction or in the social character of the individual.

Societies that lack strong external boundaries (cells 2 and 4) typically have little time to react to dangers or opportunities; of the two, societies typified by those in cell 4 are also less able to restrict the range of social interaction and personal experience; thus they are far more vulnerable to – and afraid of – outside influences and individuals who draw their inspiration and authority from outside or from hidden sources.

In Figure 1 the vertical dimension represents the degree to which a society is highly integrated. By integration, I mean the degree to which personal experience is usually contained within the framework of prescribed or permitted social interaction, and the degree to which such interaction expresses and reinforces the way the social order assigns duties and accords privileges to its members. Some societies are highly integrated (cells 1 and 2). Other societies, however, permit higher degrees of freedom (cells 3 and 4). In these latter societies, individuals gain a sense of themselves that transcends the social order. For instance, they may see themselves as potential denizens of a larger human community, of a new world order, or even of the cosmos. In extreme cases, individuals interact in ways that are intended to subvert or overthrow the social order.

In the following discussion I will argue that societies of the type represented by cell 1 require a particular sort of ritual if they are to provide a temporal matrix for their members: a ritual of transformation. Their external boundaries are relatively intact, and their social order is highly integrated. Sources of renewal must therefore come from within the social order itself. To renew itself, the society in question must be able to create new chapters or eras in time. The young must be transformed into adults in order for the life of one generation to be transposed to its successor. The single must become married if the family system is to survive. Even the dead must not be lost as a resource to so tightly bounded a community but turned into ancestors whose presence and absence can be suitably controlled through liturgical means.

Societies of the type represented by cell 4 in the model are the polar opposite of those in cell 1: neither very well insulated from outside influences by strong boundaries nor very well integrated. These societies, I will argue, require the most drastic form of liturgical remedy: rituals of restoration. Time is running out on the social order not only because its boundaries are weak or endangered but because the social order itself is not being reproduced either in the way people interact with one another or in their social character. Rituals of restoration seek to make up for lost time by restoring to a people or nation the potency or virtue of a mythic past, whether in the form of ancestral return or in the revitalization of certain values and of original vigour.

The two other types of society represent mixed types. Societies suggested by cell 2 in the model still are able to command a high degree of discipline in their ranks and are able effectively to shape social character. However, these social systems face an imminent break in their boundaries. As in the case of two armies about to engage in battle, such a break may also be conducive to disruption of their ranks, as individuals panic or fight indiscriminately, thus lending themselves to the slaughter of their fellow soldiers. Rituals of aversion, I will argue, are of the greatest significance for social systems of this type.

Societies of the type suggested by cell 3 have relatively little difficulty retaining their organizational and territorial boundaries, but because their members are quite free to engage in relationships with others from outside the society in question, these societies are permeable to outside influences. Furthermore, because the individual enjoys relatively high degrees of freedom in the choice of sources of authority and personal inspiration, these societies face possible disaffection and disloyalty from within. I will argue that rituals of purification are of the highest import for societies under these conditions.

Thus there are four ways in which ritual can help societies to transcend time. In societies that are both tightly integrated and have solidified their external boundaries, rituals will focus on enabling individuals to cross the boundaries that are internal to the social system, e.g. between families, between generations, or between the living and the dead (cell 1). Thus, as I have noted, the primary task of ritual in these societies is to transform individuals from one status to another, e.g. from child to adult, from being single to being married, and from being alive to being dead. Rituals of transformation are crucial to the creation of new periods or stages in the lives of individuals as they move from birth through marriage and death into the final status of ancestors. They are also crucial for creating a new period in the life of the society itself. When such rituals fail, therefore, the society will be vulnerable to anxiety about time. The demand for the transformation of the generations may become politicized and inform the rhetoric of social movements. Certainly the Nazi movement was highly regarded for its ability to replace the 'debauchery' of German youth with 'discipline and a sense of purpose'.[1]

The second way in which rituals can enable a society to transcend the passage of time is by enabling its members to avert impending disaster and to forestall imminent danger: the task of aversion. While this is important for all societies, it is the paradigmatic function of ritual for societies that are highly integrated but no longer well protected from their natural or social environments (cell 2). That is, what I will be calling rituals of aversion dramatize and resolve the primary task of such societies, which is to avert disaster by defending the social order from external threat and internal disruption: from panic and terror, and from passions which, if not controlled, can issue in mayhem and fratricide. These rituals create a time of grace, as it were: a sacred moment, event, or period in which the social order may be preserved and death averted. I have noted such a ritual in Chapter 3, where I will discuss the role of ritual in mobilizing an army and controlling panic and murderous impulses at a critical moment, e.g. when two armies confront each other immediately prior to battle. When rituals of aversion fail to reassure a people that it can survive in the face of real or imagined danger, however, such fears enter the public domain and may be alleviated through charismatic leadership, popular militias, youth corps, and other forms of antagonistic mobilization.

In societies which are poorly integrated but which still maintain relatively strong boundaries (cell 3), there will still be rites that seek to avert disaster (rituals of aversion) or that can create a new period in the lives of individuals as they move from one status to another (rituals of transformation). The primary task of rituals in these well-bounded but poorly integrated societies, however, is to remove disruptive and unwanted influences from the social order. Such influences may be alien people or ideas encountered through a wider range of interaction fostered through commerce and travel. These rituals will thus be relied upon to purify the social order of personal, unofficial and foreign sources of inspiration and authority enjoyed by individuals whose psyches have been able to escape from the constraints of prescribed social character. These are rituals of purification, in which the burdens and debts, the pollution and the dangers threatening the society from within can be eliminated.

During the latter part of the eleventh century, for instance, the crusades were inaugurated in precisely such ceremonies of purification and renewal. Pope Urban preached the first crusade to a gathering of nobles and clergy. Here is Cohn's fine description of the moment:

> As the assembly listened it was swept by emotions of overwhelming power. Thousands cried with one voice 'Deus le volt!' – 'It is God's will!' Crowding around the Pope and kneeling before him they begged leave to take part in the holy war. A cardinal fell on his knees and recited the *Confiteor* in the name of the whole multitude and as they echoed it after him many burst into tears and many were seized with convulsive trembling. For a brief moment there reigned in that predominately aristocratic assembly *an atmosphere of collective enthusiasm such as was to become normal in the contingents of common folk which were formed later.*[2]

The elements of purification are unmistakable. The Pope had promised to those who would take up arms in the crusade a remission of all the penalties for sin, and remission of all sins for those who would die on the crusade. For the poor who would soon be caught up in the mass movement, moreover, the crusades offered a chance to escape from the pollution of plague and famine, from villages that could no longer support them and from cities that were not yet able to sustain a large population through times of trouble. From the pollution of the past and the present, then, the crusades offered an opportunity for purification and the renewal of life. Note, however, that the enthusiasm contained in the rite of confession later animated popular movements that gave the process of purification new meaning and terror.

The social order described by Cohn appears to have been very loosely integrated, even though its territorial boundaries were intact. Thus the conditions suggested by the model (in cell 3) appear to have obtained late in the eleventh and early in the twelfth century. Cohn makes it clear that the range of social interaction in many peasant communities had been opened by trade, conquest, urbanization, immigration and emigration.[3] He also demonstrates that the social order that had bound the self to patterns of customary interaction and to traditional social institutions was already in jeopardy in that period in many parts of northern and central Europe. Beggars, mercenaries and bandits became more prevalent as individuals found that the old ties of obligation and support could not function in the new cities. In many of the old peasant villages families could no longer support an increasing population. The result was a volatile combination of heightened expectation and uncertainty, along with an increase in objective impoverishment for many who left the village for the city or abandoned the city for the highway. Under these conditions it is not surprising that the Pope should have preached a *drang nach osten* or that the poor should have visions of a new Jerusalem descending from the heavens, in which they would have an eternal habitation.

The vision of a renewed and purified body politic becomes all the more important as rituals fail to purify a people of their ills. In times of plague or famine, and in times of severe unemployment, dislocation and dispossession, the nation itself seems to be mortally wounded or fatally diseased. The demand for purification of an entire people also underlies the fascist vision:

> The biomedical vision and the scientific racism of the late nineteenth and early twentieth centuries ... contributed to the Nazi ideology and, eventually, to the killing of those who were 'genetically inferior' ... In the framework of the reversal of morality by the Nazis and to a degree the whole society, there was a reversal of medical morality. *Killing became a kind of healing – of the nation, the group, the collectivity, and the race.*[4]

The reversal is typical of magical thinking: using fire, as it were, to fight fire. To turn the tables on death, then, a ritual employs death itself through sacrificial killing, as if to defeat death at its own game.

It is when rituals have failed to purify a social system of its endemic ills that magical thinking escapes the confines of ritual and becomes encoded in ideology and social policy. To escape what Konrad Lorenz chillingly refers to as 'the degenerative phenomena that accompany domestication', for instance, a nation may take its own steps to cull the herd rather than leaving that process either to ritual or to the course of nature itself.[5] The sympathetic magic typical of ritual is more apparent, of course, in purificatory rites than in social policies, where it is disguised under a veneer of rationality.

Fears of an internal source of pollution that may destroy the entire nation are not limited to countries with a clearly fascist political movement. Take, for example, the charge that the United States of America is being destroyed from within by a fifth column, a subversive hard core, of 'secular humanists':

> Humanists control America. America is supposed to be a free country, but are we really free? ... They, 275,000 humanists, have infiltrated until every department of our country is controlled by the humanists.
>
> Humanists will continue leading us toward the chaos of the French Revolution. After all, it is the same philosophy that destroyed France and paved the way for the dictator Napoleon Bonaparte. This time the humanists hope to name

> their own dictator who will create out of the ashes of our pro-moral republic a humanist utopia, an atheistic, socialistic, amoral humanist society for America and the rest of the world. In fact, their goal is to accomplish this takeover by or before the year 2,000.[6]

The warning is very clear. To offset the threat of pollution and dictatorship by secular humanists before the year 2,000, it may be necessary to have a pre-emptive dictatorial regime, no less powerful and authoritarian than the one it is intended to prevent.

Certain societies, therefore, are relatively more exposed to influences from outsiders although they are relatively well protected from their natural and social environments (cell 3). A colonized people may still have its societal boundaries relatively intact. That is, it may be organized into communities, grow crops and pursue crafts, maintain warrior groups and enjoy a measure of autonomy even while its individual members engage in trade with foreigners and develop appetites for the consumption of goods and ideas from the colonial powers. Because the self is permitted to derive inspiration and authority from a variety of sources, the individual can develop affections and aspirations that transcend the boundaries of the social system. While social boundaries are intact, individuals may interact with one another with a certain latitude; individuals may interact with foreigners and enter into conflict with fellow citizens without offering a direct challenge to the basic standards and values of the larger society. In good times, at least, a society that is poorly integrated can allow its citizens freedom to draw inspiration from outsiders without accusing them of subversion. The social system retains its formal authority, even though the integrity of the society itself begins to be questioned.

As individuals enjoy increasing degrees of freedom in their interactions and in their souls, the social system begins to resemble an empty shell rather than a living organism. The prospect of the loss of the younger generation causes anxiety among the older members of the community; there may be calls for a return to traditional values and ways of life. As interaction increasingly escapes the confines or constraints of social organization, there may be concerns over the loss of civility and new demands for compliance and conformity. Temporal horizons are foreshortened, therefore, even though the society itself maintains effective ways of defending its borders and of adapting to the environment. The traditions of the larger society no longer seem to provide an effective guarantee of transcendence over the passage of time. To ensure a renewal of commitment and virtue is therefore one function of rituals of purification (cell 3).

Complex societies, for instance, may be poorly integrated but well adapted to their environments. Through their intelligence networks and their access to global communications they are less likely to be surprised by enemies or unable to respond to emerging dangers. On the other hand, these same societies allow their citizens to interact with citizens of other nations through travel and cannot prevent them from receiving news or sending messages through a variety of channels ranging from the telephone to the personal computer. Outside influences are therefore likely to influence individuals in their everyday lives; consider public responses to pictures of starving Ethiopians or corpses on the streets of Sarajevo. Furthermore, personal experience is likely to transcend the limits of any particular society's traditions or ideology. New Age channelling, ashrams, the consumption of wisdom and esoterica from traditional societies, and the exploration of the unconscious all tend to give individuals experiences that transcend those offered by institutionalized religion and by public or private schooling, by mass entertainment or by professionalized sources of healing and personal growth.

By their very openness to outside influences, individuals are able to find spiritual or ethical resources in peoples and places that are regarded as traditional, as primitive, or in other uses of the past. This tendency to mine the past for present purposes contributes to what has been called the 'foreshortening' of time perspectives in 'post-modern' societies, as individuals engage in a wide range of symbolic acts from meditation and the consumption of liturgical music to films on adventurous crusades to recover lost arks and ancient treasure. The same 'foreshortening' of temporal horizons occurs among fundamentalists, for whom the promise of the millennium increasingly becomes a matter less for devout hope and more for precise calculation. Time increasingly loses its mystery and transcendence, as it becomes an object for speculation and consumption. In that sense time itself becomes relatively short.

On the other hand, the existence of mass media, the constant flow of information about fluctuations in global markets and interest rates, and the vast intelligence networks of modern societies also expand the time pressures under which both the state and major corporations must live. These time pressures in turn are passed on to the individual in the form of demands for higher taxes, literacy, skills, and productivity. Physical fitness, it will be remembered, became an article of public policy after the United States federal government found a high proportion of candidates unable to qualify for the draft during the early years of the war in Vietnam.

The increased time pressures on individuals in complex societies are partly responsible, I will argue, for the increasingly widespread popular interest in spiritual resources, whether of indigenous or primitive people or of previous periods in Western society. Recordings of Gregorian chant sell by the tens of thousands, as do books promising vicarious romantic and sexual experiences set in an idyllic rural past of covered bridges and traditional virtues. Time pressures increase in a society that continues to rationalize time itself into schedules, quarterly objectives, time values, response times, and minimal times-out for individuals under stress. It is not surprising that individuals seek to engage in a consumerized ghost dance by calling on the spiritual resources of the past to cope with the pressures of the present.

Under these conditions, traditional rituals tend to develop a shorter 'shelf-life'; new rituals, called experimental or trial liturgies, are produced to make religious institutions more competitive and attractive, i.e. more up to date. On the other hand, the new rites tend to recover neglected elements in ancient liturgies: greetings, invocations, offerings, and praises that lend to the new rites an element of original authenticity. The introduction of new liturgies that seek to mine the past is thus a dramatization of the need to make up for lost time in a society that expands the range of social interaction and personal experience well beyond conventional or institutionalized limits. On the other hand, the fact that these new liturgies are experimental and under continual revision reflects the increasing need of modern societies to respond to opportunities and challenges from outside. Liturgical innovations in one country quickly become official practice in another. Rituals no longer offer a temporal matrix but instead embody the shortness of time typical of complex societies with strong boundaries but with low levels of integration. Time is short even for the very rituals that seek to restore the past and to make up for lost time.

When the boundaries of societies are endangered, however, a relatively unintegrated society faces extinction, however complex it may be. Individuals may no longer be able to engage in wide-ranging relationships or in idiosyncratic spiritual exercises without facing censure and without being put to various tests of loyalty. Such a condition obtained, I will argue, in Germany during the 1930s and 1940s. Under these conditions, I will show, the primary task of rituals is to reinforce convention, commitment and vitality through fresh infusions of the past. The paradigmatic ritual is one that makes up for lost time. The ancestors return. A golden age or the dream time of the people is restored to the present through rituals of restoration (cell 4).

The purpose of these latter rituals is to restore the solidarity of a people and to revive a sense of continuity with the people's past. In the Germany of the early 1930s, there was not only a major threat to national integration; the nation's borders had been revised in the aftermath of the First World War. There would therefore be a need for rituals that would restore cohesion and unite Germans across the artificial boundaries created by the victors of the war. Indeed, these fascist rituals appear to have been successful. In Germany during the 1930s, for instance, individuals taking part in highly ritualized programmes for social renewal may well have believed that they had experienced the 'cementing of the blood of members ... [in] a struggle to restore German glory': the words of a Nazi doctor who had entered that movement through youth groups that 'stressed Germanness and volkish views'.[7] Such a highly ritualized expression of solidarity had at best only a temporary success. As late as 1939 Hitler could claim to have restored and solidified Germany's national borders and to have returned millions of Germans to the rule of the fatherland. As Staub[8] makes clear, however, after the war began to turn against Germany, plans for the 'final solution' of the 'Jewish problem' were intensified. What was then required was the final removal of outside influences, historically associated with Judaism, and the actual cementing of blood ties through the sacrifice of tens of thousands of German youth in the military, as though national life could only be restored through the death itself. I have summarized these comments on ritual in Figure 2.

Rituals of Transformation

For a typical ritual of transformation, let us consider Maurice Bloch's recent work, *Prey Into Hunter: The Politics of Religious Experience*. There he undertakes a broad synthesis and a critical review of ethnographies from a wide range of peoples and places. Bloch's review of the Orokaiva ritual of initiation, for instance, although far too detailed for us to consider at length, is particularly useful for our purposes. As Bloch himself later summarizes it, that rite evokes 'a terrifying closeness to death on the part of the living . . . It is as if there was *an element of dare* in these stories.'[9] The point is that this ritual places the individual in a situation in which time is short indeed; the threat of imminent death is tangible. Yet those who undergo the ritualized trial pass through on the other side transformed: their souls steeled against the unbearable prospect of death itself.

Such rituals of transformation typify societies that are tightly integrated and whose boundaries are relatively well defined (cell 1). These societies have an inside and an outside, and the world of nature represents a source not only of familiar nourishment but of symbolic opposition to the social order itself. Rituals of transformation enable individuals to cross relatively well-established internal boundaries, e.g. between generations, while reinforcing the larger society's external boundaries. They accomplish this feat by impressing the social order on the individual through intensified social interaction.

Among the Orokaiva, it is not only children who are suckled at the maternal breast; pigs also are nursed by the women of the community. In the rite of initiation into manhood, pigs therefore

Figure 2

Types of Ritual and the Manufacture of Time

The degree of internal integration	The degree to which a social system is differentiated from nature and from other societies: High	Low
High	1. TRANSFORMATION	2. AVERSION
Low	3. PURIFICATION	4. RESTORATION

Type of ritual	The manufacture of time
1. Transformation	Creation of a new chapter in the life of the individual, e.g. through initiation into adulthood, marriage or the ancestral community; *the renewal of the social order over time.*
2. Aversion	Reinforcing the integration of self with the conventions of social interaction and the constraints of social organization; *buying time for the social system.*
3. Purification	Separating the present from the past by resolving grievances and expelling outside influences from the community; *the renewal of 'the times'.*
4. Restoration	The recreation of a period of original vigour and harmony in the life of the society; initiating a future that is a sharp break from the present; the restoration of a mythic past.

stand as a metaphor for the care, the satisfactions, and the security of infancy, and in fact pigs are sacrificed in this ritual by the children-turned-adult.[10] Such a wrenching apart from the nurturing and supportive world of childhood stimulates intense rage and destructive urges; these passions are effectively turned in this ritual into a form of violence directed first at the pigs, in whose slaughter the children-turned-adult terminate their own dependencies.

The violence is soon turned, however, against the enemies of the Orokaiva as the newly minted adults brandish the weapons of manhood. Not a drop of the new adult's rage is wasted but is turned into both symbolic and real aggression. There will be no undisciplined or murderous rage, but only controlled and highly selective killing. Frenzy, outside the rite itself, is literally out of order.

This ritual of transformation makes it clear that indiscriminate murder within the community is forbidden. During this rite, spirits among the Orokaiva come to a hut in the bush where the children, as it were, have been 'spirited away'. There the children learn that they are in the presence of an alien, superior and prepossessing force that can slaughter them like pigs:

> the elders organize a ritual in which the children to be initiated are first associated with pigs, creatures which are seen as very similar to them, and ... as pigs the initiates are hunted and symbolically killed by masked men representing ancestral spirits or birds. Then, the initiates are isolated in a dark hut in the forest, where it is said that they, like all those who have gone beyond death, have themselves become a kind of spirit. Finally, the children re-emerge and return from the world of spirits. They re-emerge associated with the spirits which initially killed them, as hunters and consumers of pigs.[11]

Note how space functions here as a metaphor for time. In this spatialization of time, the social world of children is assigned to the world of nature. In separating the young from their own childhoods, rituals of transformation also mark the boundaries separating the social order from the world of plants and animals. Going into the bush is like going forward through an archway; the return passage, like the return through the arch, signals the completion of the transformation itself. The passageway completed, the individual can now look back on what was once ahead, and thus a new chapter in time has been accomplished. Still ahead, of course, are the ancestors who have gone before and who will be joined in the individual's final passage through the gateway of death itself.

In the masquerade the children are not only wrenched away from their sources of nurturance and support but scared to death. Thus they can be persuaded to identify themselves with adults wearing the masks of ancestral spirits: a compromise in order to save their souls. The same strategy is often adopted by peoples who find missionaries or colonists, for example, to be an overwhelmingly controlling presence that threatens their own being-in-the-world.[12] By donning the masks of the spirits and by becoming one of them, the children can become adults, personify and act out their consuming passions, and direct their rage against those animals that represent the very passions and needs that they are seeking to conquer within themselves. This process thus reinforces the larger community's temporal order and set of priorities and exacts a terrible price: the destruction of the initiate's former self.

In order to save their souls from the symbolic (and, as Bloch notes, sometimes the real) threat of death in this ritual, the children have internalized a voice that dares them to undertake the unprecedented and the impossible: to leave home, to enter the wilderness, to face spear-bearing, masked adults, to encounter ancestral spirits, and to face death itself. On the other hand, the rite also involves them in what is for the time being mere play-acting. To be sure, only those who complete their passage through the gates of death, as it were, will also take their place in the social order. At the very least, the children are now play-acting at adulthood, although they will soon take on the roles of adult warriors. As Bloch notes, '*For a while* they truly believe themselves to be spirits and birds at the very same time that they know they are masquerading.'[13] The social order has established itself in their conscience almost like a second nature. The existential encounter with death has transformed the individual into an adult occupying an enduring place in the society. One self, the infantile, has been symbolically slain, to make room for the social character of the adult. On the other hand, however, the old self remains sufficiently intact to experience the ritual as a masquerade.

The adult warrior, moreover, still faces many tests of newly acquired charisma. Time still will tell.

In antiquity, as among the Orokaiva, ritual provided a type of mimesis in which the face of death, perhaps in the form of a mask or Gorgo's head, could be turned into the face with which one then confronts the world, no longer as prey and victim but as hunter and initiate: a form of sympathetic magic, of fighting fire, as it were, with fire. The potency of such rituals depended on their ability to mimic the magical strategies adopted by individuals in order to protect themselves from the danger of soul-loss. Speaking of the mask of the Gorgo, Vernant writes:

> We now understand better that the masks at times embody the model with which the young must identify, and at times, in the form of the savage and the grotesque, the horrible and the ridiculous, those extreme areas of alterity one must have explored in order to detach oneself entirely from them; at times, even, in the form of the Gorgon mask, that ultimate, radical form of the Other, that threat of chaos and death, which one must be able to look in the face in order to become a man.[14]

Those who have passed these tests of initiation presumably will not be petrified – will not 'turn into stone' – at the hideous prospect of the enemy arrayed in armour on the battlefield, or in the face of any other trials that life indeed may offer that try the soul. Those who failed the tests or were unqualified in the first place to take them were likely therefore to tremble, to be weak-willed, and to have no voice. Like lost souls in Hades they could not speak for themselves; indeed the class of helots were 'incapable, when asked, of pronouncing the words, singing the songs, or carrying out the movements of dance – in short, of adopting the customs that properly speaking are the privilege and characteristic of the fully human man, the full citizen'.[15]

Thus the existential encounter with death not only tries the individual to determine whose soul will not be petrified or lost in the face of death; the trial of the soul also becomes a test that determines who will be accorded social priority and who will be relegated to the ranks of the inferior. The weight of social obligation not only hung heavy on the soul; there were penalties for not carrying one's social weight. Thus many trials remain to determine whether the new warrior can indeed stand the test of time. As Vernant observes of Sparta, for instance, social honour could as easily be lost in a lifetime as gained: 'The threat of disgrace and dishonor constantly hangs over the heads of all.'[16]

The cure, however, is tantamount to the disease. In acquiring a Double, e.g. by donning a mask, the individual's sense of his or her own being-in-the-world or presence is obliterated, and control is monopolized by the mask one is wearing. Modern notions of taking a particular role in society, e.g. becoming sworn in as a juror, barely touch upon the depth to which the individual's own self can become displaced through such ritualized oath-taking. Here Vernant is talking about a trance-like state of possession in which the self is virtually lost. These existential transformations of the self are therefore exceedingly risky; they may be experienced as a form of the death of the self, incurred in the process of acquiring a new self that is, as it were, 'second nature': social rather than natural.[17] It is therefore crucial that the ritual of mask-wearing result in the affirmation of the self as a being that has survived an encounter with death itself:

> The face of Gorgo is the Other, your double. It is the Strange, responding to your face like an image in the mirror (where the Greeks could only see themselves frontally and in the form of a disembodied head), but at the same time, it is an image that is both less and more than yourself . . . what the mask of Gorgo lets you see, when you are bewitched by it, is yourself, yourself in the world beyond, the head clothed in night, the masked face of the invisible that, in the eye of Gorgo, is revealed as the truth about your own face.[18]

Note that there is no suggestion in Vernant's analysis that the Greeks are 'primitive' or 'traditional' in their use of imagery. One could easily, for instance, substitute the head of Christ for the head of Gorgo in the above passage by Vernant. That is, for centuries Christians have contemplated a head of Christ that is disfigured by a crown of thorns (rather than by snakes). Blood emanates from the places where his head has been cut by the thorns, and expressions of mortal agony mar his revered features ('the masked face of the invisible' – Vernant). Moreover, Christians have been urged to identify with Christ in his suffering so that they can see in him their eventual mortification and participation in 'the world beyond'.

To create a new period or era in the life both of the family or community and of the individual is the function of rituals of transformation. For instance, the marriage of Psyche to Cupid takes place only after Psyche's family has a funeral for her, and she has symbolically died to the order of the family which she is leaving. (Psyche goes through a metamorphosis of the innermost self and of her passions; thus she takes on the character of the moth whose transformation from the larval stage is drastic and total: a virtual death of the former in order to take on the freedom of the latter. Unlike the bat, which clings to old attachments, the moth soars on lighter wings to a new abode. I will return to this subject in the final chapter.) The family itself also goes through a crisis, since the family is composed of members each of whom is irreplaceable, so that when a daughter leaves to get married it is also the family that undergoes a sort of death.

At moments of transition it is not enough to temporize, to buy time, in the face of an imminent threat to the social order. Neither is it enough to renew the times by ridding the society of a threat to its own purity. The danger to the community is not merely immanent but can become irreversible. The individual's own life and character are about to be changed so drastically that there will be no way for the individual to return to his or her old position in the family or the community. Children once initiated into adulthood cannot return to being children; the married cannot return to their families as if they had never married and joined another family; neither can the dead return to life and take up their old rights and duties. An era in the life of the individual and of the community is ending; a new one is about to begin.

Rituals of transformation create a new chapter, as it were, in the history of the individual and of the community. If aversive rituals buy time, and purificatory rituals initiate a new round in the cyclical passage of time, rituals of transformation represent more of a rupture in the flow of time: a new beginning that nonetheless takes place within the life both of the individual and of the community itself. It is as if rituals of transformation were indeed making time rather than merely buying or renewing it.

In rituals of transformation, the individual temporarily experiences a self that transcends the social order. While the society does accomplish a victory over time, for the individual there is only a hint of such transcendence. After all the individual simply goes from one web of obligation to another: from childhood to adulthood, from the single estate to the married, from the company of the living to the society of the dead. Even in their new positions individuals are still members of the same society and share its history. It is only a new chapter in the life of the individual and of his or her immediate family and community that is being written in these rituals of transformation. The book, as it were, remains the same. Nonetheless, a new time period has opened up, and it begins with the day that someone died to their old life and began a new one as adult, as spouse or as ancestor.

Nonetheless, these rituals of transformation do open up the possibility that individuals will experience their own being apart from the social order. It is not only a new identity that has opened up through wider circles of interaction, as in the case of pilgrimage. For a moment of transition the soul hangs in the balance between an old status, now gone for ever, and a new one not yet acquired. In this hiatus, of course, passions may come to the surface and a new identity be acquired, both for the young initiate and for the bride or bridegroom. In these moments, however, the individual hangs very briefly in a sort of limbo and there gets a fleeting glimpse, as it were, of his or her own soul.

Certainly when fascist youth were initiated into their movement and took part in the parades and songs of a new and more virile generation, there was no going back to a despised regime and way of life. They had stared into the face of death, as it were, and been transformed by that encounter into individuals who now transcended death. Time would not run out on them or on the nation that honoured their sacrifice and their prowess.

However, in a society that lacks integration and strong

boundaries, the ordinary rituals of a society will fail to work their magic on a new generation. At such times that generation may then create its own rituals of transformation. Sternhell makes it very clear that in the Europe of the 1930s the standard means for transforming youths into adults were not working:

> Everywhere in Europe one found the same thing: fascism was an affair not of veterans but of a younger generation that rose up against the established order – against society generally, but also against the family, against school, against sexual restrictions, against a way of life whose constraints that generation rejected.[19]

Rituals of Aversion

Here we continue to consider rituals that are performed in social contexts that require tight co-ordination between the psyche and the way individuals interact with one another: co-ordination that will implement and perpetuate the structure of the organization itself. More specifically, however, we focus on the type of social context suggested by cell 2 in our diagram (Figure 1); there the boundaries of the social system are threatened with real disruption either from outside or from within. The primary case in point will be an army on the threshold of battle in the physical presence of its foes. There is no safe or protective distance between the two armies; indeed they are within reach of each other's weapons. Therefore the army itself is threatened with disruption from within the ranks either from panic or from the indiscriminate release of aggression. Under these conditions, as I will shortly point out, the army may perform a ritual the purpose of which clearly is to avert the threat posed by internal as well as by external dangers.

Violence destroys the tight integration of psyche with social interaction, and of interaction with the structure of social organization itself. Kertzer notes, for instance, that

> Certainly one of the most striking, and yet most common, aspects of human warfare is that people must wear the symbolic markings of their side so that all participants know

> whom to kill and whom to protect. These symbols of bodily adornment are supplemented by a panoply of other symbols and associated rites that serve to demarcate which side the combatants are on and to provide them with a rationale for killing.[20]

Even with these markings, however, it is possible for panic and terror to result in indiscriminate killing, as soldiers begin to swing wildly and kill anything in sight. It is to avert this danger of a holocaust, I would argue, that rituals of aversion impose their discipline on the passions.

Take, for example, an ancient Greek military ritual, in which a sacrifice is performed just prior to battle. One purpose of the ritual is to ensure that even in the heat of battle the soldiers remember their place in the ranks, distinguish between friend and enemy, and keep their passions under control. If the ritual fails to ensure that the formations will be kept in order, some individuals may flee while others start swinging wildly and killing their friends as well as their foes. To prevent such a fatal outcome is the purpose of the sacrifice performed just before battle. That is why I will call rituals of this sort 'aversive' rituals. Their primary function is to preserve the unity between personal experience, interaction and the social order: to keep people in formation even when their deepest passions are engaged.

Here is Vernant's description of the sacrifice of a goat performed at this terrible moment:

> Both the circumstances and the procedure of this preliminary sacrifice underscore its specificity. It is performed in front of the troops, at a definite time that both Xenophon and Plutarch mention explicitly and that is confirmed by all the sources we have. It takes place not at a predetermined time of day, but 'when the enemy is already in sight' and the two armies, in battle order, face each other before launching the attack. This is a critical moment in a situation that is liminal in every respect. The battle is readied, on the point of beginning; the wait, before the charge is sounded, is for the sacrifice to Artemis to yield favorable omens. The sacrificer – the

> Spartan king, the Athenian polemarch, sometimes assisted by a seer and sometimes replaced by him – usually performs the ritual in front of the troops, in the border area, the no-man's land separating the two armies. The psychological tension is at its highest at this moment when everything is poised on the brink to shift from the orderly and harmonious formation of the phalanx to the bloody confusion of the fighting, from the safety of standing shoulder to shoulder with one's mates to the danger of encounter with the enemy, from life to death. Everyone is torn between hope and terror. Though no longer in the tranquil world of peace, the men have not yet entered the terrible realm of combat. Everything depends on Artemis. The goat that is slaughtered in her honor decides and releases the attack. The goddess must approve and almost guarantee that, as battle is engaged, the good order of the hoplites in their ranks does not transgress a boundary and plunge into the savagery either of massacre or of rout. Located at the margins of the savage and the civilized, Artemis presides over the crucial moment, as the young men begin an action that might blur the distinction between the two worlds. In order to make the move without jeopardizing this necessary distinction, it is essential to define the limits of each world, and to accentuate the distance between them more strongly than ever so as to keep them separate – all this at the very moment, whether it be in warfare or in hunting, that the danger of confusing the two is greatest.[21]

In this paragraph Vernant has made a contribution to a current debate over the origins of ritual and has introduced Victor Turner's quite suggestive notion of liminality. It is not that ritual has its origin in the hunt or in warfare alone; it is that these moments are 'liminal' in every sense of the word. They are critical moments in which boundaries are likely to be crossed with fateful and perhaps fatal consequences for society and the individual.

Death, mass hysteria, the abandonment of the ordinary means of caring for the self and the community: all these can occur when potent images are enough to undermine an entire community's confidence in its own presence in the world.

The brink of war is thus a time in which the soul may be lost because the conventions and constraints that normally protect it are likely to be breached. In war the troops can either be captivated and overwhelmed by what they take to be the superior and controlling presence of the enemy, or they can lose their self-control under the impact of extraordinary and murderous passions. What they need is a 'controlling presence', to use De Martino's term for the soul and its surrogates: a shaman or an Artemis. The edge of battle is a critical moment of testing for earlier transformations. It is also a critical moment in which individuals may forget their place, get out of line, pull rank, fail to follow orders and keep discipline, or otherwise ignore and destroy the integration of the social order:

> At the meeting point of the two sides, at the critical moment in a liminal situation, the *sphage* [long e; = sacrificial omens – RKF] permits or forbids attack on the enemy, and so it involves the boundaries between peace and conflict, life and death, the splendor of youthful manhood and the blood-soaked corpse. The sacrifice also marks the limit between civilized order, where every soldier has a place and an assigned task to fulfill, and the realm of chaos, given over to pure violence, as among wild animals who know neither law nor justice . . .[22]

So long as interaction is confined within the net of the social order, I will argue, enormous pressures are placed on the innermost self of the individual. These are pressures for conformity and control: for control of the passions and for conformity to the formal and informal expectations of the society in question, even in the face of death. That combination of selfhood and passion which comprises the military soul is thus forged under very strenuous conditions and must be counted upon to hold up even in the face of death.

The sight of the enemy, then, is like a recognition of one's self: an emissary of death heralding one's own death and destruction. To confront the opposing army was therefore like staring into the face of the angel of death, hoping against hope that it would pass over one's own head and destroy another. Under these conditions the Greeks also offered sacrifice: '... a goat, whose ambiguous place at the edge of domestication consecrates it particularly to Artemis; its blood, spilled during the actual sacrifice, does more than the blood of other victims to evoke that of the warriors who will lose their lives on the battlefield'.[23] Indeed,

> The goat sacrificed to her shares with her an ambiguous, pivotal position. The goat symbolizes beforehand the human blood that the brutality of battle will cause to be shed, and at the same time diverts the threat onto the enemy; the goat sacrifice also protects the army, now in battle array, from the danger of falling into either the confusion of panic or the horror of a murderous frenzy.[24]

In panic the soul is lost because it has been seized by the power of an overwhelming presence. In frenzy, the soul is lost because it has been destroyed, as it were, from within by the power of uncontrollable passions.

Thus a ritual seeking to buy time by averting disaster also succeeds in intensifying the experience and significance of time. First, the moment prior to battle is filled with the added significance and meaning of a search for omens. Second, the very pace and duration of the time immediately prior to battle is interrupted by the ritual. There follows a delay that becomes a period of intense waiting. Third, the sequence of what normally comes first and second, before and after, is reversed; the soldiers find themselves being attacked while they await the omens, and they must hasten all the more, when the signal is given, to regain the initiative. Through this heightened period of waiting, and through the reversal of normal sequences, ritual intensifies the individual's experience of time in the presence of a powerful enemy despite the pressure of nearly uncontrollable passions. (The parallels with the Passover are more than formal. Both call for the sacrifice of an animal before a venture in which it would indeed be possible for the soul to be lost in either frenzy or panic.)

It is therefore not surprising that some of the earliest images of the soul are those of the warrior. The hero in battle has a fearsome eye, and his armour shines so brightly that the enemy is weakened at the very sight. If the warrior's soul weakens or leaves him, however, he becomes an easy prey even for the weakest foe. The first signs of the soul, then, afford the glimpse of a source of strength and energy that can also be fleeting and ephemeral: a phantasm or shade.

When rituals fail to avert chaos and death, religious movements may seek to enable individuals to strengthen their own souls, to face unbearable prospects, to confront overwhelming and controlling presences, or to control disruptive passions. However, such movements may well disturb social priorities, ranks and status hierarchies precisely in order to enable individuals to preserve and strengthen their souls. The possibilities, as we shall see in later chapters, are several and fairly complex.

Rituals of Purification

In this part of our discussion we will be focusing on social contexts in which the psyche begins to be liberated from various social pressures. These pressures in turn are somewhat lessened, in the contexts about to be considered, because social interaction no longer is a way of expressing and testing the authority of a particular form of social organization such as the traditional village or the army. The more interaction escapes the net of the social order, I will argue, the more difficult it will be for a society to hold death at bay. Young men will escape the confines of the village and the clan, marry women from other clans or peoples and threaten the integration of the social order itself. As outsiders come in, they will bring disruptive habits, viewpoints, sexuality, germs and genes into the community. Patients will discover other sources of healing; students will find foreign sources of learning and unorthodox wisdom; members of the household will find alternative sources of support and competing objects of affection; citizens will find alien loyalties. All of these possibilities represent the potential death of the social system in question.

Under these conditions (Figures 1 and 2; cell 3) some social systems seek to achieve higher levels of integration. Efforts are focused on the formation of social character to bring it into conformity with habits of deference and with the requirements of civility in social interaction. Other efforts are focused on the ways that individuals interact, in order to bring behaviour into conformity with the requirements of such social organizations as the school and the church, the corporation and the army. What Nikolas Rose calls administrative and technical strategies for 'Governing the Soul' replace conventional techniques for ensuring conformity and compliance, a point to which I will shortly return.[25] To prevent a wider range of social interaction and of personal experience from threatening the larger society's institutions, a social order may become increasingly vigilant about maintaining or revising its rituals of transformation. In this way it can ensure that contact with outsiders, for instance, does not threaten marriage and the family or the orderly succession of the generations; in the same way the right to be numbered among the ancestors may be increasingly restricted to the native-born, in order to offset the increasing number of immigrants in the society.

If people can associate more or less freely outside the confines of the social system, even though the boundaries of the social system itself are relatively intact, then the whole social order will become dangerously polluted by outside influences. Although there may be strong formal boundaries separating the society in question from its neighbours, the informal contact among peoples may prove threatening, if not actually subversive. Deviant ideas and ways of acting, foreign allegiances and strange passions, threaten to undo the social order from within. Indeed, it will be difficult to distinguish influences that are internal from those that are external in origin. Under these conditions it is too late to engage in aversive rituals; the camel's nose, as it were, is already under the tent. When danger is immanent, more potent liturgical medicine is required. That additional potency, I will argue, comes from rituals of purification.

This additional class of rituals will flirt with danger or impurity only to dramatize the fact that in the end the social order will have been cleansed of the sources of impurity and disorder. Individuals interact with others in ways that threaten the integration of the social order, only to see cohesion restored. During such a rite, women, for instance, may be singled out to perform a polluting task, such as handling corpses, but at the end of the rite the women themselves will have been purified from such contact and restored to their customary place in the social order.

Just as the way people interact with each other is at first disrupted, only to be restored to normal constraints, so the psyche, after a flurry of liberation, is restored to a comfortable harmony with social convention. Dangerous passions may be acted out in a dance with warlike gestures or erotic movements, at the end of which the participants return not only to their customary interactions but to their accustomed places in the community. *In this cleansing the time of pollution is separated from the present by creating the past.* In the announcement that the old season or year has been finished, a new one, the present, is allowed to begin. What was once the future becomes the present. In this way rituals of purification make time by renewing it.

There may or may not be a scapegoat in such ceremonies; sometimes an animal, at other times a person, is singled out to represent the source of pollution. Such a victim is then disposed of with more or less ceremony. Scapegoating, however, is only one way of purifying a system of pollution; dramatic enactments of dangerous interactions with outside forces or potentially uncontrollable passions are another. The point is to rid a community of alien and thus dangerous sources of pollution by ensuring that interactions reinforce rather than undermine the social order itself. Rituals of purification thus renew the times in the face of dangers that are immanent, whereas aversive rituals buy time for facing imminent perils to the integrity of the social order.

When interactions escape the net of the social order, of course, personal experience takes on new dimensions. Individuals find themselves harbouring dangerous ideas, entertaining strange possibilities, feeling unheard-of stirrings in their souls, and encountering threats to their identity. At some point in the gradual splitting of relationships from the social order, it will dawn on individuals that they themselves may be outside the customary web of duties. When interaction, so to speak, develops a certain degree of freedom from the social order, individuals will find that they can imagine themselves in another context.

In difficult times, members of a society may experience themselves as surviving outside the social order and even, in many cases, outside the web of ordinary social interaction. It is not accidental that, in American society, groups of survivalists have taken measures to outlive a nuclear war or the collapse of the natural environment, while many individuals also have experimented with forms of religious experience that require withdrawal and isolation, such as meditation, spiritual journeying, channelling, and other forms of esoteric practice.

In antiquity it was the shaman who normally encountered the wild or uninhabited areas outside settled communities, but shamans were often joined by individuals seeking escape from the dangers immanent within their communities. Prior to the civil war of 66–73 CE in Jerusalem, I have noted, the streets were filled with assassins who were indistinguishable from the crowd of pilgrims. Not only was the social order at risk through the disruption of rituals, but social interaction was filled with perils to the individual pilgrim. It is not surprising, I will argue, that many individuals took to the desert or sought the company of shamans outside the ordinary range of social interaction. There they gained an experience of the self that was not wholly confined to the social order or contingent upon routine social interaction. At these moments, individuals achieve a momentary transcendence over social life.

Rituals of purification, therefore, may include certain periods of time in which individuals are nominally free to enter into close contacts with aliens and strangers, as well as free to explore emotional experiences in a greater range and depth than is normally required or permitted. For instance, pilgrimages may well become occasions on which a wider range of social interaction begins to enrich personal experience in ways that disturb a social order.[26] Individuals on pilgrimage step out of their normal obligations to the household or to the community and expand their network of acquaintances to include individuals from other communities and countries. Indeed, on pilgrimages individuals may well come to see themselves in a new light, think of themselves as sharing an identity with others who hitherto had been alien, and find it difficult to re-enter the ordinary web of work and duty.

No doubt that is why pilgrimages ended at cultic centres

where purificatory rites dramatized the relationship between one's place in the community: between one's rights or duties and the prescribed range of social interaction. For instance, in Jerusalem of the first century Gentiles found their place at the Temple in a particular courtyard, and there was space reserved also for women, men, Levites, and priests, while the altars were washed in the purifying blood of thousands of lambs. Thus the community gained a new lease on life and started again the annual cycle of purity, pollution, and repurification.

Rituals of Restoration

A society is in some difficulty, of course, when individuals are relatively free to engage in relationships with whomever they please and to explore alien sources of inspiration and authority for the enhancement of their souls. Under these conditions it is difficult to fit social character into conventional relationships and to make those relationships perform in the way required in work or politics. A society is in even greater difficulty, however, not only when its integration is threatened but when its boundaries also become weak and permeable. Then it is difficult to keep people, ideas and money at home, and subversive influences, foreign capital and values, and hostile armies beyond the borders. Under these conditions of weak boundaries and minimal integration, a society is indeed running out of time (Figures 1 and 2; cell 4).

When a society faces a threat to its very existence, rituals of restoration are used to bring back the potency and harmonies of an idealized time of origins. The Ghost Dance of the Sioux is representative of many such rituals that restore ancestral potencies to a colonized people whose survival is at stake in the face of a prepossessing, alien and superior power. What is being restored is a time that was lost; what is being created, however, is a new dispensation, a new epoch or era, to replace the old one that is passing away.

Rituals of restoration are thus a dynamic and extreme reaction to the possibility that the society itself faces imminent extinction. By restoring a period that is immune to the mere passage of time, rituals of restoration in effect inaugurate a new era in which it is the world outside the social order that is running out of time. Such a restoration was imagined in the *Sybilline Oracles*: prophecies that had widespread popular currency second, if at all, only to the Book of Revelation. As Norman Cohn notes, the figure of an eschatological emperor was central to these oracles and was prominent in popular expectation at various periods in Western history.[27] Such expectation was heightened by rituals of inauguration which promised the restoration of an ancient kingdom. For instance, the coronation of Charlemagne in 800 CE may well have marked the beginning of the expectation that an Emperor, the Last Emperor, would restore Jerusalem and the East to the hegemony of the West. Norman Cohn goes on to remark that, when Charlemagne was crowned Emperor of the Romans, not only was the old Roman Empire symbolically restored, but that 'Thenceforth it was possible for the Emperor of the Last Days to be imagined as a Western monarch and it remained so even though Charlemagne left no territorial empire behind him.'[28]

Certainly the symbolic restoration of the Roman Empire in Charlemagne's coronation set the stage for other restorations and especially for the recovery of Jerusalem itself. According to Cohn mediaeval folklore surrounding Charlemagne eventually came to see him as the first crusader still alive in some mountain fastness.[29] The return of Charlemagne, the recovery of the royal road to Jerusalem, and the restoration of the holy city to the West, all would occur in the beginning of the end times. Indeed, Christianity would triumph in Jerusalem as had once the Roman Emperor himself.[30] In the crusades, expectations aroused by rituals of inauguration escaped the liturgical framework and animated thousands of peasants, whose armies recognized no boundaries and conformed to few social constraints.

Note that when the beginning of the end times was believed to be at hand, the crusading armies of vagabonds and the poor turned to exterminating not only Muslims but Jews. I would suggest that, once Christians harboured the same dreams of restoration as the Jews, there would not be enough room in the cosmic drama of the end for both to survive. What had sustained Jews had been in fact their anticipation of being restored in the end to full possession of Jerusalem.[31] Only one people could possess the holy city, the mother of the people of God; all brothers with a claim to access to that maternal city would have to be eliminated. One foundation for the fascists' extermination of Jews in Europe thus occurred when Christians, believing themselves the true people of God, seriously undertook to restore Jerusalem to their own possession. When time begins to run out on a social order, social space comes at a terrible premium. As Cohn makes very clear, the 'premium' was 'human sacrifice'.[32]

Rituals of restoration perform the tasks of purification and transformation by reviving a past in which both the young and the old were made potent by their dreams and visions rather than endangered by them: a time when the living and the dead could be members of the same society without dishonouring or disturbing one another; a time when women could be relied on to preserve patrilineage, and the desires of the young were satisfied with what the society itself had to offer. Once restored, such a society can have social intercourse with strangers without being consumed by desire from within, and it can go into battle knowing that every blow will be directed outward against the enemy.

Finally, rituals of restoration may fail to bring back ancient heroes, periods of national supremacy, and the purity of a chosen and pious people. In *The Pursuit of the Millenium*, Cohn recounts the development of revolutionary tracts in northern Europe during the centuries immediately preceding the Reformation: tracts in which the restoration of the ancient German kingdom under Frederick would not only be restored but would initiate a millennial *Reich*. In this restoration, the world itself would be transformed. One such tract, the *Book of a Hundred Chapters*, although itself never printed, captures the themes that were widespread both in folklore and in prophecy in the fifteenth and sixteenth centuries. It is a *Mein Kampf* written by an anonymous revolutionary; notes Cohn:

> In these phantasies the crude nationalism of a half-educated intellectual erupted into the tradition of popular eschatology. The result is almost uncannily similar to the phantasies which were the core of National-Socialist 'ideology.' . . . There is the

same belief in a primitive German culture in which the divine will was once realized and which throughout history has been the source of all good – which was later undermined by a conspiracy of capitalists, inferior, non-Germanic peoples and the Church of Rome – and which must now be restored by a new aristocracy, of humble birth but truly German in soul, under a God-sent saviour who is at once a political leader and a new Christ. It is all there – and so were the offensives in West and East – the terror wielded both as an instrument of policy and for its own sake – the biggest massacres in history – in fact everything except the final consummation of the world-empire which, in Hitler's words, was to last a thousand years.[33]

The Limits of Ritual

While ritual may manufacture the sacred, rituals have no monopoly on charisma. Indeed, through charisma individuals claim their own sources of authority and inspiration. Take, for example, the once and future Emperor, Frederick II, himself a charismatic figure, who personified how rituals can fail because of their own successes. It was Frederick II who not only recaptured Jerusalem but criticized and defied the Church and the Papacy: so much so that he was not only 'excommunicated as a heretic, perjurer and blasphemer' but also was the reason why the Pope placed Germany under an interdict. During an interdict, Cohn reminds us, not only is the administration of sacraments forbidden, but the entire people faces inevitable damnation should they die before the ban is lifted.[34] Frederick's defiance of the Church not only heightened his charismatic appeal; it stimulated the appearance of other charismatic leaders who claimed to be able, for instance, to absolve sins.

Thus charisma defends the individual and in this case the people from the potency of a rite of interdiction. It was in this tension between the hereditary charisma of the ecclesiastical or political centre and the charisma of heroes from the periphery that a wide range of popular movements developed: movements that galvanized class and ethnic hatred, regional ambitions and national identity. When rituals fail to bring the day of promised purification, it is up to charismatic heroes to guarantee the expulsion and massacre of the people's enemies and to ensure the transformation of the young, the unmarried and the dying.

Claims to charismatic endowment, however, entitle the individual to cross the usual boundaries placed by the social order on the affections and the loyalties of the individual. Of the many reasons why individuals may interact in ways that transcend these limits, claims to charisma rank relatively high. The gifted touch whom they please: never mind prohibitions on avoiding polluting contact with menstrual women, lepers and the dead. The charismatically endowed may also love whom they please, regardless of the customary prohibitions on the range or object of the affections. Distinctions of class or gender, race or generation matter little to those who, endowed with extraordinary grace, consider themselves entitled to more than ordinary satisfactions. Charismatics typically expand the range of interaction and the limits of their personal experience; their followers may enjoy expanded freedom, but still in lesser degrees than the charismatic leaders.

Rituals seek to contain the genie of charisma in the liturgical bottle. They are dramas in which customary limits on interaction and personal experience may be stretched but yet finally honoured. An unsavoury human is touched, dressed in fine garments, chastised and pushed over a cliff, and the city returns again to its precincts purified of the polluting effects of age, disease, unbridled sexuality and unwanted sources of personal inspiration and authority. Warriors fight their own battles and find their own booty, just as shamans have their own visions and see their own omens rather than the ones vouchsafed through ritual. While the ritual order seeks to set limits on the range of free association, shamans seek out whomever they wish. Their range of personal experience also vastly expands their range of interaction. Shamans see people who are miles away; in turn shamans are thought to be able to be in two places at one time. Clearly the shaman breaks the frame not only of social interaction but of personal experience.

In the tension between charisma and liturgy individuals expand the limits of their own self-awareness. The followers of these charismatic leaders are therefore capable of enlarging their range of free association and personal experience. Even the followers can be numbered among those who, chosen or favoured by the gods, do not honour customary limits on their affections and loyalties. Charisma is the antithesis of ritualized attempts to preserve the cohesion of a system and to shore up its boundaries.

Every generation, for instance, numbers at least a few individuals whose claimed endowments appear to exempt them from the rituals of transformation. These charismatics are tested by unseen spirits rather than through the prescribed trials of the spirit and the flesh. Perhaps they refuse the honours of the initiate in order to be tested in the wild or in the desert like the shaman and the seer. Perhaps they refuse the transformation of marriage and seek initiation into the company of the celibate; thus they refuse to participate in the rituals by which the larger society regenerates itself. They have other priorities of their own and thus fail to give honour to those held in the highest esteem by the family, the community or the larger society. Those who have gone before, and those who sit in the preferred seats at civic ceremonies, are not the ones to whom these especially endowed individuals give the highest honour.

Charismatics' social character escapes the net of any observable social interaction. The recipient of the divine gift of grace is in conversation with unseen sources of personal inspiration and authority that cannot be contained in any network of social interaction; on the contrary, the charismatically endowed create their own relationships, set new limits on their associations, and prescribe new rights and duties for themselves and their followers. Not for them are the usual rituals of transformation, in which individuals are rigorously tested to see whether they will adjust their priorities to the ranks of social honour. The charismatics prefer the dramas of the soul to test their claim to priorities that transcend those of the social order.

It would be simplistic, however, to suggest that the expanding self-awareness of the individual is not at risk in the tension between liberating, charismatic experience and captivating rituals that impress the social order on the psyche. On the contrary, it is well to remember that there is something enthralling about magic, and individuals lose the sense of their own being in the presence of powerful personages. Magic is indeed a source of help to the self that is otherwise subjugated to social controls and overwhelmed by social pressures, but magic also tends to perpetuate the helplessness of the self and to keep it in bondage to its own sources of authority. With every liberation from previous slavery come new commandments, as it were, to keep the emerging sense of self under fresh control. Charismatic experience nonetheless endows the individual with new priorities and claims to recognition, expands the individual's range of personal experience and association, and offers private means of foreseeing and forestalling imminent dangers.

Individuals endowed with charismatic gifts thus enjoy a heightened sense of their own priority in the social order and in the cosmos. In the same way charismatic leaders may refuse to honour the priorities of the social order and reject the rituals of transformation by which the young become elders and the single are married. At various times Christian celibates have represented not only an alternative lifestyle, as it might be considered in modernity, but the announcement of the beginning of the end of the social order based on the patriarchal household. They may consider themselves perhaps to have been transformed by suffering; they are now entitled not only to spiritual rewards but to places of honour and to satisfactions that previously had been prohibited. The charismatic is impatient with rituals of transformation that eventually permit children to sit with adults and enjoy adult rewards; the charismatic may not wish to wait for ritualized admission to a higher status in the household, to the pleasures of the marital bed, or to the higher bliss enjoyed by the departed. Religious movements reflect and mediate the tension between the society's ritualized techniques for orderly transformations of the individual, and charismatic claims to authority, rapture and everlasting life. The claims of members of the early Jesus movement to be destined for positions of authority in a new Israel would be a case in point, especially if they had been transformed not through circumcision but through the gift of the Spirit.

Those who do not wish to wait for access to pleasure and authority no doubt wish time itself to speed up; conversely, those who claim extraordinary entitlements by virtue of having received special graces have additional reason to intensify the meaning and passage of time. Claims to spiritual priority require a high level of commitment to being the first, as it were, to enter the future. One cannot lag behind in the spiritual race, to use one of Paul's metaphors. One must be ahead of one's brethren in giving evidence of zeal and virtue; otherwise one's claims to priority will no longer be self-evident. This intensification of time means that there is not a moment to waste. It is not sufficient merely to fend off a dreadful day of judgement or to seize the moment; one must move forward at all times, and therefore in all places, to give evidence that one is indeed the bearer of charismatic gifts.

The intensification of time by the charismatic is countered by the larger society's capacity to manufacture sacred time. As individuals continue to seek release, recognition and enhancement from their own sources of authority and inspiration, the social order continues to set new limits on their aspirations and on their association with others by proclaiming days and weeks of solemn obligation. Individuals may receive assurances of their own purity from charismatic sources, but entrenched interests, such as the clergy, will continue to try to regulate the opportunities for purification through their own calendar of salvation: not on any day, and not on the day of the individual's own choosing, but on days of holy obligation. If time is to be renewed, it will be under the auspices of the priests or the chiefs rather than of the shaman or seer. Certainly the early Jesus movement exhibited tension between those who felt that the life of the soul depended on freedom from ordinary obligations, on the one hand, and those on the other who argued that the life of the spirit could be enhanced within the limits of domesticity.

· 2 ·

RITUALS OF TRANSFORMATION: GUARANTEEING THE FUTURE

The individual's desire for personal transformation and freedom is thus a fundamental threat to any social system. At least, this has been an axiom of sociologists since Comte first proclaimed himself able to fulfil the ancient functions of the clergy in a world that no longer believed in a Christian god. Those functions, he wrote, were to overcome the 'individualism' and 'self-centredness' of moderns all too absorbed in their 'private interest' and far too little concerned with 'public morality' and 'the social point of view'.[1] His was a now familiar harangue against 'habits of the heart' that distract individuals from the public good into a world in which they are the sources of their own inspiration. The possibility that individuals would at last find their own souls and live life on their own terms is the spectre that has been haunting sociology from its origins in conservative European sociology.

Too much a modern individual himself to believe in a god that could be worshipped according to traditional Christian formulae, Comte was also too much an élitist to wish to see individuals think for themselves and become their own sources of inspiration. Were they to do so, he feared, the authority of the larger society itself would come into question. Failing the military-feudal god who could trample one's enemies underfoot, and failing the abstract god of the deists, whose absence was beginning to be noted, what moral order could persuade the average individual to make the necessary sacrifices to sustain the larger society's institutions and to distribute its benefits? The only way to transform human desires, notably the sexual, into social duty was through the labyrinths of sacrifice. That much was certain, at least for those who subscribed to the notion that society and the community take ontological and moral precedence over the individual. Such a notion was a widely shared assumption in Western European social thought. It is also the core assumption underlying fascist ideology.

In the name of what god would modernity offer its sacrifices? Who would be the victims? Certainly Comte did not predict the rise of fundamentalism; just the opposite would have been expected as individuals learned to take responsibility for themselves and their social institutions. Nonetheless, I would argue that certain aspects of modern fundamentalism perform useful functions within a secular society, i.e. the inculcation of helplessness and of a fatalistic willingness to be sacrificed. One thinks not only of the fatalism of those who believe that the world is headed for an unavoidable disaster, nuclear or otherwise, but of those who long for a day in which they, too, will be caught up in a day of Rapture.

Modern societies are host to a wide range of expectations of transformation. As Strozier noted, the more well-to-do fundamentalists looked forward to a day of transformation in later generations: perhaps during their grandchildren's lifetimes.[2] The poorer fundamentalists did not want to wait for so long: 'The poor and disenfranchised ... whose lives approximated the suffering of early Christians, yearned for the transformation and renewal so basic to apocalyptic theory.'[3]

August Comte, the nineteenth-century philosopher credited with being the first sociologist, however, also counted on a vast and universal 'Sympathy' that would enable humanity to adore itself, become its own providence, and limit its own destructive tendencies.[4] The transformation of humanity was to occur through its own political imagination. That was before the destruction of the Warsaw ghetto.

Others, too, hope for transformation in the here and now. According to Paul Boyer, for instance, as Pat Robertson sought to soften his apocalyptic notions and fashion himself as a credible candidate for the presidency, he adopted 'a breathtakingly optimistic postmillennialism' in which individuals could be transformed into the likeness of Adam and Eve in the present and 'enjoy the millennium here and now'.[5] In either case, however, premillennial fatalism or postmillennial optimism locate the source of moral authority and of political initiative outside the individual in a divine realm whose advent or gift can only be hoped or prayed for in a posture of devout anticipation.

There is indeed a peculiar congruence between Comte's notions about modernity and the current wave of fundamentalist enthusiasm for the end of time. Comte believed that one could not sacrifice for a collectivity alone; something higher than one's own society would be necessary to elicit enthusiasm for sacrifice: some 'Great Being'.[6] Emile Durkheim, the French sociologist (1858–1917), notes Preus, was also concerned that 'society' continue to be able to produce citizens willing to undergo 'privation and sacrifice' and to submit to a discipline that was 'contrary to our most fundamental inclinations and instincts'.[7] How else could modern societies ever reproduce themselves from one generation to the next? The problem was just that: to ensure that society could endure despite the tendency of the self to demand recognition and satisfaction in this life, as well as the next. Nothing less than the continuity of Western social order was at stake. There could be no help offered by individuals or their instincts; on the contrary, the individual – for Durkheim – was both the creature and also the potential enemy of social order. How, then, could individuals be induced to live lives that run counter to their innermost inclinations?

The answer to that question, for Durkheim, was in the derivative sort of divinity that individuals acquire when they come together in more or less solemn assemblies. In crowds, in revivals, in the gatherings of the clan, Durkheim would expect to find individuals transformed and transfigured. It was in these settings of 'collective effervescence' that individuals would discover their connectedness with others; they would become new beings, with a collective sense of the possibilities lying before them and an equally collective sense of their new-found dignity. In opening up new worlds, old ways of life would seem to be dead, obscene, beneath contempt. The sacred would become the realm in which a new, corporate sense of identity would be defined; the profane thus would be the world left behind.

For Durkheim it was the individual, alone, unreconstructed, deluded about his or her place in the world, that was the source of profanity and danger. In the collective occasions of the group or the community the lone individual would be challenged to rise to new duties. There alone true charisma – grace – was to be found; only when many were gathered together in the name of some deity or other – some totem – would the individual receive a new and imperishable dignity. The fascist potential in Durkheimian thought and ideology is evident.

What concerns me here is the proclivity to sacrifice that these collective occasions induce or intensify in the individual. Not yet fascism in the modern sense of the term, as a developed political system or ideology, still the demand for sacrifice and transformation represents a fascist prototype: a set of rules and rewards, of promises and challenges, that a society lays out before individuals who are willing to be thus constrained in the search for their souls. At the heart of this sacrificial complex is the promise of an extraordinary transformation, which lifts the individual above the ordinary: a transformation not unlike the ecstasy that individuals sometimes feel when carried away by the enthusiasm, say, of fans in a stadium or devotees in a revival. What is required of the enthusiast is nothing short of a total commitment; what is promised is never fully specified and remains exalted, elusive, and as transcendent and ephemeral as the feeling of elation in certain assemblages. Later the crowd will disperse into small units, organized around more distant goals, and these groups will also have to co-ordinate their activities with others over time around more proximate ends; then enthusiasm will be replaced by the far less ecstatic, more routine and continuous activity of the professional and the bureaucrat.

This is what Max Weber, the German sociologist and Durkheim's contemporary, had in mind with regard to the rationalization of charisma. Grace or charisma becomes 'rationalized' when the individual's expenditure of an extraordinary spiritual endowment stretches over long periods of time. The professional, for instance, often performs in a solitary fashion without the more visible collective supports of the group itself. Something like professionalization shapes the conscience of the individual endowed with collective charisma who is later required to make many small sacrifices through the continuous exertion of carefully calculated and controlled activity. That is the 'fate' of charisma, Weber reminded us: to be dissipated and finally dissolved through many activities over the arduous and long haul. What for Weber was the 'fate' of charisma was, for Durkheim, a consummation. How could Western societies survive unless these collective passions were not spent but channelled into the disciplined sorts of duty and action that require 'privation and sacrifice'?[8]

Society, for Durkheim, becomes indeed the fundamental cause. It is 'society' which supplies the necessary, if not wholly sufficient, basis for individual self-realization. The collectivity simply shapes the form of the individual's unconscious desires until they seem to require a fulfilment that embraces the individual's entire social universe. Through ritual the individual's new-found being becomes apparently inseparable from the corporate life of the group or community itself. For Durkheim, however, 'seems' is not the right word; individuality 'is' nothing more or less than a case of the collective consciousness. Societal rites transform the raw material of human nature into authentic individuality. The realization of selfhood is a mere secular unfolding of collective ecstasies, from which the individual returns transfigured by the passage from the natural into the social order. That is, society for Durkheim requires high levels of integration, so that the psyche conforms to the conventions of social interaction, which in turn reflect the priorities and prerequisites of social organization.

The fascist overtones of Durkheim's thought are implicit, yet evident. The question facing Durkheim and fascist thought is how individuals are to be persuaded to make sacrifices, to undergo privation, all for the sake of a society that requires high levels of integration. What is required, of course, is a transformed humanity. The solution is quite simply to harness the individual's unconscious drives: the person's grandiose dreams, the energy, the hunger for association and respect, and the yearning for love and security. To harness those energies requires the transformation of the individual through collective ecstasies, through the rites of the whole community, and by the symbols of the society at large. The fascist commitment to asceticism, to sacrifice and to the acceptance of a life of disciplined striving requires totemism, even when the totem is the national flag or a heroic tomb at the nation's centre.

For Max Weber, individuals were transformed less through

collective ritual than through attributions of charisma. Charisma was a relationship between those, on the one hand, with claims to extraordinary graces, and those, on the other hand, who honoured such claims. Charismatic relationships were simply one way that some individuals could get others to do their bidding. When institutionalized at the centre of a society, therefore, charisma could be a potent and conservative force that could inspire an entire nation to heroic acts of self-sacrifice. Weber was entirely suspicious of what he called the 'aura' that surrounded the nation with hints of a greater glory and of a spiritual authority emanating from its (mythical) past.

This authoritarian development, he argued, is a result of the conservative forces inherent even in the most revolutionary forms of charisma. Even charismatic rebels on a mission to reverse the world order still claim heavenly sanctions and divine authorization for their missions. It is the popular belief in such claims, and in such heavenly authority, that in the end enables the successful charismatic movement to press its demands for sacrifice upon its adherents. The sacrificial demand, however, is present from the outset, since charismatic leaders require of their followers unstinting and unreserved devotion.

There is a tendency, then, for the sacrificial demands of the old order to be reproduced, however transformed, in the new. The Czar becomes a Stalin; Caesar becomes a new Lord, a Kyrios who demands nothing short of the sacrifice of an entire life. The charisma of the political centre becomes domesticated in the humblest household, where the local patriarch is a pale reflection of the distant king. The arms of the monarchy hang over the sanctuary, even when they are the arms of a rebel prince only lately become a king. The movement of revolutionaries in the hills of Cuba produces a new tyrant who silences all opinions but his own and pacifies or stupefies a people by depriving them of the rights to speak for themselves and to consider a future other than the one he has planned for them. The fascist potential is carried from one generation to the next in the demand for sacrifice. Leaders transformed by charisma require that their followers be transported from the mundane to the extraordinary by feats of devotion.

Conservative sociologists since Comte and Durkheim have

continued to ratify the fate of the individual psyche, i.e. its inherent tendency to seek subordination. American sociology, no less than the European, sought to locate the individual within the larger society rather than in a privileged realm of the individual's own discovery or making. In their landmark study of *American Sociology* Vidich and Lyman point out that Comte had his American admirers.[9] They too, like Comte himself, wanted to see the individual make sacrifices for the good of the emerging society. A Southern Presbyterian divine transplanted to California, Joseph Le Conte, prophesied that every advance in social organization from the local community of blood-relations to the nation itself is progressive because something of the individual is surrendered to the social system.[10] For a later admirer of both Comte and Le Conte, Josiah Royce, there could be no higher expression of individuality than 'loyalty to the community'.[11] Interestingly enough, these reflections on the vocation of the individual to sanctify the larger society with devotion and sacrifice were often – but not exclusively – reactions to the experience of California, where divergent peoples and classes brought not only conflict but the possibility of integrating the more parochial and limited forms of community into a larger whole.

The demand for sacrifice, however, was widespread in early American sociology; nowhere was it more deeply entrenched than at the University of Chicago under the leadership of Albion Small. As Vidich and Lyman point out:

> Small's basis for the new national consensus, a modern secular but covenanted community, required the *conversion* of America's materialistic individualism into altruistic ethical teamwork ... In this vision of society, the highest form of altruism was the subordination of self to society, *'the obligation to make one's self and all that one can be made as a factor in the functioning of the whole'*.[12]

While it would be something of an anachronism to suggest that these sociological advocates of individual sacrifice for the sake of the collectivity were fascist, nonetheless their thought, and to some extent their despair over the direction taken by American society, laid the groundwork for later, equally despairing, critiques of 'individualism' in American society. It is these more recent critiques which provide the sociological justification for campaigns of national revitalization and the restoration of traditional pieties and commitments.[13]

Finally, as Vidich and Lyman go on to demonstrate, it was also in California that these sociological teleologies were secularized, largely through the work of George Herbert Mead, who found that communication, the interaction of individuals with each other, and an open-ended series of social interactions were all that could be hoped for; farewell to notions of a *telos* that subsumed the fate of individuals in an all-embracing social order marked by moral seriousness, harmony, inclusiveness, and justice. There would henceforth be no more sociological guarantees that everything will come out all right in the end. Nonetheless, according to Vidich and Lyman, even Mead was intent on 'the integration of the individual into the covenant, in which the generalized other becomes the moral arbiter for the self'.[14] With such repeated stress on the need for the individual to sacrifice any individuality other than a selfhood that could be realized in service to the nation and the state, American sociology laid the groundwork for a profoundly conservative reaction to modernity and for calls for the transformation of the self for the sake of the revitalization of the society.

The irony of the sociological attack on individualism is not lost on Vidich and Lyman, who see in American societies a tendency to produce individuals who lack an inner core and who have become adept at play-acting:

> the individual presents the external signs of acquiescence to the standards of a given group, without necessarily having internalized those standards. Each of the relevant groups evaluate [sic] the performance and accepts skillful self-presentation as proof that the person does possess the qualities expected. The individual does not develop a unified self with a secure ego and a strong superego – rather, a person develops skills of personification.[15]

The appearance of commitment is thus scrutinized with an eye for flaws in the individual's performance, because the self can personify sacrifice even when the individual has not been transformed.

In several modern societies during the past two centuries there has been a series of what Rose calls 'moral panics' about children: panics regarding youths who do not respect their elders, who disregard property rights and engage in violence, and who do not make fit soldiers.[16] Every society with claims on the attention and allegiance of its citizens needs to distract individuals from the pursuit of their own personal salvation or pleasure and to turn that pursuit into socially constructive purposes. In societies that are regulated largely through rituals, one can observe the young, for instance, being transformed into adults who are willing, even eager, to take up the tasks of adulthood: to fight, resolve disputes, tell stories and raise children. In societies where rituals for the transformation of the young into adults have not been able to reach the entire population or have failed to make the necessary transformations, one can observe alternative means for ensuring the safe and effective succession of the generations.

In place of rituals such as confirmation or other rites of initiation, societies such as Britain and the United States of America have developed a panoply of quasi-governmental, professional agencies for ensuring the transformation of children and youths into adults fit for citizenship, work and the military. Social workers, doctors, psychologists, educators, scientists and lawyers all have taken a part in defining what is normal for children, in suggesting techniques for producing normality, and in isolating what is, by their expert standards, to be considered abnormal, pathological, and thus unsafe for the larger society. Certainly this extension of control through expertise has also served a variety of professions and of other entrenched interests. The state is particularly interested in ensuring a useful and compliant citizenry. Males have interests in perpetuating their hegemony over women and children, just as females have interests in preserving their prerogatives: not to mention a wide range of philanthropists and moral entrepreneurs with an interest in defining problems that their own services alone are meant to address. Thus has developed a wide range of what Rose aptly calls 'technologies for the government of the subjectivity of citizens'.[17]

Colonizing the Soul

Behind the drive to ensure the development of an individual who would be useful and compliant, of course, was a widespread fear that children would not turn into safe or adequate adults. Eugenicists, Rose reminds us, were keenly interested in those who seemed intractable: the mentally deficient, who were 'kith and kin of the prostitute, the tubercular, the insane, the unemployable, the vagrant, and the libertine'.[18] Rose goes on to point out that the cities were seen as centres of such degeneracy, and in the heart of all this darkness lay the family. There, in the incapacities and conflicts of adults, lay the seeds of defective children who could at best only reproduce their parents' sins. To prevent the transmission of fault from one generation to the next required the intervention of an array of social institutions, co-ordinated by the courts, which could bring expertise and social control to bear on those families whose failings were not beyond redemption. In this way the larger society could be assured of an orderly and perhaps even of a happy succession from one generation to the next. Official interest thus extended from the most dangerous or defective children to those who were merely troubled or whose development might be slowed and arrested by inadequate parenting:

> Abnormality had its roots in the interplay between the desires of the parents and the desires of their children, in the medium of love itself . . . A constant scrutiny of the emotional interchanges of family life was required, in the name of the mental hygiene of the individual and society. As the new psychology and the child guidance clinic produced a new means of representation of the psyche, the possibility opened up for the emotions and desires of all parents, not merely those of the socially troubling variety, to be inscribed within the field of social regulation.[19]

Note that these technologies, however, achieve something of the same authority over the inner self that might be expected from rituals. Some might insist that the use of various agencies to control the family and to regulate child-raising is not comparable to traditional forms of socializing the young. Nonetheless, the authority of professionals in defining what is normal in child-development and what is proper conduct by parents has had a profound effect on what individuals actually believe is right and on what they think they want to achieve or become:

> Parental conduct, motherhood, and child rearing can thus be regulated through family autonomy, through wishes and aspirations, and through the activation of individual guilt, personal anxiety, and private disappointment . . . Through the connections established between the norms of childhood and images of family life, parenting, and motherhood, the psyche of the child and the subjectivity of the mother have been opened up for regulation in a new way. It has become the will of the mother to govern her own children according to psychological norms and in partnership with psychological experts. *The soul of the young citizen has become the object of government through expertise.*[20]

In the succession of the generations, furthermore, time is of the essence. Timely intervention is required so that the child will not deviate from the range of what is considered normal for each stage of development. The succession of the generations, through the development of children, could be conceived 'along the dimension of time in a unified sequence'.[21] Guilt would be assigned to parents less for transgressions against some law than for failing to enable normal development to take place at the proper time or for burdening the young with the parents' own dissatisfactions in life.[22]

The problem, then, was both to break the negative tie linking the generations and to create an orderly sequence and succession between the generations. To break the negative bond is necessary, lest the failings of the parents be visited on their children over the generations. However, to cement the tie between the generations is also necessary if the society is to be able to resupply itself with citizens and to reproduce its institutions and values over the years. To encompass such a contradiction has been the function of rituals, which dramatize the coming of age of the young into adulthood in terms both of a radical break with the past and of a continuous line of descent from one generation to the next. Rose is convinced that a regime of courts, schools, agencies and experts has succeeded in producing in the hearts and minds of parents a desire to achieve the norms established in the clinic and the laboratory: a religion, so to speak, of normality.

> The wish to achieve the ideal was a source of pleasure when it was satisfied, but it was also the incentive to seek anxiously for guidance and assistance from family technicians when the register of the actual diverged too much from the register of the ideal. Love and pleasure, far from representing the spontaneous and asocial humanity within us all, were to become the dimensions through which these new technologies of government could achieve their purchase on reality.[23]

Rule in any form, I would argue, makes the individual doubt personal forms of inspiration and authority, and such rule will persist so long as the desire for personal transformation seeks continuity with the past.

A similar contradiction, i.e. between a desire for continuity and the demand for a radical transformation, can be seen in fascism. Even the earlier critics of fascism, notes Sternhell, saw the contradiction between a demand for reform and an attachment to the old society.[24] As Sternhell goes on to note, fascists wanted to redeem the nation and yet purify it of its alliance with conservative, reactionary and exploitative elements; they wished to fulfil the goals of Marxism without either giving primacy to the economy or viewing the world through the eyes of materialism. Clearly they wished to revolt and to triumph, but they proclaimed the need for disinterestedness and even sacrifice. While insisting on the need for energy, on the use of force and even on brutality, they also venerated self-discipline and self-sacrifice.[25] As Theodor Reik observed years ago, it is the hallmark of the masochist to harbour sadistic fantasies of triumph while insisting on paying for future satisfactions over a lifetime of suffering and self-sacrifice.[26]

There is a generic fascism, then, which goes well beyond the particular Western experience of fascist political parties and systems. It is based on the notion that one's community, people or nation constitutes a domain of purity and salvation and is therefore vulnerable to corruption both from outside influences and from within. As one French fascist observed, 'If we question the German principle that a superior form of humanity has the right to subjugate an inferior form, why do we have colonies?'[27] Indeed, that is why I have used the notion of colonization to describe the systematic effort in Western societies to subordinate the family to official and expert forms of surveillance, guidance and instruction in the service of perfecting each new generation.

Transformation and Its Discontents

Conversely, the experience of being subject to spiritual formation by a dominant generation, class or nation leaves a profound impression on the psyche and self-understanding. Indeed, Freud spoke of the super-ego as being the equivalent of the state within the psyche itself. In the American experience, furthermore, colonial subjects in America flocked to their pastors for reassurance regarding their souls in the seventeenth and eighteenth centuries. Clergy and, more recently, professionals have become particularly adept in instilling doubts about the individual's own perceptions, insight, knowledge and expertise. To be colonized is indeed to become unsure of the potency and value of one's own experience, tradition and way of life.

No wonder, then, that this new form of professionalized and official authority has produced its own population of the discontented. If Rose were entirely right in claiming that the souls of parents have been effectively made subject, along with their children, to official and professional standards for normality, one would see a high rate of consensus over what constitutes a normal child and an adequate path to adulthood. It is precisely the lack of such a consensus, however, that is driving politics in the United States of America and fuelling the millenarian enthusiasm of the radical Christian right. Granted that there is a large constituency for expert opinion and a widespread desire to see the young transformed into good citizens, there is also a pervasive discontent with the agencies that seek to shape the psyches of the young and instruct parents on child-raising. Much of that discontent, furthermore, focuses on the role of the schools and of the media as purveyors of expert opinion on what constitutes normality and morality. Certainly the conflict over whether homosexuality should be presented in the classroom as an acceptable, however alternative 'lifestyle' and the controversy over the role of sex education in the public schools signal a high level of opposition to the intrusion of the state on the psyche through the channels of expertise and of the mass media. If Rose is right that 'the soul of the young citizen has become the object of government through expertise', it also appears that the soul of the young citizen has become the target of a variety of opposition groups and movements from anti-abortionists and evangelicals to neo-conservatives and the Republican right.

Of course, the dangers of opposition to official modes for transforming the psyche are not new, and neither is the demand for psychological freedom. Norman Cohn, for instance, describes a mediaeval heresy, known as the Free Spirit. Lasting over five hundred years, the movement consisted of 'a quasi-mystical anarchism – an affirmation of freedom so reckless and unqualified that it amounted to a total denial of every kind of restraint and limitation'.[28] Its doctrine was the most revolutionary of all the mediaeval heresies and inspired the Taborite and other movements of liberation. As Cohn goes on to argue, moreover, this movement for total freedom underlies the Nietzschean 'imagination of many of the "armed bohemians" who made the National-Socialist revolution'.[29] *There are indeed fascist impulses for the total transformation of the social order in the individual's demands for total emancipation.*

Underlying these demands for transformation of the social order, I would argue, is the failure of rituals that ordinarily would transform the young into adults, or the single into the married, or the dead into an honoured place among ancestors. During the Middle Ages, as Cohn points out, many of the millennial movements indeed promised to marry poor women and prostitutes to men of wealth and power; the marital order would be saved through a reversal of the usual prospects. As the ordinary prospects for transformation from single to married status failed, large numbers of women were left without legitimate income or any means of support at all. Under these conditions the populace may seek to reverse the ordinary rituals of transformation in order to make them serve the purposes of their own redemption.[30] When rituals of transformation fail to turn the single into the married and the young into adults in a fashion perceived to be continuous, fair and orderly, it becomes clear that the social order is having difficulty in reproducing itself. When a society's days are more clearly numbered, it will be increasingly vulnerable to a wide variety of movements that seek to speed up the clock or to make up for lost time.

The Transformation of the Living and the Dead

Some rituals seek to transform the dead into ancestors who, though still members of the community, can be relied upon to be present only on demand. The ancestor is the mirror image of the individual who wears a mask on demand for important social occasions but understands that he or she is merely masquerading. The ancestors are on call, as it were, for serious but temporary services to the social order. Thus the dead are also associated with masquerades and are allowed into the company of the living only on certain occasions. Not only is it important to keep the dead at a relatively safe distance from the living until their help may be needed for fertilizing the fields or winning battles – thus funeral rites seek to guarantee that the dead will come when called upon to restore the vitality of the community and of its flocks or fields – it is also important for the dead to be honoured if the living, who claim to be their descendants, are to acquire or maintain social honour in their own communities. These claims to social honour, of course, are embedded in rituals of transformation, i.e. in formal occasions when the status of the dead, and hence of the living, is recreated and reaffirmed.[31] Transformation thus occurs under the auspices of the dead.

The dead are also the arbiters of transformation. On the one hand, the dead represent a superior power, without which crops would fail, fields and even wombs would be infertile, and the living would be cut off not only from their past but from their future. On the other hand, the dead are often experienced as fearsome and intrusive, alien, malignant and dangerous. Under these conditions, I would argue, some funeral rites and rituals in honour of the dead will seek to limit their intrusions and, at least for an annual season of liberation, purify the society of the presence of the departed.

A case in point is found in Olivia Harris's fine account of funeral rituals among the Laymi: an ethnic group living an agricultural and pastoral existence in highland Bolivia.[32] The Laymi avoid their graveyards at all times of the year except at the beginning of the planting season, when the services of the dead are once again required to ensure fertility and success in the fields.[33] Most of the time the Laymi are quite unabashed about showing their aversion to the sick, the dying and the dead. They constantly eat and drink intoxicating substances to ward off the devils plaguing the sick. Not only do the Laymi find corpses repulsive and fear that the deceased's ghost may leave the corpse and attack them; they find ghosts envious and malignant and despatch the spirits of the dead with vigour at the end of graveyard ceremonies.[34] So important are these rituals that the Laymi think ill of those who stay away from funeral services. The efforts of every member of the community are required to set limits on the interaction of the living with the dead. The Laymi are clearly a society in which the psyche, like the spirits of the dead, is supposed to stay within the limits of prescribed relationships, for the sake of preserving the organization of the society itself.

The Web of Contradiction

The auspices of the dead tie the community together and ensure its continuity. But as arbiters the dead are an individuating – a dividing – factor as well. That is one reason why the Laymi would think of the ghosts of the dead as envious and malignant. The dead cause division and invidious comparison. It is through descent from the dead, for instance, that the Laymi distribute land and property. Each line of descent, notes Harris, is distinguished from another through a lineage that derives from the dead, and the dead are therefore honoured when a household is being established, as well as at times when the Laymi celebrate 'rights of access to community land'.[35]

Because the Laymi are a tightly integrated society, it is necessary to find ways to discourage accumulation by particular individuals, households, or lineages beyond what others might expect for themselves.[36] The claims of individual lines of descent to land and houses are therefore offset by a larger grouping, based on the juxtaposition of families in a given area; consanguinity is superseded by contiguity. Rituals of transformation, by which the dead are assigned to a place in the community, must therefore encompass the contradiction posed by the dead: on the one hand, individual lines of descent from the dead dividing the community into property-owning lineages and households; on the other hand, the dead being a source of continuing identity and vitality for the community as a whole.

The sacred space of the graveyard is thus the place where dangerous passions can be acted out, as well as being the place where the dead can be encountered in safety. The graveyard is thus the sanctuary of the Laymi. Harris sees the graveyard as a place where sacred time is created: time which unites the living and the dead across the generations. Indeed, the graveyard stands as a symbol of the entire society of the Laymi, like the goddess Pachamama, who combines in herself sacred time and space.[37] The graveyard further stands as a symbol for a community which is not only tightly integrated but enjoys clear boundaries. It is the space in which transformation of the living into the dead can be safely enacted through ritual. However, the fear of the dead as being envious or greedy reflects the passions for consumption that remain unsatisfied in so strongly communal a society as that of the Laymi. Indeed, some of these passions, e.g. for the acquisition of land, are fought out in symbolic battles in the graveyard at times of collective mourning.[38]

Only when the dead are properly transformed, by being placed within their own sphere of influence, can the community constrain its own destructive passions and strivings. That is because interaction between the living and the dead opens the way to the dramatization of passions for land and for consumption. Therefore, according to Harris, property is distributed among the living only after care has been taken to separate the living from the dead through such rites of transformation as crossing a stream over which the spirits of the dead are unable to pass.[39] Rituals of transformation manage these contradictions by setting a season for weeping and struggling in the presence of the dead, followed by a season of serenity and joy in their absence.

Rituals of transformation do not always succeed in creating a new chapter or season in the life of the community, so that the community can put its problems to rest. For American fundamentalists, for instance, the rituals of mainstream churches have failed to transform them from children into adults; new baptisms and conversions are required to complete the transformation. Some fundamentalists, notes Strozier, nonetheless still have a 'perilous and fragile new set of self structures, something well short of a transformation'; they therefore need repeated assurances that their own lascivious and violent tendencies have been beaten, like swords, into ploughshares.[40] In the end, however, fundamentalists are only certain of transformation in the beginning of the millennium. Only in the rapture, and when they enjoy the support of 'the resurrected saints', will they be able to transcend the tribulations of those still subject to their passions and the striving of others.

Visions of a final period of struggle and transformation reflect a desire as well as a fear: the desire for one's departure to be coterminous with the end of the world as one knows it. Individuals and communities typically do not run out of time simultaneously, except, of course, in the massive upheavals and genocides that produce the death and dislocation of entire populations. The Laymi also have a ritual to resolve this latter contradiction, viz. that death comes as a cyclical event within the life of the community but arbitrarily to each individual. Among the Laymi, the older members of the community attend the corpse, while the younger ones roll bones until a number comes up: an expression, perhaps, of their own understanding that death comes at a time and place of its own choosing.[41] Thus, in a tightly integrated society, this understanding of the contradiction between communal and personal fates in time is played out in a game on the periphery of the rites by which the community acts out its own responsibilities to the dead.

In far less integrated societies, this tension between communal and individual fates may be expressed in a wide variety of cultural channels. Some films, for instance, dramatize passages in time which link the fate of the individual with changes in historical events which would otherwise have occurred quite independently of the person in question. Fundamentalists dramatize through a variety of media their desire for a personal fate which transcends and yet occurs simultaneously with the end of the social order. They may yet have their way. The possibility of nuclear horror dramatizes a fate in which the deaths of the self and of the social order are coterminous.

Rites of transformation thus encompass a series of contradictions: between a society's need for continuity and its internal divisions; between the need for auspices and for arbitration of differences; between the need for a common fate and a separate existence. The rites themselves therefore are filled with ambiguity and contradiction. Take, for example, Jonathan Parry's account of the cremation of the Hindu householder.[42] On the one hand, notes Parry, the householder who dies and is cremated in the proper fashion engages in 'a sacrificial act' which regenerates not only the householder himself but the entire cosmos.[43] It would appear that the funeral rites themselves have achieved the transformation of the dead into a member of the ancestral community, while guaranteeing the continuity of the social order. On the other hand, Parry argues, however, 'the cremation rituals of the householder hold out only the promise of a renewed existence which is itself impermanent, and in which the immortal soul is unbreakably chained to a particular transient form'.[44] There is here an uneasy peace between the desire for a common fate and a longing for a separate existence with its own timetable.[45]

What begins as a failure to control the time of death must be changed into a voluntary offering, a sacrifice, on the part of the deceased. What has been experienced as being beyond the control of the community must be transformed into an act in which the community reasserts its control not only over death but over individuality. Death as an event in which time has run out on a member of the community, and by implication could run out on the community itself, must be transformed into an event in which the community renews its storehouse of time. As an event that interrupts the continuity of time itself, the advent of death must be turned into a moment that evokes the origins of time itself and thus renews, as it were, the flow of time. Time must be made once again to seem like an ever-rolling stream.

This compromise with reality is not only mediated by ritual but elaborated in religious belief and interpretation. At what Parry calls 'a somewhat esoteric level of theological discourse', his informants explained to him that the corpse is really a sacrificial victim that is killed by the chief mourner in the lighting of the fire at the base of the pyre and in the breaking of the skull of the deceased.[46] Indeed, death occurs only when the spirit is released through the cracked skull. Until that time the body was that of a sacrificial victim and not of a putrid and polluting corpse. Thus an element of control is asserted over death, which becomes a killing, and over dying, which becomes a voluntary sacrifice on the part of the deceased. Even the pollution that might seem to accompany the corpse is not present until the act of cremation itself.[47] Thus the ritual reasserts that the fate of the individual and that of the community are coterminous.

In this rite, time does not begin to run out on the individual or the social order at the moment of death. On the contrary, at that moment the deceased re-enters and recreates the divine act of self-sacrifice which created the cosmos itself. The renewal of heaven and earth thus takes place at the very moment at which time itself would seem to be running out on both society and the individual. Cremation, according to Parry, because it is carried out according to a sacrificial pattern that originated in 'the primal act of Prajapati who produced creation by the sacrificial dismemberment of his own body ... therefore represents the renewal of time'.[48]

Of course, not all the members of the community can die in such a way as to add to the communal storehouse of time. As Parry points out, help is available in countervailing rites for children, the diseased, and others who have been unable to offer themselves as a sacrifice to the gods either in their life or in their death, and whose death is therefore 'untimely'.[49] An effigy is created, which bears the stigma of pollution and is offered in sacrificial fires as a substitute for the corpse of the unworthy dead.

(In a brief digression, let me note that other communities also have used effigies in various rites to honour the dead. Jorgensen notes that, among the Western American Indians, the Northern Paiutes were 'the only Great Basin Paiutes to practice a bundle of rituals called Mourning Ceremonies that included the burning of clothed stick figures and cremations in honour of the deceased ... and were the only natives of the Great Basin who sought the return of the dead'.[50] The point of this comparison is to suggest that honorary cremations and the use of effigies may have been necessary conditions for ritualized control over the presence and the absence of the dead.)

Magical Defences Against Social Obligations

The requisite devotions place heavy obligations not only on those who must die according to a prescribed pattern but on the bereaved. What Parry calls the 'prolonged austerities ... by which Visnu engendered the world' are reflected in the obligations of those who make the pilgrimage to Benares on behalf of the dead, in the purification of the chief mourners, and not least of all in the purity required of the average householder who must prepare for a 'good death'.[51] As I have noted, moreover, individuals who find the burden of such social obligations tedious or even overwhelming may very well turn to shamans for relief: for a counter-magic that overcomes the consequences of their failure to meet the requirements for a good death. Certainly funerary rites often place the individual under extraordinary obligations from which magical relief may be sought through the aid of shamans.

In seeking help from certain shamans, moreover, the devout are fighting fire with fire. That is, they are using the logic of sympathetic magic to overcome the threat posed by the spirit of one who has died a bad death. Those whose death is untimely threaten the community as disembodied spirits or ghosts, whose presence may indeed be very troubling to the living. Conversely, certain ascetics called Aghori are themselves troublesome spirits and are sometimes called disembodied ghosts. They are often regarded as mad, and they are polluted by their close contact with animals, prostitutes, dead bodies, and the unhappy or malevolent spirits of the departed. Like other shamans, moreover, they are thought to transcend the limits of space and time, being able to be in two places at once and living as though they had already transcended time. Thus they consume fetid and putrid matter and are reputed even to eat the flesh of corpses.

The dialectic that I have suggested is therefore relatively simple to trace. The rites of transformation by which a society seeks to reassert its control over death establish stringent norms for purity and impose heavy social duties on the mourners of the deceased. For help in – or relief from – meeting these norms individuals turn to a shaman who appears not only to have transcended the threat of death and to be liberated from the norms for purity but also to have acquired a soul that can stand the test of time and enjoy its own immunity to death. The presence of such shamans poses a threat to traditional religion, in the sense that individuals now have opportunities for access to their own sources of inspiration and authority.

The shamanistic character, therefore, is one way of perpetuating and acting out the compromise with reality which is represented in dreams and rituals. Partly delusional, partly realistic, that divinized character is a form of defence not only against the fear of death but against the force of desire and overwhelming pleasure. It is a way of hedging one's bets about death, as it were, by living a circumscribed life. For instance, the ascetic along the Ganges is thought both to enjoy forbidden pleasures and also to transcend death, but he lives within severe limitations. Thus the ascetic takes on the risk of pollution by death and overcomes it by the most immediate and direct acquaintance with the bodies of the deceased. The ascetic (in the case of the Aghori), as Parry noted, often considered himself to be a disembodied spirit: a soul that has transcended physical limitations and death itself.[52]

Not only does the ascetic come to the aid of pilgrims and mourners by his austerities and ministrations. The ascetic also embodies the possibility of becoming a soul that can escape the ordinary obligations of social life, resist social pressures, and stand the test of time. Thus the ascetic may enjoy a large popular following of individuals with aspirations for achieving a spiritual life of their own. Jesus is but one example of an ascetic who ate and drank in ways that others considered irresponsible. He was of assistance to pilgrims, wandered across fields, worked and consumed on the sabbath, and in various ways expressed his transcendence of social constraints. On the other hand, he was believed by his followers to have transcended death. To his detractors, however, he was a dangerous male from the periphery and the personification of alien and occult powers, i.e. something of a witch, since he represented patterns of consumption and an autonomy of will which could disrupt or even destroy the social order. It is not surprising, therefore, to find that Parry has observed academics and professionals among the most devoted followers of a particular mad ascetic along the Ganges.[53]

If the Aghori ascetic seems too unfamiliar to be fully comprehensible, consider Strozier's comment on the fundamentalists' belief in the return of Jesus at the Second Coming:

> The Second Advent . . . is by definition to fundamentalists the event that marks the end of human history and inaugurates the sufferings of tribulation that are then followed by the hope of the millennial rule of Jesus on earth. The 'end' stops our historical time and ends evil, but it marks as well the 'return' of Jesus and the 'beginning' of the millennium.[54]

The one who, far from being consumed by death, consumed death itself in his own resurrection, will return to consummate history, destroy death for all his followers, and inaugurate a period of struggle which will lead into the millennium. As in the case of the Laymi of Bolivia, the dead return and struggle ensues, but death itself is overcome in a new season of fertility, of life, and of abundance. Indeed, Strozier points out, the millennium is seen by many fundamentalists as a period of unprecedented growth and productivity.[55] In the meantime, however, it takes death to overcome death: heavenly fire to quench the fires of hell.

The Failure of Rituals of Transformation

Let us return to the example of the Bolivian Laymi. Indeed, Harris recounts the various ways in which colonial powers have intruded first upon the Inkas and lately among some of their descendants in these valleys of the Andes.[56] Initially it was the Spanish, and more lately it has been the Christian missionaries, who have impinged upon the boundaries of the Inkas and their Laymi descendants. Now the peasants' union opens up new possibilities for social interaction, as does the Bolivian state not only through the Army but through such legislation as the Agrarian Reform Act of 1953.[57] Although Harris does not go into detail on these points, certainly the intrusion of the army, of the unions and of agrarian reform will expand the range of social interaction and alter the extent to which the Laymi experience the control of the state as direct or indirect. Rituals of transformation typically fail, I would argue, either when a society is no longer able to maintain its boundaries or when it is no longer able to maintain a high level of integration between the psyche, social relationships, and the demands of the social order itself.

Funeral rites are particularly open to subversion. Kertzer notes, for instance, that one group in a Tunisian village, who had been enriching themselves through economic changes arising in the larger society, still lacked social status or power in their own community.[58] This group then hit upon the strategy of using funerary rites to enhance their own claims and to devalue those of another group that had hitherto monopolized ancestral honours. The dead, as we have noted, make powerful arbiters of a group's future. Kertzer also notes that the Likud party in Israel has used funerary rites to enhance its own claims to power by celebrating the virtues of one of its ancestral heroes.[59] Whenever the place of the dead among the living is being altered, whether by adding names to the list of honoured dead, by dishonouring the dead, by placing them either at too great a distance or, conversely, too close for comfort, a society has difficulty in maintaining its continuity and control over the generations.

Rituals of transformation, like other rituals, are thus vulnerable to the influences of the market, which bring new opportunities and resources into a community, just as they are susceptible to manipulation and control by various interest or status groups in a community. Nonetheless, they retain their character as rituals of transformation so long as the social character of a person is being altered, whether by the transition from one status to another or by some other symbolic gesture.

The rituals by which the young are turned into adults also are vulnerable to outside pressures and to manipulation by particular status groups. Cohn notes, for instance, that in many of the millenarian social movements of the Middle Ages, images of fathers and sons were 'fused', especially in images of the enemies of the people.[60] Antichrist was portrayed both as a rebellious son and as a deceitful and cruel father figure: both rebel and tyrant. Many of the millennial movements, as Cohn frequently points out, appealed primarily to those who had little inheritance to give or to receive.

The succession of the generations and the reproduction of a patriarchal order requires property, the stability of local communities, the success of families, and the possibility of sufficient continuity that the younger generation can and must be inducted into the roles and statuses of the older generation. When these statuses are fragile or broken, and when the young have little therefore either to gain or to lose from intransigence, the codes for transforming the young into the old are broken. In their place, as Cohn suggests, were a variety of fantasies concerning charismatic leaders who were transfigured into spiritual or immortal beings. I would go on to suggest simply that the demand for waiting that is implied in the orderly succession of one generation by another no longer makes sense when there is little or nothing for which to wait. Under these conditions millennial movements, which promise an imminent new order, do have an abundant and widespread appeal. Both the fundamentalist and the secular citizen of modern societies know that time is continuously running out, although they have very different reasons for this apprehension. It is an apprehension that can lead the devout into passivity and the secular into making the most of the time remaining. There is thus a peculiar fit between the demands of modernity of a population inured to waiting and sacrifice, on the one hand, and, on the other, the learned passivity of the fundamentalist whose fate, however superior to that of most mortals, is still in the hands of God.

The attempt to control and to monopolize the sources of inspiration and authority is only a proto-fascist tendency that may never mature into a fascist social system. Nonetheless, such control is a necessary, if not sufficient, condition for the emergence of fascism. Of course, no society can afford to allow its members total freedom in their search for private sources of salvation. To find one's own soul could have revolutionary consequences if one does so under other than officially approved auspices. Thus the search for what at times may be magical formulae for salvation, for example esoteric theologies, private therapies, or wisdom imported from other societies, poses a challenge to a nation's centre to provide a model for salvation sufficiently attractive to compel the individual's attention, compliance and even sacrifice.

In American society the dynamic tension between self and society is intensified by the legacy of Puritanism and by Protestant residues carried in public rhetoric, passed on through the curriculum and the culture of self-help, and by the needs of parents not only to enliven and control their offspring but to pass on their own spiritual convictions to the next generation through certain enclaves such as evangelical Christian schools. There the transformation of the self through conversion can be fostered, if not wholly guaranteed, and habits of sacrifice, both of the heart and of the mind, inculcated from the very beginning. Certainly Protestant fundamentalism has intensified the demand for personal transformation and has made time into the vehicle of personal and collective redemption.

The search for visible marks of transformation is not new with American fundamentalists. Early American Puritanism was still concerned to locate the 'infallible signs' of the 'visible saints'. The inspiration of the individual believer had to conform to the authority of the Christian community. However, in the American colonies, various revivals and awakenings gave fresh impetus to Puritan determination to take salvation out of the hands of office-holders, scholars and others who placed man-made insights and laws ahead of revelation while dictating to the faithful.

To be wholly transformed, the believer must live in a transformed society. Baptists were opposed to the practice of infant baptism, which had been introduced as something of a compromise, just as they opposed a New England officialdom that 'governed by the precepts of men, put into the hands of unbelievers'.[61] Baptists and others in New England demanded that the community of the faithful be purified and rigorous: immune to outside influences and free from domination by a lukewarm officialdom in church and state. Even the more conservative believers engaged in 'religious democratization' and elevated the pew over the pulpit, the laity over the clergy, the ordinary above the well-endowed, the simple over the fancy.[62] *The movement back to basics, I am arguing, always involves a deflation of commitments from the larger society, no matter how inflated must be the commitments to the distant and elusive promise of salvation carried by the ascetic tradition.*

Once established in a society's cultural mainstream, religious asceticism will keep alive the very doubts about the soul's salvation that it is intended to lay to rest. No transformation is complete, and no sacrifice is sufficient, to validate the self before the divine tribunal or, eventually, before public opinion. Indeed, because this preoccupation with the soul is dynamic and chronic, it can have very unsettling – and at times disruptive – effects on a nation and its people. Gaustad, in speaking of the Great Awakening, goes on to point out that in the 1740s, individuals seeking to be sure of their souls' salvation retreated in large numbers from the established churches of New England into conventicles of the saved in the search for purity of soul. These were groups opposed to the pretensions of officials and of certain clergy, and they demanded a transformation of the society commensurate with their own charismatic endowments.

In the New England colonies, during the first 'Great Awakening', individuals flocked to their ministers in considerable agitation over the state of their souls.[63] As Gaustad notes, many of these people, especially the younger ones, may have been unsure of their salvation because they had been admitted to the churches through infant baptism, rather than through full confession of faith, under the auspices of the so-called 'Halfway Covenant'. Religious asceticism, Max Weber argued years ago, is itself a source of profound anxiety over the individual's state of grace. Grace (charisma) has to be tested and proven in a variety of good works: in success in battle or examinations, in fruitful industry or in desirable traits of character. Individuals who take the ascetic cure have to work hard over a lifetime to have something to show for themselves.

Early in the nineteenth century fresh waves of asceticism sought to purify the soul from ignorance and alcohol. For instance, the American Temperance Union or Bible Society sought the transformation of the individual through calls to conversion, followed by a spiritual rebirth. Calls to conversion, tested by a lifetime of unrelenting and productive labour (with every promise, of course, of rich rewards for individual enterprise) were proclaimed from pulpits and town squares on every Fourth of July, in speeches that Bercovitch has appropriately described as American 'jeremiads'.[64] The primacy of the social order over the needs and prerogatives of the individual was impressed on the American social character, even while some, by no means all, foreign and domestic critics claimed to discern the danger of individualism.

Indeed, for those endowed with a divine mission to redeem the times through personal transformation and the sacrificial pursuit of the common good, there is simply never enough time. Protestant rhetoric, especially in the nineteenth century, exhorted individuals to make the most of the time allotted them, to live fully in the present as the 'nick of time' between two eternities (the past and the future), and to put forth the fruits of industry and successful commerce. Time is forever running out on the soul that takes its lifetime – or even the moment – as the theatre of its salvation.

There were times in the American colonies, and again, Bercovitch argues, in the new Republic, when preachers exhorted their audiences to renewed acts of dedication, as if to say that their earlier transformations could not be trusted without fresh sacrifices.[65] Previous confessions, baptisms and professions of faith could not stand them in good stead. Social credit, like time itself, is always running out, and one must return to the source of salvation in order to renew one's supply of credit and to be taken by one's peers as acting in good faith. As Bercovitch puts it, one such time of trial had come during the native American rebellion known as King Philip's War (1674):

> The preachers reminded their audiences ... that covenant renewal pertained not to works but to that absolute 'Covenant wherein men profess themselves *unable* to do any-

> thing of *themselves*,' for precisely such men must rededicate themselves. Although the new birth occurs once only, the experience of saints showed that the effects of grace might 'so decay as to need to be done over again.'[66]

Charisma transforms the individual only for the time being. Only new sacrifices can prove old graces.

The attempt to transform the individual American led to other forms of sacrifice: note again the 'jeremiads' that Bercovitch describes in pre-Civil-War America, one such sermon, given by William Evans Arthur on the Fourth of July, 1850, is clearly a summons to rededication, to receive a fresh supply of grace, and therefore, I would argue, to enter upon a new time of trial and testing, as if the believers thus endowed with grace would have a great deal to prove. After rehearsing the struggles of Puritans, the glorious Revolution, and the sage decisions of the writers of the Constitution, the sermon points ahead to the eternity stretching forward, in which time is of the essence both for the souls of the faithful and for the nation itself:

> Hence the focus on stress and self-doubt. Insecurity proves the need for order, and order, as Arthur defines it, leads to constant improvement. Hence also the private/public ambiguities of the goals he proposes: 'liberty,''aspiring,' 'fullest happiness,' 'broadest renown,' 'unclouded future,' and above all 'American.' ... Process and essence merge in the symbols of the Revolution, teleology precludes dialectics, and progress and conformity stand revealed as the twin pillars of the American temple of freedom.[67]

Note once more that Arthur's sermon is given on the Fourth of July: a day of national birth and re-birth. The Fourth of July ceremony functions, then, as a collective form of personal transformation through baptism and renewal. As we noted in Chapter 1, the rituals of fascist movements in Europe linked hopes for personal transformation with the collective dream of national renewal.

Note also that the larger society has now learned to present itself to the citizen as worthy of the emulation once received by the heroes of faith and the saints themselves. The magical rites of the evangelical periphery have been taken over by the rituals of the political and cultural centre, that is, by the Fourth of July ceremony in which the fate of the individual is henceforth entwined with the fate of the nation. As Bercovitch describes these 'Puritan techniques' of rededication and renewal, the sermon emphasizes the present as a 'nick of time' caught between the twin eternities of the past and the future. Time is thus indeed scarce and yet freighted with eternal significance; the moment is to be redeemed by a fresh dedication of energy and spirit to the task of building the republic.

The Protestant evangelist typically puts the believer under the most excruciating temporal pressures. As we have seen, Bercovitch finds evangelists speaking of the 'nick of time', in which believers must commit themselves to the salvation of their souls and of their nation. Modern evangelists have their own litany of temporal exhortations. In his study of Protestant fundamentalists, for instance, Charles Strozier has described how their conversion has transformed many of them into persons literally obsessed with the passage of time. One of Strozier's informants, for instance, was told by his dying father that 'much of life is wasted on things that don't count'.[68] The son's reaction was to become obsessed with time: not only in obedience to the wish of a dead father but also as a way of counteracting the force of death itself. For many fundamentalists, time is what wastes the individual. In the apocalypse, indeed, many individuals will be 'wasted' by being cast into a lake of fire and subjected to eternal torment: this after being put through 'tribulations' and tried before the heavenly tribunal and found wanting. What the Gorgon's head was to the ancient Greeks, the images of the apocalypse are to the fundamentalist Christian. Just as the Gorgon's head was a double for their own destructiveness, so is the apocalypse a double of the fundamentalists's own, but rejected, proclivities toward death and destruction.[69]

The violent imagery of the apocalypse thus permits individuals to believe that they have been redeemed from their own inner violence without ever having had to confront and own it. Precisely that same function is performed by rituals; individuals can perform, literally act out, their own inner violence without taking personal responsibility for it. The violence is performed while one is transformed by a role, wearing a mask, and following a collective script. When ordinary rituals fail to perform this magical bit of transformation, however, religious movements provide alternative vehicles for the transformation of the self. Thus, I would argue, belief in the apocalypse, with its horrifying images of suffering, torment and death, allows the individual to express, in repetitive conversations, Bible studies and exhortations, the inner violence that is too frightening to admit into full consciousness as part of the self. Thus fundamentalists find in the Bible's imagery of the end a double of that part of themselves which they are loath to admit and hope, by God's grace, to avoid forever. Their final transformation, they admit, depends on a transformation of the world around them: hence their radical demands for a revolution of the social order after which they eventually shall reign.

To prevent time from running out on the self, then, and to stand the ultimate test of time, the soul requires powerful magic on its behalf. What is required, Strozier suggests, is a double of the self that will indeed endure even if everything else perishes in a lake of hellish fire. That purified and eternal self, he suggests, is the new self: the person transformed by the gift of charisma into one who fully understands the hidden mysteries of God's revelation and takes them redemptively to heart. As I have noted, however, charisma brings with it not only new assurance but fresh doubts; charisma is never wholly sure of itself and therefore requires continually to be tested. As one of Strozier's informants put it, 'Even after becoming a Christian . . . things do not change overnight.'[70] New tests are required, and vigilance must be constant lest the old self return.

What is repressed, as Freud put it, does indeed return. That is one reason that rituals are compulsive as well as repetitive. Indeed, Strozier's fundamentalists had to repeat themselves in order to reassure themselves that they were on the right track. 'In fundamentalist theory, all important things happen twice.'[71] The old self does keep coming back in the form of those who are not yet saved: unbelievers, the once-born and infidels. These others are reminders of the self that is not yet fully transformed, and, as Strozier points out, radical fundamentalists like the Branch Davidians or neo-Nazis take drastic measures to rid the world of such reminders of the rejected and alienated violence in their own human nature.[72] The Puritans were too zealous in demanding that the world live up to their own high standards.[73] Their besetting sin therefore has been an 'unwillingness to compromise'.[74]

Time will therefore be of the essence for the soul that has something to prove. The self that keeps repeating a past which it seeks to transcend is destined to demand a radical transformation of the social order. Others must die, perhaps, for the fundamentalist to enter into his or her legacy of salvation and thus become wholly transformed.

Millennialism as the Secularization of Time

Here, then, is what Vidich and Lyman refer to as the 'logic of secularization': a tendency toward reductionism that lowers the level of abstraction in the promises of God to the relatively concrete aspirations of believers. I am going one step further to suggest that it is the sense of time itself that is secularized right down to the concrete moments and circumstances of everyday life. The time of salvation becomes mundane and the period of waiting is drastically foreshortened. Thus the scope of time included in the pilgrim's progress toward salvation is reduced from an uncertain lifetime to these times. If a millennial nation is to be created, it will have to be sooner rather than later. As the threat of Armageddon is warded off by a new advent of piety, the purification of the social order and the transformation of individuals prepare the way for a heaven-sent nation. *The secularization of the Christian sense of the fullness of times, the time of salvation, paves the way for a Christian fascism.*

The charismatic's grandiose and therefore insecure self is both afraid of its own violence and also impatient for an end to torment and uncertainty. The nation's piety and devotions, its sermons and sacrifices, are not sufficient to ward off Armageddon. In his recent analysis of prophecies of the end times in American society, Strozier makes it clear that the Civil War was indeed the American Armageddon. These were years of purging the nation of its sins through blood sacrifices. In these years the nation itself was to have been transformed into a unified people who would illumine, even transform the world with their democratic institutions. Not only did American rituals and revivals fail to ward off Armageddon, however; Armageddon failed to introduce the new millennium. As Strozier puts it, 'The war that seemed to settle so much for the future – the secure institutions of a national government and the end of slavery – in fact left open, bleeding wounds.'[75]

In the aftermath of the Armageddon that failed to produce the millennium, the prophecy of the end continued to foreshorten temporal horizons. Strozier's account reiterates the rise of premillennialism as a movement galvanizing the faithful to prepare themselves for the saviour whose return would initiate the millennium. Transformations were still in order, but they were to be of the heart and the soul, the mind and the body. Sometimes firm dates, such as 1914, were assigned to the coming of the end, as in the case of the Jehovah's Witnesses.[76]

The faith in revivalistic ceremonies and other means of transformation was transferred, I would argue, to the text of the Bible itself. The magic, so to speak, left ritual and entered language. There, enshrined in the text, whose words may have been flawed by transcription but whose meaning was forever sure, could be found the guarantees of faith that would stand the test of time. In the Scofield Bible, Strozier argues, the words of the text could be interpreted in notes that themselves took on scriptural authority, so that the present times and the future could lose their mystery, along with the obscure passages in the biblical text itself.[77] Time could now go on, in a present that was forever open to the future.

The failure of ritual, whether in the mainstream churches, in national ceremonies of peacemaking and inauguration, or in revival tents, has intensified demands for transformation through religious movements. As conservative Christians have become mobilized and organized, demands for transformation are transferred to the body politic. The insistent demand for a transformation of the self, the demand to be born again can also be transferred to social institutions, such as political parties and the public schools. There the faithful are to prepare themselves for the time of testing prior to the new millennium.

Thus, with the process of secularization, millennial time, which formerly was the bedrock of faith, yields to the time within which the loan from the bank is to be repaid. Weber goes out of his way to point out that time, in this reduced, purely chronological sense, becomes the measure of credit-worthiness. The puritan character, then, becomes the hard asset underlying Western commerce and industry. The word of the artisan, himself a practical man, is as good as gold: a word that, once given, can ensure a loan for the expansion of the artisan's work. Note that it is the artisan who pays back the loan within the promised time who is the exemplar of puritan character and the new virtuoso of fidelity in everyday life. Thus mundane commitments replace the time of salvation itself; eternity, the transformation of all time, has been reduced to a period of indebtedness that can be measured on the calendar. Transformation becomes a collective as well as a personal event that can be dated on the calendar in terms of specific events. This secularization of time is crucial to the formation of fascist social movements.

In contemporary American society the residues of this reductionism are everywhere apparent. Take, for example, Susan Rose's study of evangelical schools. She found that time was of the essence of the children's salvation and of the Christian community. Susan Rose puts it this way:

> Believing that Christianity is only one generation away from extinction, since each individual must *choose* salvation, the adult leadership is desperate for their children to understand the importance of the decision and desire to follow Christ: 'it is a matter of life or death – eternal life or death'.[78]

Time is therefore always running out for the Christian community for two reasons. First, each individual has only one lifetime in which to receive the assurance of the salvation of his or her soul; second, the community itself is in danger of extinction if the next generation fails to believe 'in time'. Under these excruciating temporal pressures, it is not surprising that religious communities seek ways of buying time: seizing the moment in conversion; making up for lost time by acquiring the gifts of the tradition in infusions of the spirit; and hastening the community's release from the burdens of time through millennial liberations.

Time, as we have pointed out, is indeed of the essence. Great are the opportunities for salvation, but the moment or opportunity can easily be lost. Indeed, as Rose points out, 'evangelicals believe that they must act quickly before the world seduces their young'.[79] Nonetheless, the time of salvation had been reduced to the academic year, to the separate times devoted to particular subjects, to the fragmented times allowed for separate activities, whether going to the water-cooler or working on assignments. Students in these conservative Christian schools had to have something to show for the time that they had put in; the hard assets of education were thus educational achievement, quantified and measured over and over again.

The time of salvation has thus become merely a matter of time. That is why Susan Rose found a serious attempt to overcome 'crass worldly values' with an education of the spirit that enhanced piety along with learning in the Puritan fashion. Nonetheless, it was her conviction that even these schools offered little hope for a genuine transformation of American society precisely because that society had profoundly shaped the schools themselves.

Instead of reproducing a religious community separate from the larger society, these schools in effect reproduced the dominant characteristics of the class system by providing workers for entry into the social class of their parents: some obedient workers, others more self-determining professionals or managerial types. The middle-class school was more flexible, open to discussion and revision, and focused not on keeping students in their positions but in expanding their achievement and growth as persons. These differences are about what one would expect given the children's relative chances for self-actualization in the jobs which the children could expect to acquire. Just as the middle class values autonomy because many of the jobs open to it require a measure of independent thinking and judgement, so the working class values the ability to take orders, control one's emotions, and to show respect for those in authority.

Certainly the desire for a transformed youth is not unique to fascism or Christianity, but it seems to run deeply in both and to spring, I would argue, from the same charismatic sources. Sternhell quotes a French account of youths in German work camps in 1933 constructing a 'magnificent road': 'Those handsome boys with blonde hair and bronzed skin' gave 'the impression of performing a priestly rite'.[80]

The highly charged nature of time in the Christian schools makes parents feel acutely the responsibility for raising children. It is not merely that 'we only pass this way once', but that the stakes of eternal salvation for the individual and for the community can be won or lost according to how one spends one's time. The faith itself may perish if it does not take root in the present generation. To avert such a danger to the community of faith these fundamentalist Christian parents needed more than mere affirmation and support in their roles as parents. They required protection from the 'times', which exposed their children to outside influences whose effects might endanger their young souls and the future of the faith itself. Thus these parents sought insulation from the larger society, relief from the public schools, guidance from their churches, and refuge in a curriculum and educational process that was highly ritualized. Purification was required, if the necessary transformation of the individual were to occur.

In both the working-class and middle-class evangelical communities, moreover, the teachers and students along with the parents professed that they were seeking to develop individuality. The fundamentalists did so within a strong framework of rules and regulations; the bulwarks of the self were positions and role-requirements. In developing the self the fundamentalists relied on external controls, spanking and supervision, while the charismatics relied on counselling, persuasion, support and the personal involvement of all members of the community in the educational process. While charismatics gave close attention to the contents of the soul, as it were, the fundamentalists looked the other way and gave the soul a greater measure of privacy in return for the child's performance. These compromises, Rose argues, simply reflect the rewards and constraints that the two classes respectively encountered in their own work and everyday life. The transformation of the young would enable them to take on adult roles in the same social world as their parents: either doing as they were told or thinking for themselves as their jobs might demand or permit. In this way the schools reproduced the very secular world that they had promised to redeem, transform and transcend.

Their rituals of transformation might alter the child, but like other rituals we have discussed, they would also reproduce rather than transform the world. That failure, I would argue, explains why so many fundamentalist and evangelical Christians have decided to seek control of public school boards rather than to maintain safe Christian havens in private schools.

It is not surprising that the covenant community, in its most serious attempt to redeem the times, has in fact been producing the sorts of social character the society needs for its factories and offices. As Weber reminded us, moreover, the fate of charisma is seldom a happy one. The individual is likely to become the servant of those who concentrate charisma in their own hands: parents and teachers, priests and chiefs, kings and emperors, in whose service total commitment is often demanded. Churches and schools, along with professionals, bureaucrats and a variety of experts, are the modern bearers of 'institutionalized charisma'. Thus the tendency of Christian schools to reproduce rather than to transform the world around them. The 'injury' is simply that secular provinces of education, the media and politics, present a constant threat to those who would seek to preserve the purity of their own immediate families and communities. Charisma embedded in the institutions of the centre threatens those on the periphery with spiritual extinction and the death of their own communities. The 'insult' is simply that, when the young are not transformed by the community of faith but become replicas of their counterparts in the 'world', there will be no future. After all, the secular world, by theological definition, is headed for extinction.

In these schools we therefore witness the melancholy fate of charisma. On the one hand, charisma claims to rise above time. The gift of grace enables the faithful to prevent or reverse the slow disintegration of the community from one generation to the next. On the other hand, charisma requires that it be tested in time – and over time. The schools studied by Susan Rose provided a panoply of tests: tests of knowledge and skill, tests of commitment and faith. As I have noted, Nikolas Rose has documented the widespread increase in the surveillance of the inner self by officials and experts.[81] The goal of such pedagogy is to create a social character that actively wants to be monitored and evaluated according to recognized norms for achievement and maturity. Susan Rose's Christian schools are no exception, and indeed the social pressures on the self were particularly intense in the middle-class schools, which sought to shape the inner character of the child. To the extent that they succeeded, the schools helped to shape a character that could withstand serious time pressures. The success of this ritualized educational process, however, may well have created not only a strong character but intense desires to escape from the tyranny of time altogether.

Many Christians are anxious about the future of the Christian community, not least because of outside influences, in the schools and the courts, in the mass media and the market-place, which continue to invade Christian premises. American society is changing the young faster than the old and the young together can change American society. It is no wonder that conservative Christians and evangelicals, perhaps more than most Americans, have been obsessed with time, since it is cruelly short for people of faith.

One way out of such intense time-pressures is through a millennial religious movement: a reaction-formation against temporal demands. Millenarianism speeds up the clock and makes time run out; as time runs out, moreover, the soul can face a test of its own existence and powers: a crucial test, even Armageddon, the final battle of good with evil. Millenarianism is thus an escape from the tyranny of time into a world in which souls no longer need to doubt their own capacity to stand the test of time.

The question is whether fundamentalists will spill their anxieties about time into the mainstream of American society sufficiently to unleash fascist impulses toward a millennial transformation and a radically new future. Here is the considered judgement of Charles Strozier in his recent study of American fundamentalists:

> The fundamentalist experience ranges across a continuum from Waco to Harlem, from complete surrender of the individual to the demands of a totalistic group and a charismatic leader to the empowered experience of building self-cohesion and salvaging community, with every kind of nuanced variation in between. Most fundamentalistic churches are not totalistic. Believers are too much in the world and themselves to imagine they are under some mind-bending system of control ... Adults entering these churches make free choices about participation ... But for all that the potential to move toward totalism remains. Social crisis, or a big war, or a disaster like nuclear terrorism could transform the movement overnight into a potent and active apocalyptic force, and so transform the American political and social landscape. The consequences of such a transformation are unpredictable, but it is probably not unreasonable to guess that they would not be welcome.[82]

· 3 ·

RITUALS OF AVERSION: BUYING TIME

If the modern world is running out of time, according to some prophets, it is because a day is coming in which killing will be virtually indiscriminate. According to such prophecy, the only discrimination will be that exercised by the Lord at his Second Coming, who will come just in time to remove his chosen ones from the scene of battle. After that, the sword will slay friend and foe, brother and enemy, with the blind enthusiasm of Armageddon.

The 'sword', however, has become nuclear. The prophecy of the Second Coming prior to a time of terrible destruction leading into the millennium has captured the imagination of millions of American citizens. According to Paul Boyer, well over a third of Americans polled in 1984 believed that 'biblical prophesies of Earth's destruction by fire referred to nuclear war, with 25 percent convinced that God would spare them personally'.[1] This belief, Boyer goes on to note, has had 'direct political implications' as well as indirect and long-term consequences. The direct implications appeared during the Reagan administration, when the President and several top cabinet members publicly expressed their conviction that they and the nation as a whole were living in times prophesied in biblical apocalypses. The Secretary of Defense, Weinberger, himself said that he was familiar with the Book of Revelation, believed that the world was going to end (preferably through an act of God), and that 'every day I think that time is running out'.[2] It is one thing when the people are reconciled and accustomed to the prospect of nuclear annihilation by the prophetic 'assurances' of premillennialists. It is another when those with access to nuclear power themselves believe that a day of nuclear destruction is imminent and inevitable. If modernity lacks confidence in its own means, religious or political, to avert disaster, time is short indeed.

Paradoxically, that prediction of indiscriminate slaughter derives from Ezekiel's apocalyptic vision. Boyer notes that Ezekiel (Chapter 37) foresaw a day of 'great shaking in the land of Israel'. In Ezekiel's vision, however, it is only the enemy of Israel that will be put to such confusion that '"everyman's sword shall be against his brother;" so great is the enemy's confusion that only a sixth of the attacking army survives'.[3] Israel remains steadfast and prevails. The worst that can happen, so to speak, is for murderous impulses to get out of control, so that brother kills brother in acts of internal violence. Whereas Ezekiel foresaw a day in which such disaster would have been averted from Israel and visited on its enemies, modern prophesies of a final battle offer no such hope of escape from a nuclear Armageddon, except for those few selected in advance by the Lord. Now, entire peoples will be destroyed by the policies which have been designed for their 'defence'. Nuclear war is fratricidal self-destruction on a global scale.

Ritual seeks to demonstrate and to accomplish what it foreshadows: the end of one era and the beginning of another, the transformation of the self, the aversion of disaster, or the renewal of a purified community. When ritual fails to buy, to make, or to renew time, however, rhetoric takes over. As Boyer points out, the enthusiasts of Armageddon have resisted every attempt by anti-nuclear activists, the peace movement and international organizations such as the United Nations, to deflect the hand of God from history.[4] By discrediting such peaceful initiatives and institutions, as well as by inuring millions to the prospect of nuclear holocaust, the prophets of modern apocalypse have set the stage for the fulfilment of their own worst predictions.

To put it more formally: when ritual fails, magical thinking is transferred from symbolic action to speech, from ritual to language. Public rhetoric becomes infused with references to Armageddon and holocaust as if these were inevitable rather than political, and therefore avoidable, disasters. In the case of Ronald Reagan, moreover, who had a tendency to believe in his own rhetoric, that faith was anchored in the text of the Book of

Revelation.[5] During the 1980s, Americans faced the chilling possibility that their own elected leaders might initiate the destruction of their people: the responsibility for this outcome, however, they assigned to God. The sacrifice of the entire nation thus became a quasi-liturgical act: smooth, effortless, inevitable, and, although carried out by humans, ordained by God.

Instead of courting the disasters of the last days, ritual seeks to prevent or avoid the worst dangers of the apocalypse. Cohn has demonstrated over and over again that the intent of such rituals as flagellation and voluntary poverty was to avert the judgement of God and thus to avoid an otherwise imminent and inevitable apocalypse.[6] Some apocalyptic expectations were no doubt given added impetus by real-life disasters: famine, war, plague and devastating social and economic disruptions. Nonetheless, the crusading poor of the Middle Ages first turned their weapons of prevention upon themselves in various rites of self-immolation in the hope of becoming the remnant that would survive the tribulation and judgement that was to come. These were rituals of aversion.

When rituals of aversion fail, therefore, all hell is likely to break loose. The enormous rage of the poor and the dispossessed, intensified by fears of further devastation, may be released not in symbolic acts but in direct aggression. That aggression, furthermore, may not be directed only toward targets outside the social order, i.e. toward external enemies, but toward the members of one's own community. Certainly the millenarian movements of the poor in the Middle Ages turned not only against Saracens and Turks, but toward fellow citizens: notably toward the rich and especially the clergy, but occasionally toward the members of the movement itself. According to Cohn, the flagellants not only stoned the clergy but attacked their own members who sought to prevent the massacre.[7] Fratricidal killing, in the larger sense, occurred when the members of these movements attacked their own fellow citizens and co-religionists. In the narrower sense, fratricide occurred when the flagellants killed monks who did not fully co-operate. That is precisely the danger that such rituals seek to avert: indiscriminate killing of members within the social order itself. In a very real sense, the flagellants' rites, like other rituals of protest against the Church, failed, and the consequences of that failure were widely lethal.

Averting Mayhem and Fratricide

To avert the danger of widespread, indiscriminate killing, traditional societies have had recourse to various rituals. Let us return to one example of aversive ritual that is already familiar to us from the discussion in the first chapter: Vernant's analysis of a rite described in detail by Xenophon in his *Constitution of Sparta.*[8] Performed immediately prior to a battle, the rite seeks favourable omens from Artemis in the slaying of a goat in front of the battle lines. Both armies are ready to attack, and the level of tense expectation among the Spartan or Athenian troops is at its highest while the king, with or without the aid of a seer, slaughters the goat and seeks signs that the attack should begin.

On maintaining order in the thick of battle hinges the survival of the social order itself. Every soldier must do no less but also no more than his part. If individual soldiers panic or are overcome with zeal, they will break ranks; that is, they will lose their sense of priorities and move to the front or fall behind. Of course, a rout of the army would endanger the social order itself, but so would an excess of zeal.

Vernant reports that during the sacrifice itself, the Greek armies were composed, quiet, and vulnerable. Once the signal was given that favourable omens had been received, however, the same soldiers quickly took up their arms and moved into battle, sometimes with a quiet zeal, at others with considerable fervour, but always under the severe discipline of a military command that reduces the will of the mass of soldiers to that of the general.[9] However, Vernant is quick to point out that when soldiers are caught up in a frenzy of killing, they can no longer distinguish the enemy from their own ranks. Referring to 'bestial violence,' he adds that

> Ally cannot be distinguished from enemy, self from other. In fury and madness the contagion of killing spreads. Killing

> becomes internecine, citizen slaughtering citizen, one friend another, a relative his kin. Blind and depraved, war becomes fratricidal butchery, generalized murder.[10]

Failure of the ritual occurs when killing becomes fratricidal and warfare internecine.

The antidote to frenzy, of course, is the surrender of the individual soldier's will to military authority. That self-sacrifice verges on the suicidal, even during the enactment of the ritual of omen-seeking before the battle. As Vernant makes us realize, the Greeks were often under heavy attack during their sacrifices before battle, and the soldiers had indeed laid down their arms during the sacrifice itself.[11] It is difficult to imagine Spartan soldiers allowing themselves to be killed in order to keep discipline during the sacrifice of a goat, but that is precisely what Plutarch as well as Xenophon record. On the other hand, once favorable omens had been announced, Plutarch notes, the Spartan army reacted 'like a spirited animal' and took up the fight: not, be it noted, with 'animal spirits' or 'bestial violence' but like an animal with spirit.[12] Clearly the soul had been forged in steadfast and unswerving contact with death, and those who had not been petrified were all the more able to engage fearlessly in battle with a spirit that was more than the equal of their enemy's. It was a soul, however, whose will was contained within the structure of military command.

Xenophon's account offers an important insight into the history of aversive rituals in general and of sacrifice in particular. Certainly in these sacrifices of a goat prior to battle we find critical moments in which sacrificial killing is the prelude to actual killing. On the other hand, it is clear that sacrifice was intrinsic to the ritualization of warfare. It would therefore be difficult to argue that sacrifice was derived from the hunt or warfare when both were so highly ritualized from the outset. Rather, it would be more logical on theoretical grounds to argue that sacrifice later became differentiated from warfare or the hunt and developed autonomously in relation to a wide array of social acts. Since killing in the hunt or in war turned into fratricidal frenzy, sacrifice was introduced to control passions at such critical moments. The differentiation of sacrifice from ritualized warfare was therefore a later development. In that case later forms of sacrifice, like the Passover itself, could also be regarded as recapitulating earlier experience of war and the hunt while also acting as a prophylactic against fratricide.

Clearly the primal sin of fratricide haunted other societies; Greece was not alone in fearing that it could not prevent animal spirits from tearing apart the social order. The civil war in Jerusalem, in which citizens did slaughter their fellow citizens, was precisely the fratricidal mayhem that the Passover ritual itself sought to avoid. Indeed, it is the prospect of a disaster not only to the army but to the social order as a whole that has led to the formation of militarized societies. In his study of German fascism, for instance, Staub notes that the decimation of the German people by plague in the fourteenth century, and by war in the seventeenth and nineteenth centuries, intensified the demand for the formation of an obedient citizenry along with the idealization of the Prussian military.[13]

> Influential German thinkers stressed the role of the state not as a servant of the people but as an entity to which citizens owed unquestioning obedience ... Fichte and Hegel also viewed the state as a superior organic entity to which the citizen owed complete allegiance ... Following and obeying Hitler became a source of honor and joy, expressed in the testimony of many Nazis before and after the collapse of the Third Reich.[14]

The surrender of the will to the social order, and especially of the will of the soldier to the commander, is regarded as necessary for the survival of the order as a whole. The sacrifice of the soul and of the intellect is therefore an offering, full of 'honour' and 'joy', and not merely an expedient or a strategy. The Nietzschean man of the future, of unfettered action and remorseless aggression, can purchase the survival of the people and of the nation if, and only if, he has a mass of followers without a will of their own.

This widespread loss of an autonomous will is one aspect of what has been called 'soul-loss'. For instance, Staub evokes the notion of the splitting of the self or of irrationality; he likewise refers to the domination of the individual by the unconscious or by repression, and to passivity and depression that make one unable to respond realistically or compassionately to the opportunities and threats of one's environment.[15] Witness the compliance or indifference of ordinary Germans and the apathy of those who saw no hope for survival and no reason, therefore, for resistance. At other times, however, he insists, as in the case of the Nazi doctors in the death camps, that they were not acting autonomously or out of character; on the contrary, they 'were ideologically committed Nazis who had undergone substantial resocialization'.[16] Witness the more obvious and dramatic subservience of such groups as the medical profession or the SS to the commands of authority.

The soul can be lost not only by being held captive to authority but by the eruption of powerful passions from within the psyche. One of the more attractive and effective fundamentalist preachers in Strozier's account feared that 'someone without "God in his heart", i.e. without a soul, will "push the button"': a metaphor with clear reference to the danger of a nuclear holocaust.[17] The preacher compared himself with Jonah, whose preaching to Nineveh only bought some time. Indeed, Strozier makes it clear that 'At best we can only buy some time': a position that he attributes to fundamentalists but for which he displays considerable sympathy himself in view of the actual danger of wholesale destruction.[18]

It is therefore clear from Strozier's account that some fundamentalists need to defend themselves from their own violent impulses and imagination. The pressure from passions that can disintegrate the psyche is suggested by some of the more bloody passages in the Book of Revelation: passages that continue to fascinate many fundamentalists. To defend the soul from such violent outbursts, the believer can seek a personal relationship to Jesus Christ. Jesus is thus seen as a potent defender against violent tendencies that are internal and – for many – largely still unconscious. In some cases, however, the tendencies are not unconscious at all. Strozier recounts the story of the fundamentalist preacher who compared himself to Jonah.[19] In that man's younger days he had been a gang member who had seen more than enough beatings and killings; he knew his own violent impulses intimately and, regardless of his feelings about them, had acted them out under the trying circumstances of gang warfare. His conversion and ministry were a powerful and, for the time being, successful reaction against such violence in himself and in his past. I say 'for the time being' since it is clear that the possibility of such violence continued to haunt the preacher, even as he led himself and his congregation away from destructiveness into constructive participation in the life of the city.

As a religious movement, then, fundamentalism seeks to ward off the dangers of violence from which the rituals of the churches no longer offer protection. In other words, it is apparent even to fundamentalists that their own praise and prayers may not be enough to avert the imminent danger of a nuclear Armageddon. They can only hope, therefore, for divine intervention which will liberate some of the faithful from the tyranny of time and enable them to witness the holocaust from the vantage point of the skies. When aversive rituals do fail, the usual boundaries between order and chaos, life and death, the civilized and the bestial, are easily transgressed.

When Aversive Rituals Fail

When ritual fails not only can one observe collective behaviour that a modern sociologist might call hysterical contagion or simply panic; not only does killing often cease to be symbolic and become fratricidal and frenzied. Anxiety over the future becomes endemic, and prophetic or messianic leaders emerge to divert impending disaster from the nation. In such moments longings for collective triumphs over the passage of time break out of the framework of ritual into religious and political movements with markedly fascist tendencies. There they may be acted out in what appear to be strivings for liberation. These very strivings, however, also exhibit what I have called fascist tendencies toward the resumption of order, the achievement of purity, the increased surveillance of the individual by the community, demands for sacrifice and commitment, and attempts to restore traditional virtues and primitive harmony to the nation or people as a whole.

Some symbolic protests, of course, are clearly anti-authoritarian with no apparent admixture of yearnings for subordination. Take, for example, the American colonies before the revolution. In the metropolitan centres like New York and Boston, one can find direct symbolic attacks on the king: his effigy is burnt, his statue is destroyed and buried, and his insignia are torn from buildings. Other displays of rebellion, however, are more ambiguous. In the case of the Boston Tea Party, for instance, one finds a less direct attack on the king and a more disguised assault on patriarchal rule. In that case, colonists dressed up as Indians: i.e. not only a form of disguise but a dramatic enactment of threat from the margins of the society. As Grotanelli has pointed out, moreover, rebels in England and America for centuries have disguised themselves as mythical characters or as women; slaves or native Americans are therefore only relatively recent additions to the repertoire of rebel disguises.[20] In the very adoption of these masks of subordination we find not only a disguised desire for liberation but a covert submission to authoritarian control.

If this interpretation seems questionable, consider the French Revolution, where we also find rites of anti-patriarchal rebellion. Take, for example, a ritual that honoured both the Swiss soldiers who had mutinied and the national guardsmen who also had been slain when the army suppressed the mutiny. The surviving mutineers marched in a procession behind their broken chains, along with sarcophagi dedicated to slain mutineers and national guardsmen who had attacked those symbols of patriarchy, their 'aristocratic officers'.[21] Lest the anti-patriarchal themes be missed, a statue of Louis XV was blindfolded and adorned with a red cap, the colour of blood and revolution. However, the spectacle featured statues of Voltaire, Rousseau and Benjamin Franklin, and four men carrying the Declaration of the Rights of Man.[22] On the one hand, the procession of mutineers itself was a symbolic enactment of mutiny and was interpreted as such by the more conservative patriots who did not miss its message. Its watchword was no doubt 'Liberty'. On the other hand, however, the procession carried forward the embodiment of a new, albeit enlightened, authority that would make strong demands on citizens for sacrifice, commitment and purity of the will. Although the spectacular parade in honour of the Swiss mutineers contained anti-patriarchal themes, it also employed the symbols of the political and cultural centre to reinforce demands for the sacrifice of the individual to the collectivity. When rituals of aversion fail to stave off fratricidal conflict, demonstrations and spectacles will take the place of ritual. In these more ambiguous ceremonies, it is not always possible to know where sacrifice ends and insubordination begins.

Even more visibly fascist were the processions of the more conservative among the French revolutionaries: those who favoured a constitutional monarchy. For instance, Kertzer recounts, a counter-parade against the celebration of the Swiss mutineers honoured a slain mayor, a Monsieur Simonneau, and it featured women in Roman togas and slaves carrying a statue of the law: the typical use of marginal types in a patriarchal order to reinforce patriarchal authority.[23] Another ceremony, conducted by Robespierre, enshrined Wisdom and burnt a symbol of Atheism. These demonstrations, one designed by the supporters of the new, constitutional monarchy, the other Jacobin, allowed some ambiguity as to whether women and slaves were insiders or outsiders. The boundaries of the social order had already been breached.

Patriarchies typically cast women and the young in the symbolic role of outsiders who present a threat to the system. In everyday life, women and the young may be fully integrated into the system in question, but on high ritual occasions they are cast in the role of those who represent the threat of death to the system itself. Women are double-coded in this way for obvious reasons. *In actual fact, they may be a threat to patriarchal authority, and to patrilineage they represent the threat of alien paternity.* Young people also represent the threat of uncontrolled aggression and sexuality, of autonomous thinking, and of an eventual challenge to patriarchal rule at critical moments such as the succession between generations. That is why women and the young are typecast in the liturgical role of being potential sources of negation to patriarchal social systems.[24] The fascist impulse in patriarchal societies makes it very clear that women and the young, outsiders and those who think for themselves, are dangerous indeed.

On the other hand, women and the young may be clothed in the garments or uniforms of the state and thus made to appear conformable to the new order. *Where rituals of aversion fail to keep outsiders in their place, demonstrations and social movements will assign them new social codes and locations that are at best ambiguous.* In the counter-parade, conservatives and radicals could not agree on the meaning of one symbol, a shark being skewered on a spade: some seeing the shark as the people, others seeing the shark as official or popular tyranny.[25] Even with the lines drawn relatively sharply in these rites of rebellion, there was room for ambiguity.

Rituals of aversion are compromised whenever they fail to distinguish insiders from outsiders. For instance, as I have noted, Americans were both insiders and outsiders to the French Revolution and therefore doubly suspect, like slaves. I mention slaves in this context because they also are 'liminal' figures who are both insiders and yet who represent sources of possible danger to the security and survival of the social system. Patriarchal codes signify women, slaves and the young as both insiders and outsiders. Indeed, women, the young, the uninitiated, slaves and strangers are often assigned the task in ritual of being in touch with the antisocial, the unsocialized, the unknown, the uncanny, the wild. However, this use of insiders to personify outside forces suggests the intimate presence of what is alien to a social order. The public demonstrations during the French Revolution, in making this double use of individuals to convey both the familiar and the strange, required completion by rituals of purification. Only these latter rites, I will argue in the next chapter, can claim to purge a society of outside influences and to restore the social order to wholeness.

In effective and legitimate patriarchal societies, women and the young can be temporarily cast in the role of representing the wild side, so to speak, of uncontrolled aggression and sexuality; they are allowed to represent a threat to patrilineage and patriarchy.[26] Therefore the young and women are given dramatic roles in various rites by which they are associated with aggression and death, only to have the danger they represent overcome by a return to patriarchal society. When women and the young are successfully transformed into insiders, they can be made to represent outsiders in the rituals by which patriarchal societies dramatize symbolic victories over the threats to their survival. *When these transformations have not been successfully completed, and when the social order is threatened by the loss of control over its normative and geographic boundaries, fascist tendencies are mobilized: the most obvious and tragic case in point being, of course, the Jews of Europe.*

This interplay of symbolic opposites may go far to explaining the persistent anti-Americanism in French culture. It has been more convenient for the French to represent Americans as the source of dangerous outside influences than to locate these as internal to French society. Eugen Weber points out that the French have long 'projected onto America their fears as much as their hopes for France, [and] investigating their attitudes to America illuminates how they felt about themselves, their identity and the modernization of their country'.[27]

Besides being vulgar, boring and intrusive, Weber notes, Americans have been feared by the French as the harbingers of the disastrous mechanization of everyday life, of the triumph of technology over culture, and of the substitution of money for passion. The presence of a statue of Benjamin Franklin at the head of one of the parades during the Revolution can only have intensified the concern of conservatives that greed and rationality, boorishness and a mean, calculating commercialism were about to destroy the soul of France. As Weber points out, the French in the twentieth century found their German invaders less intrusive than the liberating army of Americans.[28] The desire to keep French society from running out of time by averting the prospect of Americanization may go far to explaining Vichy. In any event, rituals of aversion have difficulty working in social conditions that confuse friends with enemies.

France was not the only country, of course, to have trouble distinguishing its friends from its enemies. As Gaustad remarks, 'Throughout so much of American history, it has been distressingly difficult to separate the "ins" from the "outs".'[29] Even during the American Revolution, American patriots were offering toasts to the King in 1776, while other patriots were cutting down the Liberty Tree, burning royal effigies, and destroying royal insignia. It was exceedingly difficult, for instance, to distinguish a patriot from a traitor when, according to Kertzer, even in 1776 some patriots (not Tories) were gathering to give toasts to the king and to celebrate his birthday, while others were burning, hanging and burying the king in effigy.[30] Under these conditions, I would suggest, particular symbols acquire new meaning, as a demand is created for symbolic tests of loyalty to one regime or to the other. The Liberty Tree, a product of the earlier riots over the Stamp Act, took on added significance both to the patriots and the English soldiers who, in trying to cut one down, sparked 'New York's largest riot'.[31]

Colonies provide a particularly good example of the difficulty of distinguishing insiders from outsiders, since they are more or less permeated by the presence of rulers who are absent. Some colonies are ruled directly, others indirectly. In the British North American colonies, for instance, some members of the population were relatively insulated from the centres of British culture and influence, while others participated directly in a market, in the educational institutions and professions, and in offices that were closely associated with England.

In colonies, of course, outsiders have already breached the boundaries of the social system. Rituals of aversion are therefore more likely to survive among those least directly exposed to the colonizers. Among those with the most direct and continuous contact with the colonizers, one would expect to find demonstrations and symbols that are more mixed and ambiguous in signifying revolt and the desire to exclude outsiders.

At the Margins: Hysteria

If one looks to the margins of America and France rather than at their cultural centres, one will find people who had not been transformed by the usual rites; and in the crisis of the Revolution their panic and passion were again escaping social controls. In the Berkshires rather than in Boston, therefore, one could find colonists who had marginalized themselves by leaving the more settled Eastern communities, and perhaps also a few English, engaged in various forms of ecstatic religion. As Garrett observes, some, like Ann Lee, were transmitting messages from heaven and leading their followers through perfection back into heaven itself.[32] Outsiders though they were, they were being promised that they alone would become the true insiders, and the current insiders would be left outside the kingdom to come.

On the margins, as I have suggested, rituals of aversion can flourish, along with liberating gestures, precisely because there is less immediate threat of direct intrusion by the forces of the centre. In France, according to Garrett, since the 1730s and certainly during the revolution, there were many religious movements quite parallel to the ecstatic and fervent, pious and millenarian movements in the American colonies.[33] He tells of one woman, Catherine Theot, who 'did penance for the nation', held public meetings, preached sermons, dispensed with the clergy and with the official rites of the Church, and announced that God was about to lead his chosen people, the French, into a new heaven and a new earth. Not only would these rites avert the worst tribulations of the new millennium; they were even more anti-patriarchal than the populist rites in Paris that had put a red hat on the blindfolded statue of Louis XV as they marched to symbolic victory. In both countries the marginal took to the woods, bypassed the local clergy, held their own services, saw visions and prophesied the millennium: all, however, with more or less total disregard to the course of the revolution itself.

On the margins, individuals can interact in ways that do not reveal or threaten their places in the larger society. They also enjoy more degrees of freedom in their personal experiences and in their sources of inspiration and authority. Contrast the role of women in the conservatives' ritual mentioned above with the role of women in the rites of these marginal people. In the Parisian spectacles, women were given the honour of wearing Roman togas as symbols of civic order, and slaves were given the right to hold up the emblems of the law. Among the devotees in the woods outside Paris, women were very visible in both the traditional and the ecstatic forms of popular religion, and in some cases took on the stature of prophets on the national scene.

Under these conditions aversive rituals are not very well suited to warding off disastrous conflict and preventing the mass outbreak of hysteria or indiscriminate killing. For instance, Garrett notes that, in the midst of the revolution, when the rebel cause was not succeeding, one church 'described its revival as having taken place "in the midst of surrounding dangers and encompassed with innumerable evils"'.[34] It was a time filled with omens, many of them bad, such as skies darkened with smoke and, of course, the bloody scenes of war itself.[35] These made a profound impression on uncertain souls and filled many with a horror that they ascribed to an impending day of judgement. These revivals, despite all the later revisionist attempts to link them with a successful revolution, were oriented not toward politics and revolt but toward conversion and averting God's millennial displeasure. As Garrett puts it, speaking not of official religious ideologies but of popular religion:

> what one does not find, anywhere, is the suggestion that these revivals and the American revolution were together part of God's providence for the world. The intellectual tradition of linking New England's political evolution to a millennial scheme of repentance and conversion, a tradition that stretched from the Mathers through Jonathan Edwards to innumerable preachers of the revolutionary era, does not seem to have become part of the popular consciousness, at least not yet.[36]

Even at the margins of colonies, however, the larger society, with its alien influence, has a potent and ambiguous effect on local loyalties and aspirations. Rituals of aversion, therefore, are often mixed with gestures of subordination to the colonial authorities. Students of various 'awakenings' in the British (and American) colonies of North America have therefore noted the spiritual uncertainties of large numbers of people, many of whom seek out the clergy in considerable anguish over the state of their souls. Lanternari, for instance, notes that during the 1920s and 1930s subjects of Anglo-American rule in West Africa showed unmistakable signs of psychic instability and poured into churches associated with the 'praying movement' (*Aladura*).[37] Like the American colonials two centuries earlier, they were critical of dogmatism and of popular magic, sought to return to the Bible for inspiration and authority, and were profoundly convinced of their need for healing and repentance. Like their American counterparts of the eighteenth century, they too were convinced of the superiority of European culture and listened to Wesleyan preachers, relied on water for spiritual cleansing, engaged in ecstatic or visionary religious practices, and sought assistance from the Holy Spirit in combating Satan and in averting illness, whether the bubonic plague or influenza. Traditional rites seemed powerless to avert disaster, and new sacrifices were therefore required: the sacrifices of a contrite heart, perhaps, and a broken spirit. I would suggest that such revivals reflect the failure of aversive rituals to expunge dangers from outside a social order, especially when these dangers are now carried by insiders, e.g. a rising middle class attracted to the alien but superior power of the colonizers, rather than represented solely by outsiders.

It is clear that aversive rituals not only place strong pressures on individuals to sacrifice; that is, they not only inculcate a sense of sin and of a debt that must therefore be paid if death is to be averted and the gift of life is not to be taken away. These rituals also confer a sense of a powerful presence that can dwell in the soul of the individual to fortify it against all disaster. It is a presence, however, that is a bit ephemeral; it can come and go with relative ease, like the 'free soul' or the phantasm. It is charisma, with all the sense of divine power and yet unpredictability that that term implies.

To fortify the soul against disasters like the plague or an epidemic of influenza, not to mention war and bloodshed, requires infusions of the spirit, i.e. charismatic endowment. There is, however, a catch to the gift of grace. It always has something to prove and requires to be tested time and time again. To reinforce the flagging soul and to instil rudimentary controls over the passions is certainly one function of charismatic leaders. Through such leaders the marginal become exposed to what David Martin has called the process of 'betterment' by which Pentecostal churches in Latin America have been making new recruits and fitting them for modernity.[38] These movements, Martin notes, are the Third World counterparts to English dissent and especially to Wesleyanism. Located on the periphery, they are ambivalently oriented toward their political and cultural centres. The orientation is positive in enabling the members of the movement to take advantage of opportunities for betterment, in every sense of the term, and yet negative in warning them to avoid the corruption and hostilities of an unconverted world headed for divine judgement.

Similar movements in West Africa in the first half of the twentieth century offered social control and betterment under charismatic leadership. Lanternari, for instance, has studied the history of one such leader: a man named William Harris.[39] While in prison for preaching anti-American messages in Liberia, he received an angelic visitor, Gabriel, and the Pentecostal gift of the Spirit. Harris's message after leaving prison was clearly millennial, pro-American and pro-European, and focused on repentance, the study of the Bible, literacy and education. In this fashion not only Liberians but Harris's followers in the neighbouring countries of the Ivory Coast, the Gold Coast, Ghana and Nigeria found themselves disposed to enter more complex social and economic networks. The soul, fortified by grace against outside influences and potential disaster, is thus readied for the journey toward the centre and its sometimes alien but prepossessing sources of enlightenment.

In this way rebellion mixes with emulation, and outsiders seek to become insiders, as religious movements fill the void left by aversive rituals that can no longer fend off disaster. The Harris movement and its offshoots in West Africa in the first decades of the twentieth century can therefore be compared with the revivals taking place in parts of New England during the years of the American Revolution. Both emphasized ecstasies and visions, both endowed their followers with abundant charismatic gifts, and both sought to fortify them against the advance of Satan and to prepare them for divine judgement.[40] Lanternari indeed confirms that miracles of healing were being substituted in West Africa for 'traditional sacrifice and magical rites'.[41] Thus prophetic movements capitalize not only on the failure of sacrifice to ward off disaster but on the successes of traditional religion in raising expectations and endowing individuals with spiritual gifts. Harris's movement in particular used the Christian message to fortify and endow the spirit with charismatic gifts even while rejecting traditional sacrifices and promising a new era of unprecedented success for his followers.

These prophetic movements seek to succeed where traditional rites have failed to ward off disaster. As we have already noted, similar West African movements developed in Lagos and Nigeria when these countries were being devastated by a bubonic plague and an influenza epidemic.[42] One such movement (the *Aladura* or 'praying' movement), began during the flu epidemic of 1918. Note, in Lanternari's description of the Faith Tabernacle, which was one of the offshoots of the *Aladura* movement, the contradictory elements of revolt against a patriarchal society along with emulation of European culture:

> Nowhere did the Faith Tabernacle touch on colonialism. Its leaders co-operated, up to the 1930s, with the colonial authorities, and made no protest against European culture in general. Actually its predominant trend, to the present day, is to imitate European cultural models and to recuperate the original Bible, criticizing dogmatic missionary attitudes and paternalistic behavior.[43]

Thus the new shamans, being Christians, not only banned the use of traditional shamans and their magic but also rejected authoritarian Christian missions. The indigenous shamans had clearly failed to protect the people not only against epidemic and plague but also from the clearly superior European culture. On the other hand, the missionaries were dogmatic and paternalistic: hardly fit models for a people seeking liberation from traditional authority. These are precisely the conditions under which traditional rites fail to avert disaster: a society with weakened boundaries, along with traditional expectations that the individual's social character and relationships will conform to the standards of the larger society.

In terms of the model I am proposing here, it is clear that these movements reflected the failure of aversive rituals to prevent disaster and were not yet attempts to purify the land of alien influences that had become endemic to the social system. As Lanternari goes on to note, Nigeria differed from colonies in other parts of Africa by being subject only to indirect rule and by being spared the effects of European forms of land tenure.[44] That is why the movements in West Africa are so closely akin to those experienced in what Garrett called the 'less developed' parts of the New England colonies in the late eighteenth century. The boundaries of their societies were being breached by economic dislocation as markets expanded. Village life was being threatened by the expansion of towns and cities where people came into direct contact with a 'superior' culture, whether that of their more educated colonial counterparts or that of the British and Europeans themselves. On the other hand, rule was still indirect, and so there were not yet multiple sources of inspiration and authority. The degrees of social freedom were still limited, and the range of social relationships was not yet as broad as it was for those in the cities where élites, both domestic and foreign, resided.

A Theoretical Issue: The Problem of Time

The presence of colonial rule, for instance, has produced fascistic tendencies in more than one colony unsure of its boundaries and therefore anxious about its potency and its ability to survive: witness the conflict in Rwanda between the Tutsi and the Hutu. More is at stake here than merely the conflict between cultures or between official and popular versions of religious tradition. What is at stake is clearly the life of a social universe that is threatened both literally and symbolically with death itself. A colonial regime does undermine the boundaries of the colonized social system. It is therefore no wonder that people were deeply troubled and felt that their souls were in danger from outside forces. The failure of rituals to avert disaster thus called for a religious movement which would enable the individual to develop powers commensurate with those of the alien within the gates. If traditional rites fail to avert disaster from the advent of outside influences, the community must provide new sources of spiritual immunity against the return of the enemy.

The burning of effigies, the sacrifice of animals, the parade of statues in armed processions, or the use of disguises suggest an evil that returns: the 'wild' or unsocialized aspects of human nature. Indeed, Burkert argues that there was a 'continuous evolution from hunt to sacrifice'. He argues on the basis of two assumptions:

> (1) some groups of hunters installed rituals that made the killing of animals for food a striking and labyrinthine affair that drew attention, affecting the life and consciousness of all members, and (2) these customs did not constitute a 'blind alley' in the evolution of civilization, but set the path for further development through the Near Eastern Neolithic to the Mediterranean high cultures. This line of tradition still seems viable.[45]

Certainly the sacrifice to Artemis is not the earliest example of aversive ritual, i.e. of an attempt to ward off the fatal consequences of possible retaliation by those at whose expense one has lived. After reviewing much of the anthropological and ethological evidence, Walter Burkert comes to the conclusion that the 'life and consciousness of all members' were deeply affected by the rituals associated with hunting: rituals that became over time rites of sacrifice. To be sure, these rituals expressed joy and triumph at the killing of the animal and at the promise, therefore, of food. However, they also expressed remorse at the killing and attempted to compensate the victim or even to restore the victim to life through symbolic means, e.g. the placing of horns beneath a statue or covering a clay figure of a bear with the bear's skin. This sacrificial offering was itself an attempt to ward off the anger of a vengeful victim of the hunt.

In the absence of successful rites of aversion, a character is required who will be unafraid of the vengeful motives of the dead. Nietzsche celebrated 'the man of the future', who engages in the slaughter of the 'millions of the bungled and botched' without a moment's hesitation or remorse.[46] War becomes itself a rite in which the destruction of the nation is averted as the superior few slaughter the mass of the indifferent or inferior humanity. The same advance purchase on a more glorious future is envisaged, I would argue, in notions of a 'rapture' that precedes the Christian millennial rule on earth. In the 'rapture', those few Christians deemed worthy of being saved enjoy the view of the ordeal and slaughter of the unworthy millions.

In this interpretation I am assuming that there is something magical in the thinking of the individual engaged in the act of killing. The future becomes a source of dread because past killing may return to haunt the victorious. Time is not naturally an irreversible and linear flow. Without the proper sacrifice the past may return with a vengeance. For instance, take Burkert's interpretation of the sacrificial offering to the victim of the hunt. Concerning remorse, he notes,

> Nothing of the like is found in chimpanzees: they apparently have no feelings of guilt, they exhibit just the faintest signs of grudge. *They evidently fail to realize the time dimension*, the consequences of the past, the demands of the future. Man, by contrast, is painfully aware of this dimension, the main characteristic of which is irreversibility. The most drastic experience of irreversibility, however, is death. This is both acknowledged and overcome by ceremonial killing. *It is striking to see how much sacrifice in ancient religion is concerned with the time dimension*: through prayers, vows, and thanksgiving with new vows, sacrifices form a continuous chain that must never be broken; any important enterprise starts with sacrifice as a first step that cannot be taken back.[47]

As an 'ideal type' Burkert's thesis works to suggest what to look for, with the variations reminding us of the need to explain the conditions under which not only chimpanzees or South African bushmen but Christians and fascists can contemplate without remorse the destruction of others. The hunter needs to buy time for an ego that fears retaliation from a source of life that has been destroyed or consumed. The primitive psyche, being empty, draws sustenance from others by identifying with or otherwise consuming them. As a result, the ego feels an obligation to make payments over time lest those who have been consumed take revenge. Many Christians, however, can joyfully anticipate a day in which they witness, from the safety of the skies, the slaughter of humans whom they regard as sources of contamination: impurities to be removed. It is only the pure, of course, who are exempted from the final sacrifice: a reversal of the traditional association of purity with the sacrificial offering. Conversely, fascist movements have seen themselves as offering a sacrifice by removing sources of impurity from the body politic.

I fully agree with Burkert that time is of the essence of ritual, and that rituals seek to overcome the problem of remorse. Remorse is not due simply to the awareness that one cannot undo the past. The past, after all, is what is created by ritual in an attempt to put death and the possibility of the victim's revenge behind one. Remorse is an indicator that the vengeful return of the victim is not only a hypothetical possibility in the future but is anticipated and partially experienced in the present. That is the difference, as Freud put it, between simple mourning and real melancholia. In the case of melancholia, the lost or destroyed object is also internalized. So it is with remorse and the need for purification. If aversive rituals fail to make time irreversible, the door of the psyche is opened to the return of the victim's image or spirit. No wonder, then, that those who are by themselves unable to put the past behind them must rely on the magical action of ritual.

In the case of rituals of aversion, the dreaded object threatens to intrude both in space and in time. The enemy may not remain outside the individual or community and in the future. Such rituals are therefore employed to forestall imminent and imaginary dangers, e.g. the approach of an alien army or the return of one's victims. The most dreaded future is the one that heralds the return of a vanquished enemy or victim seeking revenge. That there is an impulse to repeat old murders suggests that the initial bloodshed may have been a source of considerable pleasure; indeed Burkert's account of early hunting rituals leaves us no doubt on that score. Hence the rituals of aversion allow the community a chance to savour an earlier triumph even while seeking to ward off the return of the victim.

In this same article, Burkert recognizes a difference between his emphasis on hunting and the work of René Girard, who sees the scapegoat as ensuring the purity of the community through being purged or abandoned. The difference, I would argue, is not worth detaining us. Burkert is clearly talking about rituals of aversion, whereas Girard focuses more exclusively on rituals of purification. Burkert is focusing on the situation of a human band surrounded by animal predators or enemies who must be satisfied with a victim before the rest of the band can be saved. The willingness of the individual to be offered as a substitute and sacrifice for the others guarantees the liberation of the group from the threat of imminent death. This too is seen not as a helpless victimization of the individual but as a voluntary act: indeed a consummate act of self-offering and selfhood: 'the victim is outcast and savior at the same time'.[48] Whereas Girard is concerned with rituals of purification, Burkert seems primarily interested in rituals of aversion.

The formation of the individual through ritual is thus a dialectical process. With the killing of the beast, the individual is guaranteed of survival, along with the group. The continuity of the community and of the self is accomplished. The triumph over death, as well as the continuation of life, are communal guarantees of the individual's existence: an existence which is coterminous, in the early hunting groups, with the life of the group itself. Nonetheless, Burkert indicates that there is also something strongly individualistic in hunting: an opportunity for the display of cunning, strength and prowess. Thus there is a 'Lord of Sacrifice' at the ceremonial feast, identification with whom can provide further guarantees of the self's existence. The hunt and its triumphal act of killing is a moment not to be lost, but to be enshrined both in collective memory and in the heart of the individual. To lose this moment would be to lose the self once realized in decisive and life-saving action for the sake of the community.

· 4 ·

RITUALS OF PURIFICATION: RENEWING TIME

It is not always possible, of course, to direct murderous passions outward against a real or imagined enemy. Sometimes the dreaded day of judgement, in which hatred seeks to settle old scores and eliminate old rivals, is not merely imminent but immanent. Rituals are required to settle conflicts that 'threaten to poison social life and tear the community apart'.[1] As Kertzer goes on to point out, many of these rites are judicial. Indeed, I would argue, there is a wide range of rituals which have as their object the purification of a social system from the passions and dangers that threaten to poison and disrupt it from within. These dangers may be seen as outside influences that have already infiltrated into the social networks of a society whose organizations and geographic boundaries are still intact.

Whether through penitential or judicial rites, rituals of purification seek to purge the society of its own contaminants. When these rituals are owned and controlled by various élites, the stabilizing function of these rituals is most evident. When, however, peripheral or oppressed groups and communities develop their own rituals of purification, these may pose a threat to established authorities at the political or cultural centre.

In his study of millenarian enthusiasms in the Middle Ages, Norman Cohn finds entire populations obsessed with the need to purify themselves.[2] By associating themselves with leaders, whom they imagined to be 'purely spiritual beings', the 'eschatologically inspired hordes' could imagine themselves to have transcended various forms of pollution: greed, lust and mortality.[3] If these same people engaged in rape or massacre, Cohn noted, their actions were pure because done in obedience to the dictates of a transcendent master with an eschatological mission.

'They were bright armies,"clothed in white linen, white and clean".'[4]

Such obsessions with purity, and such fantasies of purification, require a certain amount of delusion if they are to be sustained. In addition to the delusions of grandeur and holiness that came from association with a charismatic leader, Cohn reports other delusions about the impurity of the clergy and of Jews:

> To these demons in human form, the Jew and the 'false cleric', was attributed every quality which belonged to the Beast from the Abyss – not only his cruelty but also his grossness, his animality, his blackness and uncleanness. Jewry and clergy together formed the foul black host of the enemy which stood opposite the clean white army of the Saints – 'the children of God, that we are, poisonous worms, that you are', as a medieval rhymester put it. And the Saints knew that it was their task to wipe that foul black host off the face of the earth, for only an earth which had been so purified would be fit to carry the new Jerusalem, the shining kingdom of the Saints.[5]

Purification is possible only when a society has boundaries that are sufficiently intact to be maintained or restored through purging the society of unwanted influences. On the other hand, purification is only required when outside influences have begun to permeate a community or society. As I have noted, a society can be made permeable to such influences when it is no longer tightly integrated. That is, individuals have the liberty to engage in social relationships that far exceed their roles within the community itself. One example of such liberty, as I have noted, was pilgrimage, in which individuals from a wide range of societies had the freedom to leave their normal obligations and to engage with each other in intense, however temporary, relationships on the way to a sacred centre. At the sacred centre, of course, those associations were subsumed by the individual's obligations to his or her own community, e.g. to pray for the departed and to maintain its sacred places.

A society is integrated, I have suggested, to the extent that social interaction expresses and reinforces the structure of the social order, and to the extent also that social character expresses and reinforces the requirements of social interaction. The relationships between generations, for instance, must follow a certain pattern if the young are not prematurely to compete with their elders for scarce satisfactions and rewards. As I noted in the preceding chapter, conservative Christian communities are particularly concerned with the formation of a social character that fits the young to take their places at the proper time within the community; one by-product of such early education is that the young are shaped in ways that reproduce the requirements of the class system.

Many communal distinctions, for instance, reflect the ways that different groups or communities imagine and shape the experience of time. Christians are those who share Sundays, just as Jews shared their sabbath on Saturdays: clear temporal boundaries that were intended to keep both communities purified from contamination by the other.[6] So long as these two groups remain relative strangers, furthermore, it is possible for one community to demonize the other as being beyond the pale of time. It is only the other community that has no grip on the hem of eternity; its time is therefore always passing away. When, however, individuals can associate outside the boundaries of their own communities, the dangers of assimilation set in. It was because German Jews were being assimilated into German society that Nazis could successfully employ images of pollution and demand national purification. Under these conditions, I would suggest, individuals, groups and communities become more inventive and extreme in their characterizations of the other community and more impressed with the dangers of contamination.

Cohn is quite clear that such drastic symbolic splitting between good and evil social universes was pathological. He does not mind using the word 'delusion' to describe the demonization of entire classes and categories of people in the Middle Ages and the cruel deprivations that ensued.[7] Cohn also traces these tendencies to locate pollution in others to a wide range of sources. Some are endemic to Western civilization, e.g. the traditional sources of eschatological hope and fantasy, such as the Book of Revelation or the *Sibylline Oracles*, and perennial class conflict between peasants on the one hand, and the clergy and nobles on the other, with burghers in between taking sides according to the dictates of expedience and circumstance.

To explain why these pressures intensified during the thirteenth and fourteenth centuries, moreover, Cohn turns to the sort of explanation which is consistent with our model. It is clear, for instance, that individuals who had been living within the tightly integrated social structures of the village, of kinship and of the feudal system found themselves able to interact with others from other places and ethnic groups through newly opened channels of travel and commerce. This wider range of social interaction, furthermore, opened up to the individual new sources not only of inspiration and authority but of insecurity. On the one hand, greed was intensified by unprecedented opportunities for investment and profit as new markets opened up in the thirteenth and fourteenth centuries, new forms of trade and exchange with foreigners were established, and the necessary financial institutions, such as large-scale banking, were developed. Jews were then stereotyped as the symbols of greed and pollution, in the form of such bestial icons as scorpions, snakes, frogs, toads and lizards: 'dirty' and dangerous animals, i.e. outside, subhuman influences from nature itself.

As the Black Death itself decimated entire villages in the fourteenth century, new demands were therefore created for purging the society of outside influences:

> Thus when the Black Death reached western Europe in 1348 it was at once concluded that some class of people must have introduced into the water-supply a poison concocted of spiders, frogs and lizards – all of them symbols of earth, dirt and the Devil ...[8]

Cohn goes on to note that those most prone to this sort of delusional explanation were those most susceptible to outside influences. They were the insecure members of overpopulated cities, the marginal workers, those least able to make a living on the land, and those who were no longer helped by the ties of kinship and social obligation that had held together the feudal social system. Those whose greed is stimulated by new opportunities, and whose fears are heightened by outside influences that disrupt what few ties and security they possess, are those most likely to seek charismatic sources of help and to demonize others as being both greedy and destructive.

When a society becomes less tightly integrated, its people become the bearers of outside influences. Individuals assimilate, as in the case of colonials who adopt the manners and ideas of their colonial masters, or Jews who found themselves at home in pre-fascist Germany. Without losing control of its boundaries, a society can nonetheless have a population that is discovering new temptations and horizons, not only in work but in love, in politics and in play. American fundamentalists, for instance, have long attacked the importation of foreign ideas about evolution, theology, or the history and criticism of the Bible: ideas to which they are exposed simply as members of American society who have television sets and whose children go to public schools. Indeed, they have attacked these influences with at least as much vigour as they previously directed against the 'yellow peril'.[9] Wider horizons permit new experiences which the society has ways to control or censor: new enthusiasms and tastes or new deprivations, new ways of seeing things and new personal identities, as well as the death of old loyalties and affections. Under these conditions members of a society may experience its days as numbered and demand its purification.

To purify a society of alien ideas or the polluting notions of intellectuals and experts, it is necessary to get back to basics, to origins, to the very elements of nature and faith. For instance, many of the fundamentalists studied by Strozier long for a day of final purification when their temptations, like their trials, will be over. Boyer, too, has noted that for many millennialists it may even be too late to save the social order or history itself; only a final struggle will purify the soul of the 'evil passions' and the 'evil spirits some thought were exorcised centuries ago . . .'.[10] For Billy Graham, indeed, it was entirely possible that God would use a nuclear holocaust to purify the earth and thus restore his creation.[11]

In a social system that is in imminent danger of disintegrating, there will be intensified demands for the discipline of the emotions and for constraints on behaviour so that individuals will interact in ways that support social institutions and the larger society itself. The more intense the demand for reintegration, the less tolerance there will be for the play of emotions, especially of those passions, such as greed or anger, which may prove disruptive to the social order. Particularly in a fascist social system, outbursts of rage and of greed may be outlawed, so that the expropriation of property and the elimination of persons may proceed smoothly and within the law. It is perhaps for this reason that Staub speaks of greed and murderous desire as 'extraneous motives' that only occasionally came into play in Nazi Germany.[12] They were extraneous only because they were being suppressed in the service of conforming social character to the requirements of social interaction. They were hardly extraneous, I would hasten to add, from the analyst's viewpoint who would seek to account for the rapaciousness with which Jewish properties were expropriated and Jewish lives consumed. In a society that carefully codes the way people speak, dress and relate to one another and to those in authority, there is little room for the overt satisfaction of primitive emotions. On the contrary, the emphasis of such a social order is on reproducing the identity and the goals of the larger society in every institution and in the minutiae of everyday life.

To achieve such a tightly ordered social system it is necessary, therefore, to discipline and to colonize the psyche. With increased discipline certain emotions become 'extraneous'; there is no room for them in a social order that seeks to become quasi-liturgical in its emphasis on prescribed forms for interaction and belief. To colonize the psyche it is necessary to treat the inward aspects of the self as raw material to be mined and expropriated by social institutions and to be returned to the self in a form that not only enriches the larger society but allows it to reproduce itself in the minutiae of social interaction and in the interstices of the self.

The experience of war has certainly intensified efforts to order the psyche and to shape relationships in terms that serve the purposes of the larger society and its major institutions. Every bit of physical and emotional energy must be mobilized for the war effort, and every hint of subversive or disloyal attitudes detected not only in the military and the state but in the course of everyday life, where loose lips, so to speak, have been known to sink ships, and where doubts may be harboured about the need for such terrible sacrifice. That is why England went to such lengths to secure the morale and loyalty not only of military personnel but of the citizenry in ways that extended deeply into the corners of private life.[13] In the decades after the war, moreover, the techniques of social science that were used to order the attitudes of soldiers and citizens have been extended to the workplace. There indeed greed and other such motives have come to be regarded as extraneous, since work has been redefined as an arena of the soul: a place where the self can be actualized in harmony and co-operation with others, in accord with the objectives of the corporation, and in service to the democratic and rational values of free societies. As Nikolas Rose puts it:

> In the psychologies of self-actualization, work is no longer necessarily a constraint upon the freedom of the individual to fulfill his or her potential through the strivings of the psychic economy for autonomy, creativity and responsibility. Work is an essential element in the path to self-fulfillment. *There is no longer any barrier between the economic, the psychological, and the social* ... The government of work now passes through the psychological strivings of each and every one of us for what we want.[14]

Rose might have added, in the famous motto of Auschwitz, that '*Arbeit macht frei*'. If that comment seems a bit harsh, consider that some of the literature on self-actualization that was used to legitimate the new emphasis on putting the psyche to work came from the experience of prisoners in concentration camps. Those who could give their lives meaning in the pursuit of some goals, as Victor Frankl pointed out, were the ones most likely to survive.[15]

No longer a colony, and with its boundaries intact, the new United States has nonetheless had a citizenry beset with anxiety about outside influences. Not only were there strenuous religious revivals seeking purity of soul and body, but new forms of surveillance over personal manners and sobriety. Such revivals, and various organizations for literacy and sobriety, sought to re-establish high levels of integration between personal psyche and social interaction, and to place relationships firmly within the context and constraints of the larger society. These new rituals of purification, however, did not entirely succeed in allaying fears of outside influences. We shall have occasion later in this discussion to return to the problem of intense fears of subversion and pollution by immigrants from Europe.

I am suggesting that the perennial American concern with pollution, with avoiding foreign entanglements, and with preserving Anglo-American virtues from being diluted by immigrant peoples, has its roots in the continued expansion of interaction outside the constraints of social organization. Like colonial subjects, Americans still seem to feel attracted to foreign imports and yet profoundly suspicious of alien influences. One reason why the chronic concern with purification may still seem to make sense, I would argue, is that many Americans continue to be uprooted from their local or ethnic communities, involved in more distant markets and more complex economic frameworks, and hard put to it to defend themselves and their communities from the influence of ideas and values which may be foreign in origin or simply alien to those of local communities.

Americans continue to associate with others in ways which strain the capacity of their social institutions to provide meaning and guidance. The growth industry in human relations, guidance counselling, and the panoply of organizational consultants and marketing experts suggests the limitations of convention and custom for giving guidance to individuals in the full range of their social interactions. The equally expansive industry in foreign and esoteric sources of wisdom suggests that the range of personal experience goes well beyond the constraints imposed by the world of face-to-face relationships. As Strozier has pointed out, moreover, many fundamentalist communities, and not only the African-American, experience themselves as nearly overwhelmed by an alien and intrusive culture, even in a society with boundaries as well fortified as those of the United States. In New York City, for instance, one fundamentalist minister tried to defend his congregation by creating 'as self-contained an environment ... as possible. It is not possible to be hermetically sealed from the world in New York City, but one can tighten the bonds within to ward off the perceived dangers without.'[16]

Among the fundamentalists described by Strozier, many have succeeded in acquiring new opportunities for wealth and satisfaction, and they are therefore confronted with temptations which they had never faced in the past. While many of the fundamentalists find the sources of danger in the world outside the Church, many more have internalized their desires and feel both profoundly ashamed and guilty. Of these, some long for a day, the rapture or the millennium, when the struggle with 'the flesh' will be over. To gain some relief from the desire for purification and from their guilt, they 'externalize' their sin. As Strozier puts it, 'God takes over one's sin.'[17] 'A striking aspect of the fundamentalist system is that, just as individual guilt and shame diminish, collective evil increases.'[18]

The very success of evangelical and fundamentalist initiatives in raising the standards of literacy and sobriety and in promoting various forms of self-discipline has placed a relatively high price on the social contract. Admission to American society continued to require a certain doubt over the goodness of one's soul and a willingness to accept the governance of tutors who ranged from evangelists and clergy through schoolteachers and magistrates. To be tolerated in the new republic required a contract not unlike the one envisaged by John Locke for England toward the end of the seventeenth century: a willingness to forswear the sins of one's past life and to have them ignored, while accepting a daily discipline of sobriety and self-examination in order to confirm the society's good judgement in allowing one to be admitted to the role of citizen. Only a lifetime of penitence and productivity would confirm one's bona fides as citizen of the republic.

It would be a mistake to underestimate the costs of such conformity to the soul. Certainly there have been popular reactions to the pressure placed on the citizen for repentance and conversion. The very success of revivals and of reform movements, I would argue, created sufficient burdens on the soul to foster longings for a final settling of accounts: for a day on which old debts would be paid, once and for all. Millennial enthusiasms, I am suggesting, have been one result of the widespread social pressures associated with efforts to integrate the psyche with the social order and to constrain interaction within the relatively narrow limits of the family, the community and the political system.

One does not have to look far for evidence of a strong reaction against the social pressures of the larger society, combined with a millennial demand for a settling of accounts under the leadership of a charismatic figure. Take, for instance, such highly organized and defiant residential communities as the Branch Davidians: the group that acted out its apocalyptic rhetoric in Waco, Texas, in ways that Strozier compares explicitly to the belief and rhetoric of Neo-Nazi groups.[19] The fascist potential of fundamentalist religion increases as the desire to ward off Armageddon is combined with the desire to create self-contained and defensive communities purified from the contaminating influence of the larger society. Indeed, the Waco community considered itself to be the avant-garde of the millennium: the harbinger of bloodshed and of fire in the final tribulation.

The Pentecostal community is likely to find itself in the position of a colonial society. On the one hand, the members of the community interact with and draw some inspiration from the larger society, and on the other hand that larger society is regarded as alien and potentially dangerous. Take, for example, the situation of Pentecostalists in South India. Like their Hindu neighbours, many of these Christians believe in spirits, but they do not have available to them the rites that would protect them from harassment by the spirits. Lionel Caplan points out that the people of South India are often troubled by spirits known as *peey*: the spirits, for instance, of suicides or others who have died abruptly and prematurely.

> Pentecostals generally point out that, while the *peey* driven out by Hindu specialists are free to attack again – possibly even the same victim – the spirits exorcised by Christian healers are driven into the Abyss (*badalam*), the reference being to Revelation 20.3, where the vision of the Last Days has Satan chained up for a thousand years and driven into the Abyss,

> where he can no longer seduce the nations. Even then, however, the victim may be attacked by other *peey* unless baptism in the Holy Spirit takes place to effect total immunity.[20]

Thus minority exorcisms may purge the impurities from a society whose rituals for purging evil are believed not only to have failed but also to have brought evil dangerously within the bounds of the community itself. Time is thus renewed in the rite of baptism as the individual leaves an old dispensation and enters the new. Even for the Baptists, however, the exorcism only works for the time being. At the end of a thousand years, the spirits will return with a vengeance.

The problem is not only that Hindu rites of exorcism may be ineffective; as Caplan notes, they also are regarded by the rival Pentecostal exorcists as vehicles for the evil influence of Hindu deities.[21] The Pentecostalists in Madras, Caplan argues, regarded the Hindu shamans' rites as 'satanic' and thought their antidotes against 'evil spells and evil spirits' were indeed 'the very forces they are meant to guard against'.[22] Pentecostalism therefore substitutes its own dramas of the soul, acted out under the auspices of its own shamans and according to its own rites of purification, to replace the rites of rival religious communities. Just as mediaeval religious movements offered their own forms of absolution to defend the psyche against the penitential system that governed the social order, the Pentecostalists have found it necessary to fight the potency of the larger society by offering their own purificatory rites. Indeed, the prophetic message of the Pentecostal community claimed that the Hindus' sacrifices not only were ineffective but were in effect a Trojan horse allowing the forces of the enemy to penetrate further into the community itself.

Such strategies are neither new nor uniquely Pentecostal. As Cohn has argued, mediaeval Europe was host to a variety of groups that reacted against the social pressures of the larger society by demanding a settling of accounts. The institutional Church demanded purification in the form of an elaborate and exacting system of penances. While burghers and artisans in the expanding cities may have found it in their interest to satisfy the demands of the penitential system and so accumulate social credit, the poor were in no position to pay their own debts or the debts of the departed. They were both subject to the demands of the penitential system and unable to satisfy them. As we have seen, many of the crusaders were attracted by the incentives offered by the Pope: the remissions of the penalties for sins or of sins themselves. Some demands for relief in mediaeval society took the form of mass movements to remove such enemies of the people as the rich, the clergy and the Jews: the sources of obligation and of indebtedness.

In some respects one can look at the crusades of the poor, shepherds and outlaws, paupers and bandits, as a similar mass movement motivated at least in part by the demand for cancelling the system of social credit that kept them on the margins of the social order. The clergy were not only the symbols of luxurious living and indolence that inspired class hatred; they were also the dispensers of the penitential system that awarded or withheld the means of acquiring merit or social credit. It would not be surprising, therefore, to find the charismatic heroes of the poor to be precisely those who had transcended the penitential system and could liberate their followers from the crushing weight of social obligation by breaking the clerical monopoly on costly absolution.

Two examples of mass movements in the thirteenth century suggest that charismatic leaders gained some of their popular force from their ability to survive and transcend the penitential system. Cohn recounts a myth that focused on a dead king who was believed to be only sleeping: Baldwin IX, the Count of Flanders installed in 1204 as Emperor of Constantinople but a year later captured and executed by Bulgarians. In popular mythology, however, informed by the *Sibylline Oracles* and ancient folklore about the once and future king, Baldwin was really transformed into 'a fabulous creature, half demon and half angel'; Cohn notes that

> Gradually a whole legend was elaborated. It was rumoured abroad that the Count was after all not dead but, having sinned greatly, was still discharging a penance imposed on him by the Pope. For many years he had been living in

> obscurity as a wandering beggar and hermit; but his expiation was now completed and he would very soon be returning in glory to free his land and his people.[23]

Indeed, a hermit appeared in 1242 in the French countryside, and was believed to be the returned Emperor, and after accepting the attribution of such charisma he soon became the leader of a mass of largely urban poor. Eventually he was unmasked as an imposter and executed, but not before his followers had succeeded in starting a civil war, strengthening the Flemish resistance to France, liberating towns from the authority of the French monarchy, and burning alive those who took sanctuary in the churches of the area. A renegade monk, believed to be a noble prince and saintly king returned from the dead, galvanized a depressed population into resistance that lasted in various forms for over a century and a half. What had delayed his return to his people was a penance that had to be satisfied, and on his return he relieved his followers from the weight of social obligations imposed by the clergy and the rich on an easily discredited social class of those literally unable to pay their dues.

Later in the thirteenth century there were other crusades of the poor, one of them led by another renegade monk, one Jacob.[24] In addition to preaching against various monastic orders as being hypocritical, self-indulgent and proud, he also attacked the sacramental and penitential system of the Church head-on. Not only did he present himself as a dispenser of divine healing and divine grace; he also claimed the authority 'to grant absolution from every kind of sin'.[25] If, as I have argued, charismatic leaders are a form of popular defence against the weight of social obligation, it would be hard to find a better example of the use of such leaders in neutralizing the prevailing system for distributing social credit.

It may be no accident, furthermore, that these revolts took place shortly after the Lateran Council of 1215, which solidified and extended the penitential system. Later in the same century, indeed, the Church promulgated the doctrine of purgatory, which gave to the dead time to purify themselves of their sins and, to the living, gave the opportunity to satisfy the unfulfilled penances and obligations of the dead. Certainly it was a system by which those who were acquiring some security in the new mediaeval cities could acquire social credit. It may also have been a means of buying time not only for both the living and the dead but for the Church itself.

When Rituals of Purification Fail: The Case of the Melpa

Up to now we have been concerned primarily with the pressures associated with effective rituals of purification. The fascist dream of a society which is impervious to the advent of death must make further sacrifices of both satisfaction and reality when rituals of purification fail to purge the community of the stain of death. Take, for example, Strathern's fine discussion of the New Guinea Highlanders of the Melpa region; it provides a particularly good illustration of what happens as a community becomes somewhat less integrated as it faces new opportunities for interaction and personal satisfaction.[26] As we shall see in a moment, one community was seized by a panic over the presence of cannibals in their vicinity: a presence that threatened to pollute the community itself. The excitement and fear caused by the intensification of patterns of consumption aroused the anxiety of one community in particular, the Hagen, over their own passions to consume. Whereas consumption had previously been seen to be the besetting sin of women, men now also were consuming far more than had been their due in the past. Rising prices for coffee beans had given the Hagen not only more money to spend but a new taste for beef, beer and four-wheel-drive vehicles. Whereas in the United States these have been advertised as the symbols of untrammelled manhood, among the Hagen these new patterns of consumption signified not merely a breaking down of one important distinction between men and women; according to Strathern, they also signified the introduction of cannibalistic European values and especially of cash and prostitutes into the local community.[27] After a period of inflation and heightened consumption, in which fears of cannibalism turned into a local panic, the people regained their composure, restricted their consumption to local products, and lost their fear of dying of insatiable desire.[28] They instituted a rudimentary form, as it were, of National Socialism.

The reference to National Socialism in this context may seem inappropriate or even frivolous. To be sure, it is a long way from the tribal communities of the New Guinea Highlands to the complex societies, class conflicts, advanced capitalism, expanding states, and ideological controversies of Western Europe in the 1920s and 1930s. Nonetheless, I make the comment here to point out the common element between the two: a powerful reaction both against outside influences and against degeneracy from within. In his study of fascism, Sternhell makes it clear that fascism sought to purify and renew societies by restoring the nation's spirit in two ways.[29] One was to give primacy to the nation rather than to subordinate it to international interests or alliances. The other was to purify the nation from the corrupting influences of money. National Socialism, and, as we shall see, the Hagen, sought to overcome similar evils: greed, consumerism and the inhumanity of a capitalist society, on the one hand; on the other hand the failure of the people to live their own life free from involvements with outsiders. In the case of nationalism the foreign devils were international alliances of the working class or wars in the name of democracy against dictatorships. At stake for the Hagen as for the National Socialists, I would argue, was quite simply the salvation of the soul of the people from corrupting influences and outside associations.

When a society's days appear to be numbered, intellectuals may articulate a sense of despair and the need for purification. Speaking of one ideologue, Mounier, Sternhell notes: 'he had . . . [a] sense of decadence, of decrepitude, the same conviction that an intellectual and moral, political and social revolution was necessary for the salvation of the French soul'.[30]

There is here something of the same 'moral panic'[31] that frightened British and American society into attempts to provide authoritative surveillance and guidance to families whose children seemed to be too untutored to take up the tasks of a democratic society, too unskilled to work in industry, or too feeble to perform in the military, on the one hand, or on the other hand too dangerous to both person and to property to be allowed to be free. Yet the panic seems to go deeper, since the fascist ideologues had no faith in the agencies of the state or in professional expertise; these, after all, were merely the solutions of a liberal or bourgeois society. On the contrary, Sternhell notes, 'no one has ever had a stronger taste for renewal than a fascist in the making. No one has ever considered himself the bearer of a future more promising, more different from the present order, more radically opposed to that which exists . . .'[32] The self-styled revolutionary, contemptuous of governmental sanctions, and avid for the moral regeneration of social life, is by now a familiar player in American politics and criticism.

It is understandable that, when rituals of purification fail, religious movements arise in order to resolve the contradictions in the social order. Strathern reports that, a few years before their panic over cannibals, the Melpa had developed a cargo cult in a period of heightened expectations for wealth and independence associated with the arrival of Europeans.[33] Their apocalyptic beliefs promised high levels of production to satisfy all desires for consumption and independence; the cargo cult anticipated free play for those of a liberated spirit and strong will. The cult failed, the Melpas' investments were consumed in magical attempts to produce money, and they sought to restore earlier rites and patterns of limited consumption. The failure of the cargo cult, Strathern notes, set the stage for the later fear of cannibals whose consuming passions and lawless wills would destroy the community.[34] In their period of inflationary expectations, they expected a period of full employment and progress in both consumption and welfare. It was in their deflationary period that they developed their fears of those who would feed themselves at the public trough.

It is not easy for a society to recognize destructive desires and consuming passions within itself and among its own members; it is far easier for a society to imagine that these passions are really external to the community, embodied in cannibals or illegal aliens. It is not the people's own greed that can turn duty into consumption. On the contrary, for the Melpa it is women who marry into the community from outside who may consume not only their husbands' vital fluids but his economic resources.[35] If it is not women, it is a magical power on the fringes of the society, controlled by men but on the edge of nature, which can assume the form of birds and, entering men through the anus, consume them from within.[36] For Bloch, as we have seen, any society conjures up threats to its existence in order to score symbolic victories over them and dramatize its own vitality; it 'figures' that a patrilineal society would symbolize threats to its existence in the form of women who marry in from outside clans, and threats to male dominance in the form of the uncontrolled sexuality of rogue males.[37]

It should be noted that the association of insatiable desire with evil is not peculiar to New Guinea Highlanders. Let us return to Caplan's study of folk religion in the region of Madras. There he found that the spirits of the dead (*peey*) are often associated with dangerously unsatisfied desires, especially in the case of individuals who have died young. Certainly such desires as lust or envy, sometimes violent and angry passions, are represented in the form of these evil spirits; sometimes the evil spirits themselves are thought to be hungry for blood or for the flesh of foetuses.[38] Even the lower gods may be upgraded forms of these evil spirits. Interestingly, these gods are considered by villagers to be relatively benign; it is in the city that they are likely to become evil and possessive.[39] It is clear that the opportunities for exchange and consumption, along with the weakening of ritualized techniques for transforming desire into duty, may make spirits once thought to be relatively benign seem demonic. *The wider the range of social interaction and personal experience, the more necessary, and the less effective, are rituals of purification.*

It is interesting momentarily to note the parallels between this reaction against the destruction of traditional society by a money economy and Marx's own metaphors for the bourgeoisie and 'capital'. Marx, too, found the bourgeoisie destructive of every traditional form of attachment and duty through the introduction of a cash economy that turned every relationship and virtue into a commodity that could be exchanged on the open market. Marx, too, extolled the virtues of solidarity among those responsible for production as a means of defending the workers' communities from being consumed by the factory, the market and the state. It may well be that the attempt to purify the social order of reactionary (bourgeois) consumerist values and to restore the leadership of 'big men' reflects the same fascist tendency as the attempt of traditional communities to purify themselves of metropolitan influences and to control the passions that, turned into patterns of consumption, could dissolve the ties between generations.

Let us return to Strathern's account of the New Guinea Highlanders. Certainly the Melpa were suspicious of consumption and sought to purify themselves of influences that could lead them into that sort of indulgence. Thus they were given to witch-hunts. It is witches who both signify the threat of death and who feed themselves on the nourishing parts of the body (the greasy remains of the dead, the semen, etc. – 'grease', among the Melpa, serves as a symbol both for what is nourishing and for what is corruptible, e.g. the decaying corpse). Witches, having wills of their own which have not been brought into harmony with the social order, can cause not only disruption but death itself. Therefore, when rituals of purification begin to fail, the fear of witches and cannibals intensifies. That is, the loss of cohesion in the social order is personified in individuals who threaten to tear the community apart with their insatiable desires and unscrupulous wills. Indeed, according to Strathern, men as well as women can be personified as witches.[40] The fascist demand for purity of will is clearly evident in this belief.

When purification rituals fail to renew time, appeal is often made to a former time purified of alien influence and filled with spiritual potency. It is a difficult feat, and in the case of the African Zionist churches appears to have been accomplished by appeal to a xenophobic religious past under charismatic leadership. The former time may have been one that is alien but potent, as in the case of the appeal to the history of Israel as a mythic past for African-Americans in slavery. Conversely, the former time may come from a purer period in the indigenous past: African-Americans again being a case in point, having drawn from their own spiritual history.

The attempt to make up for lost time by recovering a purified and potent past characterizes religious movements that seek to expunge outside influences from a culture that is on the verge of disintegrating and being overwhelmed by them. Furthermore, these movements appear under similar conditions: the dislocation of individuals from rural villages to urban centres; the disruption of traditional pieties toward the dead; the separation of communities from ancestral burial grounds; the intrusion of larger markets and administrative districts on traditional communities; the introduction of alien forms of administration, adjudication, education and religion into the larger society; and the rise of new middle classes that carry these alien cultural forms and attitudes.[41]

The choice of the purer and more potent past depends, of course, on whether such a past is culturally available. African religious movements seem to have drawn heavily on traditional forms of community and worship, whereas the Iranian revolt against Westernization drew heavily on an indigenous clerical leadership, the *ulama*, who were alienated from 'the Westernized new middle and upper classes' and in close touch with 'the mass of urban migrants from the countryside'.[42] Given the prevalence of these clerics and their access to Islamic tradition, they could lead the movement to purify the nation of alien influences and lift the burden of Western norms, e.g. of modernized relations between the genders and of competition according to Western economic and social standards. Led by Khomeini, the *ulama* could heighten 'nostalgia for a forgotten and idealized past' and proclaim 'a return to true Islam'.[43] Conversely, certain African movements adopted the cultural past of the West as contained in the Old Testament. There they found strong charismatic and xenophobic themes, as I have already noted, coded in the language of a culture that appeared to have a potency superior to their own.[44] In the next chapter we will take up in more detail the attempt to restore an idealized past.

When Rituals of Purification Fail

When rituals of purification fail, pressure mounts for a reign of terror through torture and executions. Official execution is intended not merely as a deterrent to others but as a way of removing from the social order the profound stain of death. A particularly grisly form of such purificatory rites is found in Graziano's description of the abduction, torture and execution of innocent civilians during Argentina's 'dirty war' of the late 1970s and early 1980s.[45] The state surrounded houses, even entire blocks, with vehicles, marked and unmarked, to seize individuals who were defenceless and had no reason to believe themselves the object of official inquisition. As Graziano points out, while the abductions were officially secret, they were dramatized by the panoply of officially sponsored horror.[46] The danger against which the state was claiming to defend the people had to be dramatized in order to be overcome. Thus each abduction had to be carried out with enough publicity to herald yet another case in which the state was rescuing the public from the threat of subversion and death.

The histrionics of the police suggest that these arrests and, later, the executions were highly ritualized displays of official charisma. As Graziano notes, there was an element of 'sympathetic magic' in these official acts.[47] To begin with, they mirrored the very threat that such ritualized punishment was intended to prevent.[48]

Furthermore, magic always works against itself by imparting a note of unreality or abstraction to the proceedings. For instance, in slaying an animal in order to prevent the plague from decimating the people, the priest is taking the threat of death out of its context (the advent of the plague itself) and representing it in symbolic form by killing an animal; thus an element of abstraction and representation enter into the act of extermination itself. As O'Keefe puts it: 'There is a strong sense in which abstraction does violence to reality . . . There is a sense in which magic is man's original bag of abstractions for the purpose of doing violence to reality.'[49] Again, as commentators on the state's murder of innocent civilians in Argentina and Nazi Germany have noted, the public are participants in these magical displays and in the disruption of context. They share in the violation of reality by coming to regard the victims as bearers of something like the plague.[50]

Purificatory ritual may degenerate into a spectacle, like the Roman crucifixions or *autos da fé* that staged Roman power and authority over death itself in an attempt to deter others from taking seriously their thoughts of freedom. As Graziano points out, however, public executions may be performed off-stage and thus achieve a higher level of abstraction from the original context of alleged crime.[51] Indeed, modern societies have in fact abstracted their rites of extermination so that executions have become largely private. Although a national audience is indirectly involved through the media and can be profoundly affected by the prospect of official murder, the ritual of execution as a deterrent is performed off-stage, where it achieves the potency of a collective dream or even a nightmare. If Graziano is right, the disappearance of criminals or victims behind walls, the secrecy surrounding their torture and execution, and the uncertainty regarding their fate makes the ritual even more effective.[52] The line between a purificatory ritual and a public spectacle is not always easy to draw. The more obscure it is, the more, I would argue, is a fascist tendency likely to be acted out in collective theatre.

Even when execution is abstracted, set apart in a sacred sphere, and approached only by those with sufficient sanctity to come away from ritualized killing unscathed, it still profoundly affects both the public and the private imagination. Note the use of concentration camps and detention centres to dramatize the state's monopoly of legitimate murder and its ever-present threat to the life of the populace it claims to defend. Graziano compares the rumoured killings in the detention centres of Argentina to a ritual that terrifies those who witness it, silences their opposition, and makes them not only compliant but vicariously complicitous in the act of killing.[53] It is as if the larger society were party to a secret which is in fact public knowledge. Although some within its bounds will have to suffer the pangs of death, the many will be saved. The people share the guilt of the official murders. They are not only compliant but complicit in the killing, as they maintain the 'secret' that some are being dispatched in contexts remote from profane view.

In an attempt to give meaning to the horror, the public adopts the view of the state that the victims have done something to deserve their suffering; indeed that was the common refrain among the Argentinian public.[54] Speaking of the Argentine junta's relentless pressure on public opinion through continuous, however random, arrest, torture and murder, Graziano writes:

> No Argentine was exempt from one participation or another in this drama that posed the individual against his or her own

interest and will. 'Today', as Admiral Massera put it, '*no one has the right to not rise to the heights of the burning demands of the moment.*'[55]

As Bloch puts it, ritual turns the individual as prey into the citizen as hunter through the dramatization of controlled violence.

More is needed for a public ritual of purification to be successful. Histrionics, magical imitation of the enemy, loss of control, the weakening of public checks on reality, and even passive public complicity are not enough. To be successful, fascist movements for purification must sanctify the meaning of time not only on state occasions but in the times that precede and follow its fatal rites. The citizenry must be schooled to anticipate the days of obligation, to make special preparation for them by leaving behind their ordinary pursuits and occupations, and to rise to the occasion as witnesses and participants in the drama. However, when the state takes killing into the days of 'ordinary time', as it were, any day or time can be the scene of ritualized killing. Terror becomes a permanent but unpredictable feature of the social landscape.

Under these conditions, I would argue, popular religion uses apocalyptic prophecy to encourage the public to rise to the occasion. In the days leading to the apocalypse, moments and days are discrete rather than continuous, with any day capable of being the one on which all accounts are to be rendered. It will therefore be necessary to rise to the fatal occasion at any place and at any time. Indeed, many of the exhortations of the New Testament are based precisely on this necessity to rise to an occasion which could occur at any moment with devastating consequences for those who are unprepared.

Conclusion

A society's rituals, then, may be analogous to an individual's dreams. Both have elements of reality elaborated in ways that express unresolved conflicts. Both express powerful passions which cannot be wholly satisfied. Both may reflect earlier times and contain disguised memories, whether of cannibalism or, in the case of the infant, fantasies of having destroyed the nourishing breast or the mother's body. Like dreams, however, rituals also disguise and deny the presence of certain wishes and fears, just as they provide only the most limited capacity to come to terms with the real threats and opportunities in the surrounding world. Thus rituals, like dreams, represent proto-fascist longings: ways of denying contradiction, eliminating opposition, enjoying fictitious victories, in a terrible over-simplification of life's very real dangers and opportunities.[56]

Under these conditions, religious movements may arise which seek to provide new sources of purification and, at the same time, the benefits of shamanic relief from social pressures and the diseases of the soul. As we have seen, Lanternari notes several new religious movements among colonized people in Africa. Some offered only relief from impending disaster and did not seek to purify the people or the land from the polluting effect of foreign influences. Where the people had suffered the consequences of more direct European rule and had become alienated from the tenure of their own land by European practices of land ownership or, as in South Africa, by segregation, Lanternari speaks of various Zionist churches which largely rejected the New Testament in favour of the Old, from which it could draw more direct support for a 'nationalist, xenophobe or antagonistic attitude toward whites'.[57] Where the New Testament was used, the figure of John the Baptist eclipsed that of Jesus because of the emphasis on purification and the return of the ancestors: John the Baptist being associated with the return of Elijah.[58]

That is why, in the following chapter, we will turn to rituals of restoration and the rise of revolutionary movements. On the one hand, these (Zionist) African religious movements prophesied a new Mosaic exodus from the obligations and demands of a society under the domination of whites; on the other, these same movements prophesied the expulsion of alien influence from a newly purified social order owned and controlled by black Africans themselves.

· 5 ·

RITUALS OF RESTORATION: MAKING UP FOR LOST TIME

There are times in the life of many societies when rituals fail to avert danger, to purify the social order and to transform the young. Time runs out, then, as danger becomes imminent. The failure of rituals to purify the social order makes it impossible to renew the times; the dead weight of past sins and the corrupting effects of social change make the present seem intolerable and a better future seem apparently beyond hope. The failure of rituals to transform the young into adults, to change the single into the married and the deceased into ancestors means that the continuity of the society from one generation to the next also is endangered. The society is moribund, and more than redemption is needed.

The overt triumphalism about a new reign of God in history covers a latent despair about the course of history. Drastic new beginnings on the grand scale are only required when a people has lost the means to make time or renew it. Conversely, triumphalism is often disguised by a tragic sense that one's people must suffer before entering into glory.[1] Consider Hitler's own sense that, in exterminating the Jews, he was facilitating the work of God in history and helping to usher in the millennium. On the one hand, the draconian measures indicate the historical despair of a nation unsure of its own ability to stand the test of time; on the other hand, the punishment visited on Israel may serve as a vicarious payment for the grandiose fantasy of national triumph over all enemies and rivals. Such guilt can also be satisfied vicariously by displacing it on to a double, e.g. another nation accused of being grandiose in its designs and therefore obligated to pay the price. Thus

> Prophecy writers of the 1930s and 1940s generally treated Nazi persecution of the Jews as a sad but wholly foreseeable instance of God's effort to correct his recalcitrant people, and a foretaste of worse ahead ... Ultimately Israel's suffering would yield to a glorious destiny, but first, dreadful events loomed on the prophetic calendar.[2]

Hitler, notes Boyer, shared these sentiments and felt that he was expediting the hand of God in history by his attempts to arrive at a 'final solution' of the 'Jewish problem'.

A millennial *Reich*, in other words, is not the recent invention of German fascism. The expectation that the new United States of America would be a millennial republic is at least as old as the colonialists' independence movement; for some, as Boyer notes, the millennium was believed to have begun even during the Great Awakening of the 1740s.[3] Nonetheless, there was a note of contingency in some of the early prophecies. New England *might* be the seat of the New Jerusalem, and America *might* be the 'seat of Christ's millennial kingdom' or America the location of the 'Divine Metropolis'.[4] For Timothy Dwight, according to Boyer, the thousand-year millennial kingdom was certainly slated for America, but the millennium might have to wait until the year 2000: its time now fast approaching.[5]

Not all American millennialists, however, have been so convinced about the virtues of the soon-to-be revealed American republic. Some, in the tradition of the Mathers, saw a millennium approaching in America only after tribulation and Rapture. It would be necessary to suffer first, before entering into glory. That is why, as Boyer notes, American evangelicals and fundamentalists have been as opposed to fascism as to capitalism.[6] Both are human contrivances, whereas only divine intervention is capable of producing a transformed and just social order: a new Israel. If there is to be a restoration of the people of God, it will take indeed a Second Coming.

The hope for restoration comes, I would argue, when there is no other hope for preventing a society from running out of time. That is why the evangelical and fundamentalist hope for the Second Coming anticipates precisely such a radical rerooting of the present in the past, i.e. restoration. Such anticipation is heightened, I am suggesting, when a social system exhausts its means for averting disaster, for purifying itself of outside influences and for transforming the young. Certainly the prophets of the end-times uniformly agree that there is no hope at all for averting the imminent end of the world. Boyer makes it very clear that, with the advent of the nuclear age, prophecies of a final conflagration have been made with complete assurance.[7] There is no doubt that such a disaster will soon be forthcoming, and their only hope is to be allowed to join Christ in the Rapture that immediately precedes the inevitable holocaust.[8] Boyer notes a typical pronouncement regarding nuclear holocaust: it claims that "'It is only a matter of time . . .'"[9] Time *will* run out in the end. There is no way to prevent the consuming fires at the end of time.

The Christians' hope for a a victory over time is thus based on despair that there is no way to buy, renew, or even redeem time. Boyer notes that earlier prophecies, for instance, warned that 'all the worst attributes of humanity have come to the front; all the most evil passions have been unleashed; all the evil spirits some thought were exorcized centuries ago have returned sevenfold, more loathsome and diabolical than of old'.[10] Nonetheless, one can detect even in this dire prediction a sense of trust in God's eternal purpose being worked out in history. In the nuclear age, however, some enthusiasts of the Second Coming offered no hope for a history over which even God would preside: a fact, Boyer notes, which drew critical attention from other prophets who insisted that the final nuclear annihilation would occur only after everyone had been dispatched either to heaven or to hell.[11] In either case, the end of the world and of history is a foregone conclusion; it cannot be averted through prophecy or sacrifice, through purification or through the transformation of the self. The only transformation that can do any good is the one in which this earthly body is transformed into a celestial one during the Rapture itself.

To say that 'It is only a matter of time' reflects how profoundly secularized some prophecy has become. The time is often foretold through the nicest of calculations of days and weeks, months and years, based on information gleaned from perusing not only biblical prophecies and apocalypses but also scientific and military journals. It is not the first time that prophecies of the end have become more political than theological; speaking of the movement for independence from England, Boyer notes that 'what had been formulated in religious terms now took on a secular cast'.[12] It was more obvious after 1945, however, that the theological basis of prophecy was becoming a gloss on 'an essentially secular worldview'.[13] The subject was, one might say, 'only a matter of time' rather than of sacred history.

Of any society that is threatened with extinction, of course, it is the colony that is the most endangered, for reasons that we have pursued in the preceding chapter. As I have noted, some colonies are more able than others to maintain their cohesion if not the integrity of their boundaries. We have therefore discussed some colonies in West Africa which were the scene of religious movements in the first half of this century: movements that resembled some of the more enthusiastic religious experiments in the American colonies during the Revolution. We also discussed some West African religious revivals that resembled some of the revivals in American churches prior to and during the Revolution in at least one important respect: the dread of divine judgement. It is one thing to come to terms with an alien presence when local communities are relatively intact and colonial rule is indirect. Those conditions appeared to obtain in some parts of West Africa earlier in this century, and in the more isolated American colonies. Under these conditions, some areas of the indigenous society can maintain a high level of integration between traditional forms of organization or interaction and the social character of the people. It is quite another thing to come to terms with alien influences which disturb the fabric of everyday life. *When aversive rituals are not sufficient to restore the integrity of a society, and when rituals of purification are insufficient to restore social cohesion, a society is moribund. Under these conditions rituals are necessary which not only can renew, buy or redeem time but which can, so to speak, restore a time of idealized purity and integration. These are rituals of restoration.*

Because economic relations with the colonial powers expanded opportunities and horizons for the West African subjects, it was difficult not to believe in the superiority of colonial institutions and culture. In West Africa, Lanternari notes, subsistence agriculture was being replaced by cash crops, the new economy was being tapped for taxes and tributes, and the expanding economy exposed traditional village communities to the uncertainties and disruption of a more distant and complex market.[14] Local forms of government were increasingly overwhelmed by the agencies of colonial administration. Under these conditions, as we have noted in Cohn's discussion of religious movements in mediaeval Europe, uncertainty and insecurity increase along with the expansion of desire and opportunity. New relationships undermine old obligations, and new sources of inspiration undermine traditional pieties. Even with indirect rule, there is a threat to the integrity, the boundaries, of the society and of its major organizations. In the more urbanized areas, the integration of the larger society is even more endangered by the expanding degrees of freedom to interact with strangers in various forms of exchange and, by acquiring alien culture, to have new thoughts or to think for themselves. With direct rule, the threat to the integrity of the society, as well as to its cohesion, is even more severe. These are the conditions, I am suggesting, which increasingly call for rituals of restoration.

Of course, since they were still largely British, the colonial communities in North America found it difficult to distinguish indigenous and domestic culture from alien influences. Unlike the West Africans with whom I have been comparing them, they did not have to master the Bible to become British. So long as the social order allowed individuals in the colonies to interact with the British, to receive inspiration from British evangelists, and to accept the authority of British arts and letters, the social order remained permeable to outside influences. Especially since the American subjects were part of the royal 'body politic', monarchy and British rule were felt to be internal to the colonies and not merely imposed from a government on the other side of the Atlantic. Many Americans therefore would have doubted their own souls long before they focused on the British monarchy as a source of impurity and evil in their midst. In Chapter 2 I noted that patriots were hard to distinguish from traitors in view of the fact that some patriots continued to honour the king. Kertzer puts it very well:

> A major requirement of the revolution was that the mystique surrounding royal power be dispelled. This was especially problematic because for many years American patriots had . . . largely blamed the king's ministers and parliament, rather than the king himself, for the oppression they suffered. Indeed, up to 1776, gatherings of patriots included rituals of obeisance, such as toasts, to the king, while celebrations of the king's birthday continued to inspire popular enthusiasm.[15]

Kertzer goes on to point out that after the Declaration of Independence was read in the various colonies, crowds burnt George III in effigy, buried his statue and tore off royal insignia from public and commercial decorations.[16] Two millennia ago, crowds in Jerusalem did the same thing with the eagle that Herod the Great had placed over the gate of the Temple in Jerusalem. The destruction of that eagle, like the burning of the British king in effigy, signalled a desire to restore a social system whose cohesion and boundaries were largely in tatters.

Societies may seek to break with the present by restoring a past that is to a large extent imaginary: a time of primitive vigour and harmony, of justice and equity among the people. Sternhell captures the sense in which fascism was an attempt to recreate a mythical past and thus to inaugurate a future that was completely unlike the present:

> Thus a complete break was seen to have occurred between the old world and the world of the revolutionaries. Materialism – Marxist or liberal – was opposed by a sense of the spiritual . . . the united and disciplined national collectivity replaced fragmented bourgeois society; and the young, athletic fascist replaced the flabby-muscled bourgeois. Fascism represented a physical and spiritual renaissance, a moral revolution that gave a new meaning to the dignity of the individual, who, after centuries of decadence, was recreated in body and soul.[17]

Of course, National Socialism was not the first effort to redeem the nation-state. Europe had witnessed earlier attempts to create the future from a mythical past. Zerubavel notes that, in order to destroy vestiges of Christian culture, the French Revolution instituted a calendar devoid of traditional holy days and named the months after the wind and the rain, snow and the harvest, just as German fascists later sought to 'replace the traditional names of the months with pagan archaisms associated with seasonal aspects of nature'.[18] As Zerubavel points out, both the French revolutionary and the later fascist attempts to institute new calendars were strenuous efforts to secularize culture, in the sense of removing its Christian references and signposts.[19]

Such attempts to restore the past, I would argue, were a sign of despair not only over the present but over the possibility of beginning a genuinely new future. Thus it was not only the primitive harmonies of nature that were being restored, but the power and virtue of ancestors and of founding events: 'the foundation of Rome for the ancient Romans . . . [and] the march on Rome for the Fascists'.[20] Conversely, when Napoleon restored the Gregorian calendar in 1806, collective memories of a Christianized past were also being recovered.[21]

Those who are perhaps the most vulnerable to such despair are the poor, whose hope for a better life depends on a sense that justice will be done, that grievances will be redressed, and that there will be in the future new opportunities for acquiring property and dignity. The poor have less reason and less ability to wait than those whose social and emotional eggs are contained in many baskets. Time is running out faster for them than for those whose social and economic worth has not already been exhausted. Nonetheless, the enthusiasts of the end also come from the middle classes and – in some cases – from the élite. Indeed, in his study of millenarian movements of the Middle Ages, Norman Cohn notes that many of the devotees of radical leaders often donated their jewels to the cause on demand.[22]

On the whole, however, the time horizons of the poor are much shorter than than those of the rich, and the poor know it. That is why so many of the millenarian movements studied by Norman Cohn embody the beginning of the end of the social order in some charismatic personage: a messiah or mystic in whose person the new age was believed already to have started. In the twelfth century, for instance, the area around Antwerp and Utrecht was disturbed by the presence of a particularly attractive and compelling leader, one Tanchelm, even whose opponents gave him credit for appearing as 'an angel of light'.[23] Among his followers were those who wished to be emancipated from tithes, dues and other levies: feudal payments for a protection no longer desired or needed. Thus not only the poor but the burghers of these cities joined Tanchelm's movement.

More was at stake, however, than the clearly material interests of his followers, who brought an element of devotion suitable only for a divine being; Tanchelm not only presented himself as a messianic king and betrothed himself to the Virgin Mary; he distributed his bathwater as a substitute for the Eucharist.[24] Cohn notes that Tanchelm's influence survived his death (perhaps at the hand of a priest) in 1115.[25] The nobility and the Church understandably saw in Tanchelm's movement the beginning of the end for the social system. Under these conditions dominant religious institutions may seek to provide the magic for which the populace craves; once under élite auspices, magic no longer threatens the prevailing distribution of wealth and power. It was only when the Church recruited a holy man of noble origins, known as a healer and wonder-worker, that the poor began to return to the allegiance of the Church.

The messianic movements on the periphery often are a double of the religious institutions of the centre. These popular movements often model themselves on the ideals of the centre, thus producing populist leaders that claim to represent true holiness or to possess the powers of absolution monopolized by the centre. These claims are clearly competitive, however, and if they go far enough may in fact supersede those of the centre. That was precisely what the ecclesiastical opponents of Tanchelm most feared. *The time remaining for the social system, then, is often the result of a contest between the centre and the periphery for ownership and control of magic.*[26]

In the hands of the poor, charismatic means of purifying the social order and of transforming the individual may be accompanied by the claim that a vital and harmonious future has already begun: an ancient paradise indeed restored. Magic, however, not only buys time for the individual overwhelmed with social pressures, but, in the hands of professional or propertied élites, buys time for the social order. The advent and proximity of the end are negotiated in the form of ritual. Sternhell makes it very clear that the potency and appeal of Nazism for the masses was largely through its use of ceremony and ritual; indeed fascists were apparently quite self-conscious about their expertise in the deployment of ritual for the fascination and recruitment of the people.[27] Sorel, for instance, 'insisted on the religious element in fascism and nazism'.[28] Thus fascism attempts to transfer populist charisma to the political and cultural centre in order to co-opt the magic of the periphery.

The notion of a millennial kingdom or *Reich* is thus not merely a reaction to modernity but has rather well-developed cultural roots in Western folklore and ideology. As I have noted, the theological roots of enthusiasm for the end were more evident in the Middle Ages; then a wide variety of populist movements envisaged the restoration of a period of harmony, vitality and justice. Some expectation focused on the return of Frederick II, the German emperor who captured Jerusalem in the thirteenth century. Frederick II became the focus of a myth about the once and future king who 'would *return* at the end of time to reform the government and establish righteousness'.[29] Cohn describes one very popular tract, in which the anticipated return of Frederick II emboldens an army of the poor to kill persons of wealth and high status both in the Church and in the secular world: the Pope, the clergy, the 'great men', even the 'little students'.

> As soon as he has risen from the dead and stands once more at the height of his power, he will marry poor women and maidens to rich men, and *vice versa* ... He will see to it that everything that has been stolen from minors and orphans and widows is returned to them, and that full justice is done to everyone.[30]

This is restoration with a vengeance: restoration, because a powerful and just social order, embodied in the person of

Frederick II raised from the dead, returns; with a vengeance, because old scores are settled. Only thus can a new age begin.

That is precisely the point: the millennium, the new age, is an article of faith not only that the past can be recovered but that the future can indeed begin. Only with such a restoration will individuals be transformed, the social order be purified and calamity be averted. In modern societies, millennial aspirations are more clearly futuristic; the new order will represent a radical break from the old. Even in fascism, however, with its emphasis on ushering in a bold new future, it is past glory that is being recovered and restored. Glory is, after all, the halo effect or aura that heightens the significance of an object. It is mythical and dangerous, since its charismatic residues falsify secular reality and may give a nation delusions of uniqueness and superiority.

The Loss of Mystery or Enchantment in Modern Societies

> 'Aura', Benjamin (1979a, pp. 250–251) writes, 'is a strange weave of space and time'. The auratic cultural (or natural) object is characterized thus by its 'unique appearance', its 'semblance of distance', and its 'duration'. The demise of aura, which Benjamin (1975b, p. 239) attributes not just to the inclusion of mechanical reproduction, but also to the activities of the avant-garde of the 1920s and especially to surrealism, is correspondingly characterized by the overcoming of uniqueness, the need to bring things closer to people, and transcience.[31]

In societies that are secularizing, religion loses its aura. The churches become one interest group or institution among many, each seeking to influence public affairs, define issues, recruit supporters, shape public opinion, provide recipes for personal growth and happiness, and – not least – pay the salaries of their professionals. Politicians, doctors, journalists, writers: each group becomes more visibly a protagonist of its own interests. Their fall in public esteem is merely one indicator that the aura that may have dignified them in the past and that made them seem both unique and somewhat inaccessible has made them familiar and not beneath contempt. The military may suffer less than most this loss of aura; they may be called upon, in fact, to restore a fallen society to a measure of grace.

When social processes become visible, social structures tend to lose their mystery. What may have taken place in back rooms among politicians may still occur in relative secret, but modern societies have listened to enough recorded conversations to know what has been going on. Investigative journalism has made the politician, the corporate executive and the celebrity familiar characters better known for machination than for mystery. Even the process of scapegoating has become visible and familiar; there is little opportunity for collective self-delusion in a society whose rhetoric consistently points to the process of 'blaming the victim'. 'Disenchantment' captures the fall from grace in both senses: a loss of mystery and aura along with disillusionment. Fascist tendencies, however, seek to recreate an aura behind the nation-state which could offset the processes of secularization that turn the unique and the transcendent into the quite ordinary and mundane.

The Merging of Religion and Politics

Aura, however, does not always die completely, but leaves residues that fascinate or haunt the public imagination. In studying the city of Springfield, for instance, Demerath and Williams time and again found people suggesting that religion was a powerful force behind the scenes.[32] While city politics were ostensibly governed by the Constitution and by local statute, nevertheless the Catholic majority and in particular the bishop were still thought by many in the community to be *éminences grises* behind the throne in city hall. Try as they might to find examples of collusion between the bishop and the mayor, Demerath and Williams in fact came to the conclusion that the church and city government were relatively separate and autonomous realms of social life, however much they were sensitive to each other's interests and in close informal relations with each other. Nonetheless, the perception that things are not what they seem, and that religion remains a powerful but covert influence on city politics, remains a belief among many of the people they interviewed.

Such a persistent impression can be explained in part by the loss of cohesion in the modern city. Cohesion declines to the extent that the way in which people interact with one another is not limited by the constraints of social organization. The formal separation of church and state, for instance, does constrain individuals in their social, political and religious roles and relationships. The disjunction between formal organization and the conduct of actual relationships also creates a split between social appearance and social reality. For instance, power works precisely by not making a public appearance, especially where issues are controversial. This sort of power succeeds by keeping certain options and issues off the public agenda. As one of the businesspeople interviewed by Demerath and Williams put it, 'Underneath everything that occurs in this community is the presence of the bishop in some form or another – never obtrusive, always appropriate.'[33] Or as another business leader argued, 'There's not much attention given to religion in this city. But come to think of it, isn't that a sign of absolute power?'[34] The authors and their interviewees agree that the church in Springfield kept a low 'political profile', but the authors do not believe that the profile was deceptive simply because the church did not 'come out of the closet' or that it exercised 'insidious' influence.[35] The authors conclude that there is no sign of conspiracy or collusion between church and city hall; certainly there was no 'major church–state cabal tucked under the civic carpet'.[36] Furthermore, only a few clergy, self-selected, put in a major public appearance on any of the issues that have attracted the most political attention in the last few years, e.g. homelessness, sex education in the schools, and black community development. Influence that is overt is far less effective than authority that does not have to exercise itself in order to set limits to what comes up for discussion on the public agenda.

What Demerath and Williams found in Springfield reflects the relative openness of social networks that range far beyond the boundaries of particular institutions and organizations. To put it over-simply, what the authors found in Springfield was a lack of boundaries between religion and politics, while the boundaries between church and state remained, on the whole, relatively intact. On the one hand, 'Springfield's officials have shown no inclination to flout the law' regarding the separation of church and state: indeed, religious leaders themselves feel increasingly isolated from 'civic decision making'.[37] On the other hand, however:

> one can find instances of virtually every proscribed form of church–state collaboration in the city, ranging from prayer in public classrooms and unwarranted assistance to the parochial schools, to religious symbols on city property and discrimination among religions by city bureaucrats and agency heads.[38]

It is therefore no wonder that religion has 'exerted considerable political influence on selected issues, indeed more influence than many social scientists might have expected'.[39] In the form of specific groups, mobilized on particular issues for a short period, religion in the city has affected the public agenda with regard to the homeless, sex education, and black community development. The point is that informal, *ad hoc* coalitions have injected religion into politics, albeit through the narrow channels offered by specific issues and contests, rather than remaining dammed up behind a wall separating the church from the state.

Some would argue that this is a peculiarly American solution to the problem posed by the persistence of religion in a secularized society; it is also a solution to the problem of how a society based on reason and law can still mobilize the type of commitment expressed in religious loyalties and the compassion enshrined in religious communities. The boundaries between religion and politics remain permeable, even though the line drawn between church and state is heavily fortified by the laws and the courts. I would argue, however, that the collapse of boundaries between religion and politics is precisely what one would expect in a society whose social structures do not define or control its social processes.

The Erosion of the Boundary between Culture and Power

The opening of relationships to wider networks is also due to the growth of new technologies of communication. As the distinction between the television, the telephone and the computer begins to collapse, so also does the distinction between making, reporting and marketing. In a world where all forms of knowledge can be turned into digital information, the differences between the media collapse. As the media begin to overlap, so do the people engaged in creating, distributing and interpreting 'information'. Telephone companies, the defence industry, utilities and the electronics industry keep their boundaries while exchanging their data and their personnel. *The Wall Street Journal*, for instance, reports that in one city the local electric company not only controls electric water heaters and otherwise reduces the load on the utility at critical periods; it also controls television and telephone services to the community.[40] As the electronic media break down the distinction between news and entertainment, 'infomercials' and journalism increasingly operate within limits set by advertisers.

The contamination of news services or films with covert or implicit political messages is only one example of the interpenetration of boundaries between politics and economics, entertainment and education, the home and the market-place. If the home has become a retail outlet and a theatre, it follows that the home is also becoming a classroom and a courtoom, a waiting-room in a doctor's office and a political cell: all receiving indoctrination from the anonymous sources of 'information'. No wonder that

> Government, which has long tried to separate the fields of broadcasting, telecommunications and information, is relaxing its grip . . . in the end, 'technology is going to obliterate the current regulatory structure'.[41]

In such a world, religion will lose its aura of transcendence. It will become difficult to distinguish religion as an institution from religion as a social process: between what religion is and what it does. Religion loses its uniqueness, comes closer to people, and becomes more transient. Benjamin was right. Demerath and Williams, in their study of Springfield, stress the increasing difficulty of knowing how to assess the impact of religion, in part because the distinction between culture and power is becoming increasingly problematical.[42]

The erosion of the boundary between culture and power can be seen in the collusion between the producers and reproducers of news, between the media and business, between medicine and industry. No one knows for sure whether medical research, sponsored by drug companies, is truthful and undistorted by its sources of sponsorship, just as no one knows whether news coverage is not contaminated by the sources of media advertising and sponsorship. Boundaries are also collapsing between various academic fields. Sociology and anthropology often reflect the interests and perspectives of dominant parties: government funding agencies, for example, or colonial regimes, not to mention the cultural interests and presumptions of educated élites. Now, polemics over the collapse of the distinction between scientific and personal narratives reflect the struggle for power in anthropological discourse.[43] When the legitimate authorities are difficult to distinguish from the impostors, the question also becomes, 'Who has the right to speak for the field?' The same question of legitimacy bedevils other aspects of social life. School officials, for instance, while claiming to be making policy on the grounds of educational theory and practice alone, appear to be merely self-serving, or exclusive, or dominated by local groups. Questions of authority and belonging displace educational policy itself.

In studying Springfield, Demerath and Williams noted that religion and politics were more closely interwined because of the break-up of the old ward system. The ethnic groups on the way up, the blacks and Hispanics, were thus deprived of the sanctuaries of the old ward system from which they could have mounted their attacks on city hall: sanctuaries formerly enjoyed by the Catholics as they were gathering their forces in the city for a move on the political and economic centre. The Catholics were left virtually unchallenged as the only group capable of dominating a citywide electoral process. In specific issues the process of de-differentiation went even further, as religion edged back into education, economic issues and city hall politics – even at the same time that the churches themselves were more separate from the political centre and from other institutions than ever before.

The erosion of traditional boundaries between ethnic groups, along with the blurring of the distinction between culture and power, threaten the integrity of the city as a social system. More is thus being lost than simple cohesion; it is the city's confidence, as it were, in its old boundaries. This is a process analogous, therefore, to the colonization which we have discussed in previous chapters. The process results in a widespread feeling that religion, and especially the Catholic bishop, had a pervasive and invisible influence in the affairs of the city. In Springfield, institutions that are formally separate, like the churches and city hall, are knit together through many informal ties. That is why some of the people interviewed by Demerath and Williams called the city a 'small community' or even a 'big town'; 'You have different boards but pretty much the same people, and the ties are more personal.'[44]

The ghettos of the city become exposed to the mass media and expert opinion. As Scott Lash has pointed out, there are still small communities within the modern city, but they have been invaded in their labyrinths, their ghettos and enclaves, their working-class districts and ethnic communities, by encroachments from the political and economic centres.[45] Just as the boulevards of Paris exposed working-class districts to the armies that came from the provinces to the city in times of insurrection, as in 1871, so the modern city exposes all its citizens to the encroachment of rational administration, high-rise buildings, functional architecture, and the pressures to join a single system of accounting.[46] Fascism in Germany was the accomplishment of a highly co-ordinated social system that brooked no resistance from traditional centres of opposition. There can be no ghettos in a state that seeks total access to every enclave.

The encroachment of the state and of mass politics, however, cannot long be resisted by what Lash calls 'oppositional postmodernism': 'the reconstruction of community, the street, and the "labyrinth," and the attempt to define the needs of communities in terms of decentralized groups of welfare recipients (pensioners, single mothers, minorities), themselves with specialized needs'.[47]

To be sure, in their study of Springfield, Demerath and Williams noted the efforts of the black community to get the downtown politicians and financiers, who have sponsored urban renewal, to have an outside accountant explain why so little of the money went to the renovation of the black neighbourhoods and commercial district. The same sort of opposition has been voiced by James Fernandez, the former New York City Superintendent of Schools, on behalf of communities and families whose values have not been honoured in the schools of the city. Fernandez defended the rights of various sorts of families, including those headed by couples of the same sex and by single parents, to determine local educational policy in the schools, over against the centralized control of bureaucrats in the school board or urban school system.[48] The spokesmen for the communities still contained within the cities are, like Lash, calling for opposition by what is left of the labyrinth, the tangled streets of impacted communities in which meaning is first generated and produced long before it is absorbed and transformed by such centralized institutions as the mediaeval cathedral or, in the late twentieth century, the school boards and financial districts, the professions and the arbiters of public opinion in the media.

Nonetheless, Walter Benjamin's description of modernity as being antithetical not only to auras but to uniqueness is a reminder of the secularizing tendencies of the modern state that respects no aura other than its own. There are strong political currents in the United States to break down every form of ethnic protection and resistance, from affirmative action to bilingual education. Conversely, the rearguard reactions of particular communities may yet produce strong reaction-formations: attempts to restore a *status quo ante* in which possibilities for justice and new life still remain open. The same rearguard reaction and demand for restoration may produce authoritarian leaders: witness certain aspects of the religious right or of what is currently labelled 'black fascism'.

The Hope for Restoration: The Fascist Potential

Is there a fascist potential in such defensive manoeuvres by communities that are running out of time? Certainly many commentators have noted the dangerous aspects of American populism: its sanctification of ethnic boundaries and traditional communities, its hostility to the law and to abstract or general standards of judgement and value, and its antipathy to experts and professionals whose views weigh more heavily in the courts or in public opinion than the knowledge of the ordinary citizen. It is therefore not surprising that resistance by particular communities takes the form of going back to basics, fundamentals, and literal meanings. In the case of abortion, such reduction takes the form of being 'pro-choice' or 'pro-life', as if boundaries could be maintained by preserving these simple distinctions. Reduced to this level, language is concerned not with the truth or falsity of particular statements but with making the distinction between 'friend and foe'.[49] The language of enmity is proto-fascist.

Does religion still have enough transcendence, enough 'aura', to provide the basis for a social movement to restore a society whose values and institutions are presumed to be based on religious belief and practice? On the one hand, I would argue, religion has lost much, even most of its aura of transcendence by being a party to such single-issue politics. What is unique in religion is lost in the play of interest-group politics; what is transcendent is brought into close proximity with the mundane and the strategic; what is everlasting is sacrificed for the gain of temporary advantage in the struggle for public and judicial opinion. What is left of the aura may be the feeling, often expressed by the citizens of Springfied interviewed by Demerath and Williams, that religion plays a pervasive role behind the scenes in city politics: a suspicion that the researchers could not confirm. It would seem that the process of secularization would further weaken the transcendence of conservative religion as it is brought into the play of symbols and political partnerships on the way from the periphery to the centre of American politics. Furthermore, religion, if it is not reduced to the particular and the mundane, operates at such a high level of abstraction as to provide little if any guidance in the way individuals and groups make specific decisions. In either case, whether abstracted or reduced to the merely strategic, religion loses its aura of transcendental distinctiveness. The aura of religion or of traditional communities may well be diminished in a city which relies on pragmatic alliances that cut across race and ethnicity.

What is the basis of social cohesion in a society that is so loosely integrated? The emphasis on rational administration creates a demand for a data-based political argument. Proposals, charges, counter-charges and plans are required to be based on facts and evidence, but these are hard to come by in a community that keeps two sets of books, one for public – the other for private – consumption. Demerath and Williams report that the African-American neighbourhood movement called the 'Covenant' sought to challenge the expenditure of funds by the city administration in the area occupied by the black community, only to find that 'the current city administration was not eager to dredge up old memories or account books'.[50] These books, however, like others kept by the city, may have included data that had been falsified in order to justify the city's application for various grants.[51]

In a society with an 'underground economy' and a variety of creative forms of book-keeping, it would be surprising if the façades of public administration in Springfield also did not mask a variety of subterfuges and illicit expenditures. The existence of such a façade, however, adds pressure over the long term for a day of public accounting. When the African-American community group known as the 'Covenant' formed in Springfield, black clergy who had been quiescent or victimized turned into active protagonists and removed the masks of civility; indeed, as the authors put it:

> Certainly there was an exhilaration to the combat, perhaps especially for men who had operated for so long under priestly constraints – although, as one summed up his character, 'I'm an antagonist.'[52]

Their discourse, however, became more 'vitriolic' as the members of this group sought to break through the façades of public civility in order to demand equity for the black community and an accounting of the city's past failures in their regard. The members of this protest group lost their dignity on enough occasions, we are told, that their potential allies were embarrassed and their critics justified in discarding their own 'posture of public deference' to the black clergy.[53] Nonetheless, the city has been warned. Some groups in the city have long memories for old grievances; they are impatient with the façades of pragmatic political life; they speak hard words and wish to engage in hard deeds; above all they seek a day of accounting. They are likely to get it all too soon, since prophecies of a day of accounting tend to be self-fulfilling.

The reformers who wanted an audit of the city's accounts in developing a particular black neighbourhood over twenty years found themselves left holding a bag partially filled with incomplete and inconclusive data that inevitably failed to support their charges. Discourse in Springfield was governed by the city's 'distaste for public controversy and its penchant for decorous consensus'.[54] As Demerath and Williams note, public discourse was often a façade that concealed not only the actors' true motives and intentions; it also masked conflict and division within the city itself. The Catholic bishop 'sometimes seemed more interested in stating his positions than implementing them'.[55] That sense of decorum, I would suggest, probably owes as much to the role of liturgy in the city as it does to the lifestyle of the urban élite. After all, the mayor's term is inaugurated with a Catholic Mass, and painful disturbances are as unwelcome in the liturgy as they are in public life in a city accustomed to having things go smoothly and without painful interruption.

Community life, then, has two sides. On the one, social life is filled with temporary alliances forged to deal with specific issues. Old enmities based on race and class are displaced for the time being as individuals and groups make partial commitments to one another for limited, strategic purposes. The discourse of such groups may be more or less civil or vitriolic, but the alliance created does not endure or run deep into the life of the community. On the other hand, beneath the surface of such temporary alliances remain traditional neighbourhood, ethnic, racial or religious communities with long memories and long-standing suspicions and grievances. If there is an aura to the life of a city, it comes from the persistence of these spirits among the people. To mobilize them into a political force that promises to restore the aura of past glory and to deliver a day of accounting is to inject the fascist dream into the body politic.

To survive at least as a community of memory or hope, a community may well seek to restore a glorified past in a millennial *Reich*. That is in part because religion can no longer easily provide the enduring and substantive guarantees of cultural identity that an ethnic or regional group requires when its survival is endangered. Whether the impulse is African-American, conservative Christian, or tribal-Teutonic, the impulse to ensure the future by restoring the past is protypically fascist.

Religion as a Sea of Abstractions

Social interaction itself no longer sets limits on what individuals can think and do; their sources of inspiration and authority are drawn from sources that far exceed the face-to-face community. The people of Springfield, no doubt, consult self-help books, imbibe wisdom from alien sources, and develop political sympathies that far exceed the range of their local associations or of their community's organizations. Take, for instance, Hart's research on the religious and economic views of ordinary Christians.[56] Hart wants to resist the kind of labelling and categorization that has made the sociology of religion fruitless and, in his opinion, at times absurd. Hart assumes that in American society one's gender – and one's religious affiliation – do not preclude a wide range of choices in other areas of social life. 'Individuation', as it is sometimes called, has produced a society in which religion is of apparently little direct relevance to a wide range of choices.

Through a process of what is sometimes called 'disintermediation', individuals do gain their own access to experts, officials, to specialized information, professionalized opinion, opportunities for investment in distant markets, foreign sources of capital and culture, and deviant or alien sources of religious inspiration and authority.[57] The local school no longer mediates the larger society to the local community; the school is one theatre in which national conflicts are played out on a local stage before audiences who have already become exposed to and polarized by conflict at the national level. As social integration becomes relatively loose, traditional communities find themselves recruited as audiences and clienteles for opinion brokers, by protagonists of various issues, and by national organizations, focused on one issue or another, that need to develop 'base communities' at the local level in order to claim a following. What is lost in this exposure of the periphery to the centre is a sense of local ownership and control of such strategic institutions as the school, the churches, or the bank. The future of the local institutions is tested in the stock or commodities markets or in the market of public opinion. Thus time begins to speed up for the local community as it becomes more current.

It takes the trained eye of a sociologist to find a broad pattern of consistency discernible in what would otherwise appear to be a labyrinth of choices and opinions.[58] Hart's general argument claims that religion is a source of guidance, and of very flexible control and constraint that informs the decisions and views of people in work and politics, in privacy and yet also in the public sphere: an order that helps to control, however indirectly, an individual's path through the labyrinth of everyday life and its multiple choices, preferences, opinions and decisions. In other words, religion still sets limits and provides direction to the social system, although from a relatively high level of abstraction. He is certain, for instance, that at some level of abstraction a persons's beliefs and values do help to make sense: that they do guide, even if they do not wholly govern, a person's decisions in the world of work and consumption. Where he finds discrepancies between a person's beliefs and actions, he attributes them to the individual's background, upbringing or other aspects of an individual's situation: to the 'givens', as it were, of social life rather than to the realm of choice and decision, to nature, as it were, as opposed to culture.

Because religious meanings and direction are so abstract, however, they do not provide explicit guidance in concrete conditions. That is, religion functions more or less like money: a medium that can be converted into choices and decisions in many different situations. Although individuals are freed from the constraints of any particular context, including the constraints that might be imposed by one's own religious beliefs themselves, they are swimming in a sea of abstract formulae like 'pro-choice' that offer little concrete guidance on what choices to make in specific contexts under particular conditions. Having the right to choose an abortion or a religious denomination does not help very much in making the actual decision. *The sea of abstractions can also feed proto-fascist longings for leaders who will make the hard choices and will substitute very hard deeds for mere words.*

Furthermore, contexts themselves are no longer 'concrete', local, specific or highly exclusive. Any time or place is invested with meaning from quite distant times and places. Both the distant past and the distant future can impinge on the choices that one makes in a modern society. The events enshrined in a religious tradition, along with anticipations of the future, can impinge on the present quite forcibly; witness the effect, for instance, of commemorations of Columbus's landing in 1492 on the shaping of public policy regarding native Americans. Current discussions of the national debt are couched in terms of the burden of debt on future generations. In the same way distant peoples impinge directly on the choices and decisions of individuals and governments; witness the effect of the media's coverage of starvation in Somalia and Rwanda on public opinion and on public policy. Time is always intensified in late modern societies, as the past and the future, the far distant and the most immediate situations come together.

Precisely because time is of the essence in a late modern society, decisions have to be made on relatively abstract considerations, like national security or religious belief; there is little time for all the data to be gathered and added up. Lives are at stake, and there is precious little time for decision-making. That is one reason, I would argue, why abortion is of such enormous symbolic and expressive significance in many late modern societies. The abortion issue allows for the dramatization of many aspects of modern societies: the loss of protective communities and of traditional values; the collapse of traditional boundaries and conventional controls; the need to reduce abstract beliefs and values to specific directives; and the increasing shortness of time in modern societies. Something is indeed being lost that can never be recovered. Abortion is a particularly good example of an issue that creates alliances for the time being across traditional lines that in the past have separated religious communities from each other and from non-believers. Like other issues in the 1980s and 1990s, however, it will flare up and subside along with the alliances that have formed to bring it into the home through the media and back into the voting booth.

Volatility

With 'disintermediation' comes an increase in 'volatility'. In the simplest terms volatility is the rate at which cheques are written, cashed, and returned: a measure of the flow of money. By volatility I would also include a wide range of observations: the time elapsed before bonds (and decrease in employees) are 'retired', for example. Volatility concerns the rate of turnover among personnel, the increase in 'tempo', and the rate of change in everything from the money supply to public opinion, in the time served in prison or in the duration of magazines, companies, and other ventures. Time runs out faster on people and places, on policies and personnel, on friendships and affections, when other considerations, like fiscal restraint or corporate 'downsizing', are given priority. Everyone becomes expendable. Even long-standing liturgical forms are discarded and replaced by new ones issued by ecclesiastical authorities on a trial basis as temporary alternatives. Not even prayer retains the sense of being imbued with power and authority from a spiritual distance, of being transcendent and permanent. Worship loses its aura.

With increases in volatility, there is a more rapid turnover among issues, ideas, agendas, leaders and ideologies. The shelf-life of a social movement like Moral Majority will be at the most a few years, in contrast with churches that manage to persist in good times and bad. An increase in volatility is precisely what Demerath and Williams found in Springfield: special interest groups formed around specific social issues or problems, with highly intense rhetoric and heightened emotional commitment.

These movements engaged in abrasive acts for a relatively short period among a limited number of people before finally subsiding.

Even the churches themselves are therefore not immune to increased volatility. Their members come and go, with attendance patterns that do not yield increased membership in the congregations or higher rates of affiliation with their particular denominations. In their involvement in city politics, furthermore, the members of one congregation or denomination have interests and affinities in common with members of other churches and denominations, even across the lines that in the past have segmented Protestants from Catholics and Jews. These traditional forms of segmentation are yielding rapidly to class divisions and to groupings with particular moral climates and cultural interests. The result is a series of temporary alliances for the sake of achieving specific goals in, say, the schools or local politics, or on occasion for electing a candidate to national office. Social life increasingly is carried on with the tacit acknowledgement that the end is near.

Volatility, however, is not the hallmark solely of the churches or of religion; it permeates American society. Take, for example, the experience of literally millions of American workers whose jobs have been terminated or exported. Even the ones who find new jobs, more often than not at the cost of moving themselves and their families to unfamiliar places, are not happy in their new situations. Mobility is unsettling. In one General Motors plant, for instance, many of the labour conflicts have been ascribed to the high percentage of workers who have moved to the plant from their homes elsewhere: forced to do so by cutbacks and plant closings elsewhere in the General Motors system, these workers, too, account for much of the time lost to divorce, alcohol, and drug addiction.[59]

It is not only blue-collar workers who are volatile; even professionals find that their firms and practices may not provide a firm base for their careers. Adding to the volatility of professions are law firms like Myerson and Kuhn: started from scratch, hyped through public relations and capable of attracting the most mobile – and expensive – lawyers in the profession. In the course of two years the firm flourished and then headed into potential collapse. In a trend toward increasing 'disloyalty', lawyers move from one partnership or firm to another with unprecedented ease and frequency.[60] Not restricted to the professions, volatility also affects management. Managerial posts have now been altered to accommodate the 'interim executive', whose skills are hired for limited purposes over a short period of time lasting as little as a few weeks.[61] Volatility becomes an aspect of American social structure: built in, as it were, expected, institutionalized. Temporary workers and some of the firms that hire them are increasingly 'terminal'.

In this respect the market for professionals, blue-collar workers and executives comes to resemble the market for securities. The liquidity of financial markets has no doubt increased enormously throughout the 1980s and early 1990s: large amounts of stocks being bought and sold with extraordinary convenience and speed. 'Critics contend computer-driven trading strategies have injected dangerous new volatility into the stock market . . .', but this volatility is also a function of the 'liquidity' of securities offered that makes even huge transfers of capital possible within a very short span of time indeed.[62]

The same volatility, however, affects not only the market for securities and employees; it dominates the public discussion of social issues and legislative agenda. Public interest in the 'war on drugs', for instance, escalated about 800 percent within the span of a month following the appointment of a drug czar, William Bennett, by the Bush administration and the declaration of a 'war on drugs'. Within a month or so news coverage – and public interest – had returned to normal.[63] In very much the same way public interest in issues like sex education and the homeless comes and goes; churches that stake their claim to relevance on these intense but short-term mobilizations around specific social issues condemn themselves to having a limited and very temporary interest to a constantly changing set of audiences and publics. As Demerath and Williams remind us:

> There is no question that most religious institutions have become internally more democratic in recent years, especially as greater influence and participation has been extended to women and minority groups, and less arbitrary power is

> invested in ecclesiastical authority. But it is possible that this surge in internal democracy may result in declining external effectiveness. Precisely because of the decline of religious authority and the difficulty of mobilizing an increasingly active and diverse constituency, many religious institutions have become less politically united in either means or ends.[64]

The Church used to be a reservior of social credit that could be tapped for particular purposes and commitments. As that reservoir runs dry, the time horizons affecting any social issue are correspondingly reduced to the near term or even to an ephemeral present.

On the one hand, the churches, the more separated they become from city hall and the local political parties, can offer only a vague sort of symbolic legitimacy to the beleaguered politician, who turns increasingly to the local business leaders for support and financing. On the other hand, the politicians, in turning to the churches for support, find themselves drawing upon a reservoir of social credit that has already been spent on a variety of specific issues. The treasury of merit, as it were, has little in reserve to offer the community in a time of crisis. *To put it another way, the community cannot count on the Church to keep it from running out of time.*

Demands for a day of accounting may be softened and postponed if a religious community can enable the society as a whole to buy time by remembering its origins and traditions and by recalling its historical vision for the future. Churches whose membership is volatile and whose interests are focused on single-issue politics will have little to offer in the way of expanded time-horizons when pressures for a settling of accounts intensify, as they inevitably do when times are bad. *What has been lost, and not only in Springfield, Massachusetts, is an institutional reservoir of time.* The more the churches become one more voluntary association engaged in interest-group politics, the more they, too, are seen to be mundane and temporary. Political promises, like other forms of social credit, however, rely on having at least a measure of time in which to make good. Time is as much the essence of a political promise as it is of an ecclesiastical oath or benediction: simultaneously a way of buying time and of shaping the future. When time is short, and social credit is at a low ebb, the future will not begin. That is why fascist impulses intensify the demand to initiate the future by restoring an dealized past.

In a community such as Springfield, still based on the family and ethnicity, political assets usually come from the candidates' identities as Irish or Italian, Asian or black, and from their ties to specific families. As Demerath and Williams point out, however, these credits do not last very long when politicians are known to be insincere and fail to keep their promises.[65] By the same token, such credits are quickly exhausted when politicians are inept and fail to stave off crises of one sort or another, such as the economic collapse of the central city. Sheer effectiveness, the ability to accomplish goals and keep promises, to preserve the fabric and enrich the opportunities of the city, becomes essential for keeping power in a secularized city or nation. The only reliable assets are effective actions.

The Church and local government are not the only institutions who are running short of hard assets. In a biting essay on 'the over-leveraged ethos of . . . corporate leaders', Alan Webber (editorial director of the *Harvard Business Review*) notes that the 1980s witnessed a spate of self-advertisements by chief executive officers of major corporations in the form of autobiographies and news stories. The basic asset of the corporation was claimed to be the chief executive officer and his or her leadership; the CEO personified the corporation and determined its character and commitments. It was not long, Webber writes, until

> Many that focussed heavily on an ego-driven culture found themselves beached-stranded on too much debt, too many undigested, ego-driven acquisitions, too much style, not enough substance.[66]

One of the basic assets of any society, of course, is not merely character but memory and information. Recent complaints of cultural amnesia as a disease affecting the American body politic go to the heart of the matter; a society that does not know its own past or can scarcely remember its basic commitments has no core, no treasury on which to draw when expediency, calculation and the quarterly report fail to provide adequate guidance for the future. One of the more chilling of recent anecdotes on the subject concerns a major politician who claimed on national television that the United States had been allied with Hitler until the Japanese bombed Pearl Harbor.[67] Not only Americans, however, but the Japanese have engaged in cultural lobotomies; witness the average Japanese textbook that fails to report Japan's invasion of China and of Indochina in the decade preceding Pearl Harbor.[68] The churches are not the only institutions whose members have forgotten – or never knew – its basic history and foundational documents. *Time is perennially running out on institutions and societies with poor memories, foreshortened histories, and futures that cannot begin.*

To the extent that ethnic, regional or racial communities survive, they can provide a sense of time that can relieve the present of the demand that it initiate the future. On the other hand, these same communities are the custodians of old grievances that, under trying conditions, may issue in demands for a day of accounting. As these same communities get caught up in the politics of a modern society, however, they begin to lose their aura of transcendence. Furthermore, time pressures increase as alliances become temporary and as constituents increasingly demand results. As the presence of the larger society increasingly invades the institutions and neighbourhoods of traditional religious, racial and ethnic communities, moreover, their days begin to be numbered.

It would be surprising, under these conditions, if there were not an increasing number of social movements seeking to restore the vigour and harmony of a more primitive communal past: an outpouring of Farrakhans and Dukes, Limbaughs, Norths and Buchanans on the central stage of American politics.

· 6 ·

RITUAL AND THE ELEMENTARY FORMS OF FASCISM

Rituals, even well-established ones like the Church's penitential system, can thus defeat themselves by their own successes, by stimulating longings for liberation not only from time but also from the weight of social obligation. Under certain conditions which I have called optimal for each ritual, however, these rituals can continue to work reasonably well. Since rituals are based on a combination of longings for timelessness and magical control, however, rituals have to be repeated. But rituals fail for other reasons that have to do not with delusion but with reality. The outside world may impinge upon or actually invade the social order. People may come to live, work and do business with others who are not part of the social order that is defined and expressed by the ritual in question. Individuals may have personal experiences for which there are no customary channels for expression and which are therefore regarded as illegitimate or dangerous. Under such conditions rituals will inevitably fail to carry conviction or impose control, and performances will become more self-conscious, artificial and tongue in cheek. Under these conditions, I will argue, fascist tendencies will find expression not in rituals so much as in spectacles or games, and fascist movements will seek a new social order purified of outside influences, in which the young are transformed and dangers averted once and for all.

Ritual's compromise with reality is always partial and uneasy. What has been excluded from the compromise with reality threatens to intrude itself once again both on ritual and on the social order: destructive impulses, indiscriminate and uncontrolled sexuality, insatiable hungers, autonomous mental activity, delusions of grandeur, and magical thinking that informs even the apparently most rational policies and procedures. Outside the order expressed and imposed by ritual, therefore, lie a host of potential enemies. That is why I speak of rituals as imposing a proto-fascist solution to the problem of time faced by all societies.

The compromise of ritual with reality is most obvious and vulnerable in one respect, namely that individuals run out of time before the demise of their social systems. The lack of synchrony between self and society, of course, begins with birth and only ends in death. When infants first experience the gulf separating mother from child, furthermore, they may experience anxiety or even depression; there is a primitive panic that attends the discovery that one is outside the timeless matrix of the womb. There one first had lived without any sense of danger to the self. In moments of extreme regression or of temporary bliss, individuals recover that original sense of unity with the mother in the feeling that Freud called 'oceanic': a psychic eternity. Infants also sense time running out when their nourishment or comfort is delayed. Waiting is experienced not as merely frustrating or even enraging but as a threat to life itself. This primitive sense of helplessness threatens the very survival of the fledgling self; the passage of time at this level of emotional experience is therefore filled with the apprehension of the death of the ego.[1]

It is to avert that disaster and if possible to restore the primitive, timeless unity of the self with its original matrix that certain rituals have developed as ways of buying time and making up for lost time. When they fail, the impulse to make time last forever, and the fear that time is running out, spill over into everyday life and the larger society. I would argue that American fundamentalism, for instance, has grown in part because of the failure of ritual in the mainstream churches. That default has left literally millions of individuals feeling that time is running out. Not a moment either of this life or the next is to be wasted. Danger – even nuclear holocaust – is imminent, as is relief from the struggles and burdens of the world. On the way to the millennium, there will be terrible conflict, from which only the purified and the transformed will emerge as the bearers of God's will.

Compared with a society's purchase on eternity, the individual's own share of time is limited and precarious indeed. So long as a society's institutional house is in order, for instance, the society will long outlive the individual. What chance the individual has for eternity will therefore be mediated through official channels, e.g. through institutions like the observance of the sabbath or other holy days. Individuals know or believe that their days are numbered and will come to an end long before the social system reaches its own conclusion.

There are societies, moreover, which declare their own war on the very essence of the individual. In the Middle Ages, the very success, I have noted, of the Church's rituals of penance created the need for a counter-magic of absolution and remission that belonged to the people themselves rather than to clerics, so great was the burden of the penitential system and of the Church's authority over the soul.

The reaction against an overweening penitential order continued, of course, during the Reformation, but that reaction was hardly universal or single-minded. Notwithstanding his appeals for a more humane pedagogy with a minimum of terror and coercion, even John Locke asserted the need to reinforce persuasion with the threat and occasional administration of blows to the body of the child. In colonial America and also in Germany prior to the Second World War, child-rearing practices justified the breaking of the will of the child through corporal punishment, albeit in the name of saving the child's soul.[2]

Indeed, the means by which societies ensure that they will not run out of time may be so impressive or coercive that the soul of the individual is enthralled or crushed. Under these conditions individuals will experience themselves as moribund:

> Deep feelings of hostility and insecurity result from such childhood treatment. People are seen as dangerous. The result may be an anti-social value orientation, which has to be carefully controlled, may be largely unconscious, and gains expression only when the group or authorities clearly define permissible objects of hostility.[3]

Staub goes on to document what he calls 'substantial psychological reorganization' on the part of those who are active participants, merely compliant, or even passive sufferers in an authoritarian regime such as Nazi Germany.[4] What he does not report on, however, is the extensive use of psychological insights and practices to ensure the compliance, tractability and efficiency of individuals in the German army prior to 1941, even after specifically psychological military units had been disbanded.[5] In order to avoid running out of time, modern societies increasingly have placed pressure on the psyche to 'come up to speed', as it were: to synchronize the wishes and needs of the individual with the roles and requirements of an increasingly co-ordinated and complex social structure.

It is paradoxical that the sense that one's own time is short is therefore often caused by social institutions whose function it is to perpetuate and renew the larger society. The very rituals that require individuals to postpone their desires for gratification or for the settling of accounts may succeed in enabling a society to reproduce itself or avoid disabling conflict, but these rituals may also place considerable burdens on the psyche. Those burdens, I will suggest, are experienced by the self as time-pressures: e.g. as a sense of imminent danger, of a need for a break with the past, an insistence on beginning the future, or as a yearning to make up for lost time.

When they succeed, therefore, a society's rituals often enjoin the soul to number its days, to be aware of the shortness of time, and to prepare accordingly for a last judgement, as if to make the individual rather than the social order responsible for the sense that time is running out and that one's innermost self is therefore endangered. When they fail, such rituals are incapable of delaying demands for gratification or for a day on which old scores will be settled. Those demands, when translated into the body politic, are one source of fascist tendencies.

When a society's rituals fail, some may not be willing to postpone the satisfaction of their demands and may therefore refuse to subscribe to the prevailing distribution of time. They may claim, for instance, that they have received a vision of the approaching end, a day of trial or of judgement, in which the society as a whole, with very few exceptions, is headed for eternal disaster. Such visions typically reverse the prevailing distribution of time, by making the individual's purchase on eternity far more certain than that of the society as a whole. Prophecies of the apocalypse, for instance, typically turn the conventional tables and envisage the society coming to its end long before the end will come for those who share the apocalyptic vision. To mediate this tension between the personal and societal construction of time has been one function of religion and particularly of sacred ritual, but when such mediation fails, individuals may seek their own remedies in this life without waiting for the next.

Of course there are perennial discrepancies and tensions between the way individuals experience time and the way time is constructed for them by social systems. Individuals do not always honour the sequences by which individuals move from youth to adulthood or from the single to the married estate. Some experience themselves as gifted or are seen as precocious; others may claim the benefits and authority of a divine commission and may be seen either as divinely inspired or as merely grandiose. Some may claim the right to marital satisfactions without benefit of the clergy or of the state, while others may seek exemption from the burdens and responsibilities of marriage by claiming to be wed to a higher authority. The temporal sequences of such individuals are difficult to synchronize with those of the larger society. Religion has typically provided an alternative set of times and seasons that an individual can observe with impunity: alternative vocations, seasons of the soul, and roles for virtuosos that are exempt from the calendar of sacred and secular obligation.

There are other ways in which individuals may experience their own time as being out of harmony with time as it is officially constructed and publicly understood. Societies have set times for putting the present into the past. These may be times for settling old grudges or for making atonement for past sins. Alternatively, these stated occasions may be times for mourning the dead or for placing the dead firmly, once and for all, in the collective past. The official calendar, whether religious or secular, limits the occasions on which individuals can seek satisfaction for old injuries and insults.

Some individuals, however, are not inclined to accept the official status of limitations on the past; their memories and grievances are not so easily assuaged. Others are not willing to wait to redress their grievances or to postpone them. They wish old losses to be redeemed on a timetable that differs markedly from that of the larger society. These demands for renewal or for redemption from old grievances place an enormous strain on the society's capacity for purification. Such demands are easily translated into mass movements that settle old scores with the club and the axe and that take the means of restoration into their own hands. When rituals of restoration fail, religious movements provide a cure for impatience that is often difficult to distinguish from the disease.

Thus individuals may turn to popular sources of spiritual assistance, to charismatic leaders and magicians or sorcerers who can enable the individual to feel potent rather than helpless, or full rather than drained of energy and empty. As I have tried to show, however, these defenders of the soul are also part of the disease and not only of the cure; they, too, can be intrusive or enchanting and thus displace the innermost self.

The Intensification of Social Pressures on the Individual: The Effect of War

As Nikolas Rose has argued, the attempt to 'govern the soul' of the individual citizen has been spurred in modern societies by the experience of two world wars. Not only must the soldier's fighting morale be sustained, but so must the average person's psyche be controlled sufficiently to produce an efficient workforce and a loyal citizenry. The demons of a modern society are thus 'unhappiness, inefficiency, incompetence, maladaptation, and antisocial conduct' rather than the more bizarre forms of mental illness.[6] Thus, trained professionals are required whose rituals will suffice, in Rose's apt formula, to 'govern the soul'.

Even those who are employed, then, in the service of the psyche are required to serve the interests of the state. Conversely, the citizen's own psyche must be impressed with the legitimate urgency of the larger society's demands for order, commitment and sacrifice. Through psychological testing and through a vast machinery for assessing and shaping public opinion, Western democracies from the Second World War to the present have sought to ensure the formation of a social character responsive to societal demands:

> Citizenship had acquired a subjective form. From this point forth, winning the war, and winning the peace, required the active engagement of the civilian in the social and political process, a shaping of wills, consciences, and aspirations, to forge social solidarity and individual responsibilities in the name of citizenship and democracy. As citizenship became a psychological matter, the psyche of the citizen was discovered as a new continent for psychological knowledge and for the deployment of the professional skills of the technicians of subjectivity.[7]

The rituals of the professional, however, are up against a potent source of commitment in what has come to be called the 'primary group'. Rose recounts in detail a discovery by the new cadre of sociologists and psychologists working for the military during the Second World War: that the immediate community of the soldier was a far more effective source of morale and support than propaganda could ever become. It was in fact a rediscovery of the primary group, as Rose points out, since the industrial sociologists had already noted the impact of small working groups on worker satisfaction and on the rate of production. Workers, like soldiers, were responding far less to the dictates of management or of self-interest than to the promptings of the group with whom they went to work every day.

Revolts Against Social Pressures on the Individual

Beneath the surface of bureaucracies, then, in the interstices of factories, and in the heart of apparently chaotic inner cities one finds small, vital face-to-face groups with their own way of doing things, their implicit understandings or codes, and their techniques for controlling their members. These groups may foster or sabotage the goals of the industry, of the military unit, or of the city; in either case they are the key to its future. Indeed, many of the 'advances' in management have sought to give these groups more autonomy and responsibility while bringing them into line with the goals and objectives of the corporation itself. The point, however, is that these groups have lives of their own which are not easily subsumed within the purposes of the larger society. To co-opt such groups so that they will serve the purposes of larger units like the corporation or the state, it is necessary to mimic their magic.

Victories over the individual's primary loyalties and defences, however, will be won at considerable cost to the individual. At one time or another, a society will require commitment to battle, the sacrifice of one's childhood and of one's original family, and often the strictest repression of consuming passions. Demands for courage, sacrifice and purity can indeed become so oppressive that the individual is threatened with the death of the psyche: with what some anthropologists and psychoanalysts still call soul-loss. Some individuals will turn to magic to defend the psyche against the overwhelming weight of obligation, while others will defend themselves against crushing social expectations by accusing others of witchcraft. The revolt against social duties may also take the form of rebellion against tyranny itself. The very success of rituals in buying or renewing time is won at the price of spontaneity and freedom; these are sacrificed to a social order that impresses its own priorities on the soul and demands a certain purity of heart.

Examples of the revolt against the power of ritual to impress the soul could be drawn from many social orders. To begin with, however, let us return once again to Norman Cohn's study of religious movements in the Middle Ages, *The Pursuit of the Millenium*. Many of these movements, I have noted, were a protest against the extraordinary weight of the Church's penitential system: a weight impressed on the soul in rites of confession, contrition and penance. Cohn describes one free thinker, Amaury of Bène, who was condemned for his ideas by the Pope and forced to recant: a ritual of shaming and humiliation that may have cost Amaury his life; 'he took to his bed and shortly afterwards – in 1206 or 1207 – he died'.[8] The Church had the power to crush the soul and thus to kill.

Amaury posed a threat to the Church in part because his ideas had found a following among the Brethren of the Free Spirit. This group, like many other libertarian movements of the thirteenth and fourteenth centuries, no longer subscribed to the Church's penitential rites and thus neutralized the power of the Church over the soul. According to Cohn,

> This doctrine amounted ... to an assurance of a universal, though impersonal salvation; and the more consistent of the Brethren of the Free Spirit did in fact hold that heaven and hell were merely states of the soul in this world and that there was no afterlife of punishment or reward.[9]

As Cohn goes on to point out, the Brethren of the Free Spirit were not merely attacking the Pope and the Church but the power of society over the individual. They equated the conscience with purgatory, hell, and the Devil, and considered salvation to be relief from the pressures of the conscience on the soul.[10] Cohn finds contemporary analogues of this 'mystical anarchism' in modernity, notably in the drug culture.[11] The secularization of social pressures does not weaken the need for psychological defences against what we have come to know less, perhaps, as conscience and more as the super-ego or ego-ideal. On the contrary, I would argue, these pressures are all the more dangerous because they are pervasive and diffuse rather than concentrated in the Church.

Whenever the psychic vitality of the individual is threatened, time is experienced as very short. In part this intensification of the meaning and duration of time is an expression of the danger to the inner self. The imaginary shortening of time reflects both a wish and a fear that the end of the self (and in fantasy, therefore of the world) is in sight. No doubt the sense of hurry is based on a profound wish for release from suffering. All these aspects of the intensification of time can be found in many of the other protest movements that Cohn describes. Each turns out to be millenarian, obsessed or enthralled by the prospect of a Second Coming and of an end to suffering and repression.

Notably, I would add, each mounts an attack on the Church's monopoly over the means of grace and of rites of penance. Flagellants not only beat themselves and disparaged the sacraments; they claimed the right to hear confession and absolve from sin.[12] Many undertook voluntary poverty rather than flagellation in order to escape from the Church's monopoly over the dispensation of such grace as the absolution from sin. Some, like the Brethren of the Free Spirit, sought to recover magical powers in order to defend the soul against the crushing weight of the conscience; they believed that the perfected soul, in fact, was 'incapable of sin'.[13] In all these strategies, however, time itself was of the essence: each moment counting toward a salvation that would soon be revealed in apocalyptic events.

Rebellions against such overwhelming social pressures carry forward an old dream under the auspices of new authority. That is, the old dream of living in a social order that is proof against the passage of time does not die; on the contrary, that dream animates the hope for a new social order purified of former tyranny and disloyalty. While fundamentalists in the United States, for example, are eager to see an end to the social order as they know it, they foresee an interregnum and a new millennium in which 'the best and truest will survive'.[14] In the new order the soul or *pneuma*, as it were, can freely breathe. Therefore the revolt against old tyranny quickly imposes new disciplines: calls for loyalty and sacrifice; a new surveillance over the individual to ensure purity of heart; and challenges to rise in the defence of the new society against its enemies. *Fascist tendencies therefore not only shape rituals that preserve the status quo but also inform religious and political movements that seek liberation.*

It is crucial, if the self is to develop a life of its own, for the self to be sufficiently separate from others so that its life does not hang in the balance of every relationship. The self needs its own inner time-zone, as it were. For every withdrawal of emotional investment from others, furthermore, the self pays rather dearly. Children – and adults who are regressing – tend to look back on their sources of nourishment, security and support, like the child who is learning to walk but looks back to see if the parent is still there. In this turning back to recover the sense of a presence which is now absent, Freud found the compulsion to repeat. It is as if the child, and later the neurotic adult, cannot trust his or her own perceptions or powers sufficiently and needs to bring forward the presence of individuals who were originally experienced as bigger-than-life, omniscient and omnipresent.

The psyche that does experience this drive to repeat the past, however, is quite literally running out of time: fleeing from the present, wasting time, and seeking to recover a timeless past when wishes used to be transformed, as though by magic, into deeds. Rituals, which indeed are obligatory and must be repeated, temporarily exempt their participants from the flow of time. For the liturgical moment one can abandon the present, delay the future, create and restore a mythic past, but only for the time being. Time out, as it were, must be paid for by redoubled commitment to being in time. The alternating rhythm in Western societies, between weekends and weekdays, in which the duties of the week are intensified by the pleasures of weekend enchantment, is a case in point.

Ritual, especially an initiatory rite, expresses and perpetuates a compromise between the progressive, forward-looking self that is making time, and the self that is looking back to recover the recognition and support of powerful presences that have been left behind. Individuals who withdraw love and attention from their parents as they make their way in life also pay a sort of emotional debt to them by bringing them forward. The parents are enshrined in the self in what is often called the ego-ideal and the super-ego: elevated positions from which these internal presences can monitor progress or offer guidance and correction. From this vantage point in the psyche, these superior, and often sanctified figures suppress drives for satisfaction and control that threaten their authority. In extreme cases, these presences are cruel and tormenting. While they may appear to offer love and support, they torment the self with reminders that the self has not yet arrived, lived up to expectations, or reached perfection. While appearing to offer guidance and correction, they may crush the self by depriving it of nourishment or the satisfaction that comes from being autonomous and effective. Certain rites of initiation enact the obligatory and sacrificial aspect of this compromise between autonomy and separation.

Many persons therefore find it difficult to lay the dead psychologically to rest; they remain a bit haunted. The self thus burdened by the (often unconscious) presence of the dead may consciously suffer from a crushing conscience or from a set of ideals that constantly find fault. That self, therefore, will indeed be starved of crucial nourishment and denied hope for the future; it will be literally running out of time. The self thus constrained may also feel continually late for important connections and appointments. In either case it is a connection with the self that is being forfeited.

Rituals that are done in the right way and at the right time may offer a temporary reprieve from terror over the passage of time, but there is always a catch. The rituals themselves may become a source of torment and frustration or increase the burdens of social obligation on an already fragile and overburdened psyche. That is why there is often an iconoclastic aspect to social movements that declare an end to the old social order and to obligations to the past, even while seeking to restore a period of primitive virtue to the people and nation. Fascist movements are a case in point.

Ritual is therefore a means not only for transcending or for destroying time but for creating it. Some rituals enable individuals to 'buy time', or entire peoples to ward off impending disaster. Other rituals allow individuals to enter into new stages in life or enable societies to purge themselves of potentially fatal influences and thus to renew the times in which they live. Again, some rituals allow individuals to make up for lost time by recovering the resources of the past, while other rituals enable entire societies to believe that they have transcended time by bringing all past and future generations within the scope of their celebrations. The ancestors return; future generations are foreshadowed. The past continues even while the future begins. As I have shown in the chapter on rituals of restoration, such rituals were of particular importance in the fascist movement in Germany prior to the Second World War.

The more successful are such rituals, the more they place peculiar burdens on the individual. To intensify the meaning of time also tends to add to the oppressive weight of social obligation on the soul. It is no wonder the popular religious alternatives enable individuals to avoid panic, stagnation and helplessness by giving them access to ancestral or angelic powers: thus temporizing with powerful and potentially overwhelming presences. At their most effective, rituals forge a soul, an innermost self, able to stand the test of time. When they are effective, rituals therefore present communities and societies with something of a problem: a soul that can transcend time on its own. Such a soul may also start a new community outside the confines of the old and renew itself without passing through the sequence of the generations. The born again, who believe that they can stand the test of time even on the Day of Judgement, are an ambiguous case in point, since the twice-born in American society are also the exponents of traditional obligations and issue calls for sacrifice to each successive generation. A better case in point, as I have suggested, are the mediaeval Brethren of the Free Spirit and later anarchists, mystical or otherwise, in the nineteenth and twentieth centuries. The fascist potential of a social system can be kept under control so long as the relevant rituals do their public work without imposing too heavy a burden of obligation on the individual.

To succeed in imposing the burdens of the past on the present, even the souls of the departed may be recruited in the service of future generations. The Catholic tradition maintained a relatively high level of reverence for social rank and the saints, while exhorting the laity to pilgrimage, penance and the fulfilment of their social obligations. In anti-fascist revolutions, therefore, the bodies of the religious may be exhumed and placed on public display as a move to disenchant the social universe and lift the weight of duty.

It is thus often the success rather than the failure of religious ritual that produces movements of liberation. In seventeenth-century England, the progressive impoverishment of the population, in contrast with the new affluence of a fledgling middle class, certainly drove many to despair. Added to their increased mortality, however, was the pressure of Calvinism and its doctrine that the vast majority of the people were not only unregenerate but damned to eternal torment. It is not surprising under these circumstances that many chose suicide.[15] It is also not surprising, as I have argued, that prophecy became increasingly widespread. Here is Hill on the subject:

> 'All the Lord's people are become prophets', declared Milton in *Areopagitica*. The true Church, William Dell agreed, 'is a kingdom of prophets', for Christ lives in the elect. Lower-class rejection of the oligarchy of the elect, and a common-sense suspicion that perhaps all morally good men might be saved, could now be expressed and discussed freely, side by side with the writings of more intellectual antinomian theologians who concentrated on demanding complete moral

> freedom for the elect without troubling to ask how they were to be known . . . If all believers were prophets as well as priests, all men might be saved . . .[16]

The egalitarian distribution of prophetic charisma left all on the same footing and thus undermined the élite's claim to preference and priority.

The sense that the ordinary individual has the charismatic endowment with which to prophecy, moreover, came from the very success of Calvinism in propagating its notion of an elect endowed with sufficient grace to weather the tests of time and inherit eternity. As Hill points out, 'Calvinism stimulated an individualism in behaviour and thought against which it had no external, visible objective check.'[17] The Reformation attack on ritual signified that the Church's major rites had clearly failed to purify the social order, hold death at bay, and transform the next generation. Various forms of Messianism filled the charismatic demand for deliverance from oppression and death. Under these conditions, demand for authoritarian and magical leadership escalates rapidly along with an increasing supply of claimants to prophetic status. Indeed, fundamentalism helps to create a nation within a nation: a 'kingdom of prophets' each with his or her own vision of the end of time.

When rituals of purification are successful, they can remove an anomaly from the midst of the social order: a decrepit old man, a poor beggar, a licentious woman or headstrong youth. As Hill points out, however, in the midst of the English revolution, the poor were entertaining the notion that they, too, might be inheritors of heaven and recipients of grace.[18] These 'beggars' and the 'vagabonds' presented an enormous threat to the enclaves of religious and social merit. Rites of purification only work if they are capable of turning these human anomalies into conquerable sources of negation. When these 'negative aspects' are turned into symbols of death, however, they are 'accorded a prominence which it is hard to entirely erase'.[19]

It is as if Calvinism defeated itself by its own successes in defining large segments of the population as beyond the pale of salvation. The poor, Hill noted, became the bearers of such pollution that they were often forcibly excluded from attending church, and they represented what appeared to be a mortal threat not only to the hegemony of the propertied but to the survival of the social order as a whole.[20] The attempt under Archbishop Laud to make the ceremonies of the Anglican Church into the means of progressive purification of the unregenerate masses ran afoul not only of entrenched Calvinism but of the firm belief that the poor were bestial and evil anti-Christians who would be the death of the social system itself.[21]

Under excruciating social pressures such as these, individuals develop their own forms of counter-magic to buttress their souls and to prevent themselves from succumbing to what O'Keefe and others have called psychic or 'voodoo' death. Hill would appear to agree that many aspects of Protestant revolt in the English revolution were just such strategies to prevent the soul from being crushed to death. Rather than anticipate a future of eternal damnation, some dissenters claimed to be the possessors of an 'inner light' that was more than adequate to purify their souls of Calvinist self-doubt.[22] In fact, the notion of justification by faith served just such a purpose of fortifying the soul against the crippling effect of being cursed as unregenerate and headed for damnation. Here is Hill once again:

> Justification by faith, paradoxically, is an active doctrine, active in this world. It rejects attempts to propitiate an angry God by ceremonies mediated by a priesthood. It preaches the supremacy of the individual consciences of the elect, boosting the morale of those who would believe that, against such heavy odds, they are of the number of the elect.[23]

In this sense, Calvinism's early successes in opening up the possibility of a sovereign individual conscience, opposed to all forms of sacrifice and purification as prerequisites for access to God, laid the groundwork for its eventual defeat by secular individualism.

On the other hand, however, Calvinism not only released longings for a social order that could stand the test of time but injected them into the body politic. There they could be transformed into fresh controls over the young and into renewed demands for purity of heart. Fascist tendencies, given access to the means of social control, could then create new forms of surveillance and demands for sacrifice. As Strozier puts it of American fundamentalists, 'a violation of children's wills occurs in forcing on them an ideology that makes the world an evil place'.[24] Here it is enough to note that the longing for a social order that will stand the test of time is often expressed in imagery that evokes violence and justifies sacrifice. Indeed, Strozier says that fundamentalism possesses 'a potential for violence . . . that I often found troubling'.[25] It is a violence, I would argue, that is born of the suspicion that 'death has not been successfully harnessed to the cycle of regeneration'.[26]

In preventing societies and individuals from running out of time, it is necessary also to create a societal order that spans generations and transcends individual lifetimes. Consider, for example, the Ghost Dance religion of 1869: 'By supernatural means the world was to be rid of Whites, Indian land and resources were to be restored, and deceased Indians were to be resurrected so as to restore Indian life unhindered by Whites.'[27]

I have been arguing that when rites of transformation fail to cement the link between generations, the continuity and hence also the survival of the society comes into question. Popular religious movements may then call on past generations to come alive once again and to restore the potency of the community. If access to previous generations is broken, however, the time soon comes for old scores to be settled and long-standing debts to be paid in full. Those in power can no longer temporize; their clients or constituents will no longer wait. Religious groups prophecy the imminent coming of a new social order. Individuals feel that their own days are numbered. The old despair of being remembered by the young, and the young despair of the future.

Once the continuity of the living with the dead is broken, it becomes an urgent priority to make up for lost time. Perhaps the English revolution began decades earlier as the monarchy sought to inhibit the alms and honours offered on behalf of the dead. In the same vein, I would argue that the revolution was completed as England secularized the national experience and understanding of time, began producing clocks, and devoted its national attention to the daily newspapers.[28] Individuals were soon to be on their own, related to God not through their membership in a society that spans the generations but by unmediated access to divine and natural law through their own reasonable consciences.[29] Only toward the end of the revolutionary period, when millennial hopes had been abandoned, did belief in an indefinite and protracted time-span return, and with it a sense of the need for covenants, contracts, bargains and the discipline required to make them work.[30]

Those in power are typically in less of a hurry to see the old order end and the new one begin than are the relatively destitute. As Strozier notes of the wealthy among American fundamentalists, the transformation of history at the Second Coming is a 'real but remote possibility', while for the poor it cannot come soon enough.[31]

• 7 •

FASCISM AND THE END OF TIME

This book started with reflections about the way ritual manages the succession of the generations, but when that succession is managed through the media and on the streets, the older generation finds that its own transformation into a place of perpetual honour has little chance indeed. The fantastic interchanges between the generations no longer take place with the mask and the drum but largely in the cultural creations of each new generation. There is thus a symbolic world, filled with art and films, fashion and music, that encompasses and expresses the succession of the generations, but that succession is no longer assured or benign.

Each new generation can destroy the older generation's sense of itself and of its place in the community's history and recollection. In his recent work on the psychoanalysis of everyday life, Christopher Bollas notes that

> When a new generation forms, it inevitably sends a shock through the prior generations. The passing of a time that moves oneself, one's friends, one's loved ones, and one's era to extinction arouses anxieties that thus far we have tended to conceptualize in terms of individual psychology – as in a mid-life crisis – rather than in social-psychological terms. For there are generational crises when one's cultural generativity is defined by succeeding generations that mold another vision of social reality.[1]

Bollas observes that cultural objects disappear or are put to different uses as subsequent generations appropriate or discard the objects by which previous generations defined themselves: 'tail-fins', 'drive-in movies' and 'hamburger joints', to name a few.[2]

These end up, I would add, in new films like *Pulp Fiction* as parts of a set in which sleek and violent couples stage their own scenes. The motif of violence is very clear in the succession of the generations; Bollas puts it simply enough:

> Generational violence is essential to generational identity. Indeed, only when an emerging generation clearly violates the previous generation's aesthetic can we identify the emergence of a new generation . . . In the fate of one's generational objects we see the mortality of being; we watch our precious objects as they are discarded on the rubbish heap of history, and in this sense generational creativity is cannibalistic: the new generation scraps the older ones and eats what it will of them, leaving the prior generations skeletonized.[3]

It is important that we take Bollas literally here. In the psychoanalytic setting the analyst becomes very familiar with the patient's fantasies about the analyst. On the one hand, the analyst is like a parent helping a child to emerge from the residues of the past. The beginnings of generational succession are thus re-enacted in the clinical setting. On the other hand, however, analysts listen to their patients' dreams and fantasies about eating, consuming, devouring, and thus destroying the analysts themselves.

Christopher Bollas goes on to argue that individuals live in an imaginary social world: one that they construct out of their own daydreams and fantasies, and out of their often unconscious wishes and fears. The world of everyday life is religious, in the sense of being serious, imagined, and fateful for the way individuals live their lives.

Nowhere is that world more evident than in the symbolic exchanges between generations. As the older generation sees itself through the eyes of another, it realizes that it is being consumed and discarded. Time is thus very short indeed: shorter even than the biological clock of the individual would seem to indicate. That is because we endure a social death in the succession of the generations long before our time to die actually comes.

Not only the relationship between generations but the internal life of a group of friends, the psychological space between ethnic groups in a city, and even the imagined world of a large organization: all these are experienced by the individual in much the way that a person dreams. That is because social life resembles that of the mind itself: complex, full of ambiguous and partly expressed emotions, with secrets and strivings that are often as opaque in everyday life as they are in dreams themselves. I agree with Bollas that it is therefore necessary to compare the individual's experience of ordinary social life to religion; that experience is indeed full of imagined and often imaginary presences, half-revealed meanings, portents and promises.

Fascist social movements, we have argued, are best understood as religious, and they make the same sort of appeal to the individual as the sacred. The sacred, for all that it appears to be powerful, external, constraining, and thus superior to the individual in every way, is also, and some would add – merely – a creature of the cultural imagination: part of the 'religious' world of everyday life that Bollas and other psychoanalysts have so readily observed. Some sociologists, of course, styling themselves in the Durkheimian tradition, would argue that it is the sacred that is real, because it is social, and it is therefore the individual who is the social product: a merely derivative sort of being. Nonetheless, speaking of the sacred, Durkheim called it a collective representation, but he added that it was pure fiction:

> Assuredly, this representation is illusory. It is ourselves that we, in a sense, avenge, ourselves that we satisfy, since it is within us and in us alone that the offended sentiments are found. But this illusion is necessary. Since these illusions have exceptional force because of their collective origin, their universality, their permanence, and their intrinsic intensity, they separate themselves radically from the rest of our conscience whose states are much more feeble.[4]

The above quotation from Durkheim makes it clear that social life is based on illusions. They may be 'necessary', since a society without some sense of cohesion may fall apart. They may seem powerful, external and coercive, especially if they take the form of the sacred. But even the values of others, their projects, and their sense of themselves can seem to us as a too pervasive and even invasive presence in our lives. Witness the fears of fundamentalists about secular humanists and their values. In the process of believing in these collective illusions individuals become 'radically' separated from their own beings. Social life depends, as it were, on fictions which seem essential to our very being and yet which alienate us from our selves.

Social life is thus based on fictions, but they are fictions which constitute the basis for our solidarity with one another as well as the source of our differences from one another. Although fictitious, these projects and perceptions of others do become shared. In their collective manifestation they are more or less sacred. To avenge them against various offenders is thus at least 'quasi-religious' activity: a 'metaphor . . . not without truth'.[5]

I mention these sociological truisms in order to suggest that there is something perennial about the fascist tendencies which we have been examining in this book. If these were only truisms, however, this book would not have been written. Instead, the fascist tendencies which we have been examining are not only pervasive, at least in the United States, but they have been intensifying in the United States over the past 150 years.

The mental division of the world into 'us' and 'them' is fundamental to the American experience of facing death on what had once been alien shores. In his brilliant essay, *Imagined Communities*, Benedict Anderson writes of the experience of Hispanic civil servants in central America, and especially in Mexico.[6] Some were born on the peninsula of Spain and would return to the peninsula before their death. Others, however, were born and would die in the New World. Ostensibly sharing the same work and culture, they in fact followed different paths: the one to major centres, the other more often than not relegated to provincial capitals. More importantly, the two shared a very different fate: one being destined to die in the New World, while the other could return to the mother country.

Those whose fate, so to speak, was cast in the New World would also understand themselves to be similarly affected by arrivals and departures from the Old World; the newspaper would be a source of secular communion bringing them news of these fateful events. The Hispanics destined to die in the New World, where too they had been born, thus shared a common fate that distinguished them from the emissaries of old Spain. Those in the New World would answer the question, 'Who are we here together?' rather differently from those destined to return to the Iberian peninsula. The former, indeed, were 'Americans'.

There are other ways in which an immigrant community comes to terms with its new world and distinguishes itself from those who are destined to return to the old country. Certainly the immigrants who remained in the United States, in both the nineteenth and twentieth centuries, knew that they shared a different fate from those who, having made the journey to the New World, returned to the Old. Those who stayed imagined themselves to be the true Americans: more truly American even than the settlers who had arrived years, even generations, before them. To be a true American was to be a quintessential outsider in the New World. Whether distinguished by fidelity to a language and culture or to orthodox religious beliefs and practices, these immigrant communities claimed distinctions that entitled them to share the common fate of being an American. Their communities, too, would transcend particularity and death.

The existential imagination of one community makes it dread others who stake out a claim to the same spiritual territory. The new immigrant communities both intensified and threatened the earlier 'Americans'' sense of uniqueness and superiority. Indeed, some of the immigrants were objects of dread because they owed their allegiance to a foreign power, the Catholic papacy, and were simply going through the motions of citizenship. They were thus imagined to be both seditious and subversive: a fifth column, as it were, or a Trojan horse, in the city of God. It is thus not only groups, communities, or institutions, which, regarding themselves as sacred, foster the fascist state of mind among their members or adherents. A nation can also take on a similarly sacred aura for those who most firmly identify themselves with it, and for them the outsider in their midst can be as abhorrent as the Jew in Nazi Germany.

The Christian right not only attempts to restore an idealized America of the nineteenth century but also imagines a revival of the church as a force for Americanization. Indeed, many Protestant churches of the nineteenth and even of the early twentieth century attempted to reproduce a Protestant agrarian community in a space largely occupied, if not dominated, by foreign nationals who have cast their lot in the American city and who are competing for American jobs. To the most evangelical of Protestant leaders, these foreign intrusions had been a stimulus to spiritual revivals that demonstrated the moral superiority of the Protestant community and ensured its purification from such forms of urban pollution as drink, prostitution and violence. In his study of the churches in Gary, Indiana, for instance, James Lewis notes their aversion to the people who gathered in that new city from a wide range of countries and cultures.[7] A leading Methodist minister in the earlier days of Gary, one William Grant Seaman, saw the city as filled with an 'anonymous, mobile, materialistic, hedonistic population'.[8] Indeed, for Seaman the city was filled with problems, both 'foreign' and 'industrial'.[9]

To the élitist's loathing of the poor and the foreign-born this clergyman added the paternalism of Christian charity and the Church's aversion to 'the world':

> In an article in *The Homiletic Review*, Seaman observed that many children in modern society live not in 'our cultured Christian homes, but rather in the homes of the ignorant, the poor, the shiftless, and even the vicious'.[10]

He was not alone; other clergy also wished to 'take care of any of these ignorant and dangerous elements' through a massive programme of Christian charity and uplift.[11] Few clergy, however, were perhaps as energetic as Seaman in enlisting the aid not only of denominational boards and fund-raisers but of US Steel and of Judge Elbert Gary: the latter two being the industrial and judicial faces of raw power in that new steel-making city. The Church and US Steel jointly were interested in controlling labour, the 'Foreign Problem' and the rising population of blacks in Gary. The Church's various urban ministries, settlement houses and social programmes were, quite simply, agencies of social control.[12]

The Church's dread of the larger society as 'the world' is most acute, I would argue, when the Church as an institution is most clearly identified with the interests of a dominant class facing a challenge to its vested interests. Certainly conservative Christians in the 1980s and 1990s continue to describe the poor as a major threat not only to their own class interests but to the social order itself and to the Christian way of life. Lienesch describes in some detail the views of various conservative Christian authors on the poor.[13] It is clear that these writers see the poor as a danger to themselves and to others: a danger that must be brought under Christian – and not only secular – control. Indeed, these authors quite frankly state that they are urging the Church to get into the business of social control through Christian surveillance, discipline, punishment and 'moral training'.[14] These are the politics of purification.

The point, once again, is that this strong programme in moral and spiritual reform of the poor and decadent classes is a major illustration of fascist tendencies under the most sacred auspices. About the poor, notes Lienesch, there is the stench of sin and evil.[15]

> In each case the undeserving poor are seen as culpable ... 'Men who do not know Christ and do not walk in faith are more often than not immoral, impure, and improvident ... They are prone to extreme and destructive behavior, indulging in perverse vices and dissipating sensuality ... And they are thus driven over the brink of poverty.'[16]

To the most conservative of Protestants, the urban world was a sign of the beginning of the end. Things would be getting very much worse and would culminate in the Second Coming of Jesus Christ before they began to get better.

This is not the place to try to summarize the story of conservative and evangelical Protestantism in the nineteenth and twentieth centuries. Here the point is simply that Protestants and Catholics alike have sought to answer Benedict Anderson's question, 'Who are we here together?', in ways that have created an imaginary community defended against the power of death. Such a community is, in psychoanalytic terms, a reaction-formation: a symptom of the very ill to which it is opposed. Such an imaginary community not only thinks itself capable of renewing itself from one generation to the next; it imagines that it is able to purify itself of sin and other forms of pollution even in the urban context, where boundaries between social worlds are constantly in danger of being breached. That imagined social world is a form of that social 'madness' to which Christopher Bollas has referred.

I am not suggesting that Christians are the only ones who find social life so complex that they must always regress to more primitive configurations, like that of the church 'family', where they can feel more homogenous, purified, and secure. On the contrary, as Bollas argues, this form of regression is indeed commonplace:

> it is my view that our primary adult relations in life – marital, familial, ideological, political – are necessary regressions from the logic of human development, in which transformed simplified structures are found to comfort us against the harrowing complexity of life: be it the life of the mind or life in the strange mind of the social group. Complexity displaces the pre-Oedipal and Oedipal structures: the child discovers his own mind and the solitude of subjectivity. Knowing this, life becomes an effort to find inner sanctuary from the logic of psychodevelopment, and when this generative asylum is established it allows the subject to play with the samples of reality that pass by him during his lifetime.[17]

Certainly it seems to have been the cities of a newly industrialized America that threatened Protestants' imaginary community. In the face of immigration, class conflict, violence, and a secular culture that had its own momentum without the blessing or benefit of clergy, the Protestant world itself seemed headed precipitately toward destruction. Here is one description of the period by Margaret Bendroth:

> Gilded Age Protestantism shared the growing prosperity and optimism of its time but proved largely unable to penetrate urban culture, increasingly non-Protestant, and no longer

northern European. Revivalists hoped to renew national righteousness by winning the urban business classes, but even they confronted rising secularism among men who bowed chiefly to material gods. As the discontent of the lower classes, spurred by the arrogance of capitalist robber barons, ignited violent strikes and urban riots, the churches seemed helpless to confront or to change this course of events.[18]

While urban revivalists thought to reclaim the world for Christ, there were other Protestants who, as Bendroth puts it, chose to watch 'the demise of their culture from a safe theological distance'.[19] That safety was found in the claim that, under the new dispensation of Christ, his followers would survive a Second Coming which for the rest of the world would prove disastrous. Only after the conflict between Christ and his enemies had been won, would a new millennium usher in the longed-for age. In the meantime, therefore, the imagined community would preserve itself from contamination from the urban sources of impurity and from the kinds of urban missions, dominated by women, that exposed the community to 'contagion'.[20] This is that form of shared madness which – as we have seen – Bollas finds in the life of the group.

This shared 'madness', however, is fascist in the state of mind that it fosters, and I have been arguing that it is also fascist in the sort of social movement that it inspires and informs. To be sure, the belief in the millennium may also be a sample of the sort of mental sanctuary which individuals construct for themselves so that they can 'play' with various bits and pieces of social reality. The churches provided that 'generative asylum' that Bollas finds in the mind that regresses even as it makes progress toward further complexity in adulthood. Nonetheless, from the safety of that mental sanctuary emerge demands that the community or even the country be purified of those found unworthy to receive its benefits. From the same sanctuary, as we have seen, emanate demands that the nation restore the putative virtues of the nineteenth century in its treatment of aliens and the poor.

On ideological grounds alone, we are left with a complex and confusing picture of the way that some, evangelical and conservative, Christians proclaimed their transcendence over death.

Some were more likely to be transformed from children into adults than others: women remaining in the eyes of many fundamentalists spiritually immature or inferior to men. Some were more likely than others to be protected from the incursions of death and the devil: a masculine and vigorous faith providing a spiritual armour only for those fortified in the Spirit or qualified for immunity by their gender.[21] Some would be more likely than others to prove themselves purified of sin, whether through the blessings conferred by gender or through the power of revival. The point is simply that the Protestants' collective representations or illusions (as Durkheim called them) have broken out from evangelical or fundamentalist enclaves into the mainstream of American politics, where their implications are clearly fascist.

The tendency to split the world into a community of the saved and of those too unclean to be anything but damned was reflected in the compromise solutions offered by the schools and the settlement houses. These offered Protestants an opportunity to demonstrate their generosity and practice their virtues while at the same time acting as a buffer between Protestant congregations and the dreaded urban community. Certainly aliens may well have stood in need of help and of civilizing virtues, but they were at least partially demonized – and hence dreaded – by the Protestant community:

> In their pervasive paternalism, in their continual efforts at immigrant assimilation, and in their implicit denial of the worth of old world cultures in the new world environment, Gary's Protestant settlements became active and rigorous forces for Americanization.[22]

The Protestants therefore did try to reproduce the virtues of the small town and the agrarian community in the public of Gary. Impulses not only to transform the young, to avert disaster, and to purify the community of alien influences suggest that fascist tendencies have long been contained within the Protestant community. The same may be said for the desire to restore an idealized past. Indeed, as Lewis shows, the school system (known as the 'soul' of the community and its 'greatest civic achievement') was an attempt to recreate for children the integrated life of the agrarian community, where work, play and learning had not been compartmentalized activities but occurred in the normal course of everyday life, with the schools providing only 'formal educational skills'.[23] The rural community was thus sacralized, and the attempt to restore the 'religion' of its everyday life was part of the Protestant urban agenda well into this century. Even the choice of social issues on which the churches decided to engage the city also reflected this attempt to re-create an agrarian community: prohibition and Sunday baseball.[24]

The Church needs to see its environment as deficient or dangerous in order to define itself as the symbolic opposite of 'the world'. Whereas the world is undisciplined and corrupt, the Church offers hope for purity and self-discipline. In Gary, Indiana, it was a major article in the faith of one of the major downtown churches, according to Lewis, that the city was in perennial need of the strongest efforts to save it from its own sins. Before the Second World War the clergy of that congregation took stands regarding prohibition and Sunday baseball.[25] After that war there were other evils to fight: notably political corruption. As Lewis notes, the leading Presbyterian cleric of those latter years proclaimed that 'Gary needs a great cleansing;' twelve years later he repeated the diagnosis: 'the idea of cleansing our city and county of the corruption that has run rampant'.[26]

I am not suggesting that there was no corruption in Gary or that the problem was not systemic. I am suggesting, however, that the Church was selective in its perceptions of the city and needed to focus on flagrant examples of what it took at various times to be the symbolic opposite of the gospel. Its warfare was in part instrumental but largely, I would suggest, inspired by the need to dramatize the opposition between the Church and the world. Thus the same pastor who called for 'cleansing' derided secular efforts to raise the level of civic virtue:

> During the Chamber of Commerce's Civic Week membership drive in 1927, for example, Backemeyer satirized some of the week's booster rhetoric and articulated his own vision of civic

> righteousness: 'Talk about "community service!" Talk about municipal "evangelism!" Talk about the "gospel of civic welfare!"' There is but one evangelism, the evangelism of the Cross; and there is but one gospel, the gospel of the Son of God. And Gary will attain civic righteousness only as this evangelism and this gospel grips and controls the individual lives that make up our city's population.[27]

While their pastor insisted on comparing the world so unfavourably to the Church, his congregation managed to retain its own racial purity in a city with an increasingly diverse population. In 1969 less than 1 percent of the members of First Presbyterian were black, and there was one Asian member.[28] With a drastically reduced and ageing membership, First Presbyterian finally merged with four other downtown Gary congregations and achieved a more representative ethnic and racial balance.[29]

Thus the Church imagines the community around it in such negative terms that the city becomes an object of dread: filled with corruption and lax in spiritual discipline. Indeed, the Church thrives on such spiritual opposition in order to define itself and to mobilize its members. In turn, however, the church seeks to keep its membership unspotted from a world that it has imagined to be dreadful; in this way it reinforces the tendency of the congregation to remain homogenous and to resist intrusions by others who would not fit in, whether because of racial and ethnic differences or because they lack the social and cultural credentials. Even after several declining Presbyterian congregations had merged, they were still defining themselves as people willing to reach out 'with no strings attached' to a world around them perceived not in terms of its strengths, resources and virtues, and potential, but only in terms of its need.[30] The Church would remain the place where the world's deficiencies could be corrected and its needs met, and the world would remain the place that required such completion and correction through the Church.

First, then, comes the symbolic split between the 'Church' and the 'world'; then comes the definition of the world at the negative end of the semantic range, with the Church at the positive end. At opposite ends of the semantic spectrum, therefore, it is possible for the Church to see the world not only as negative but as its very negation. The Church must cleanse the world if it is to remain the Church. Eventually the 'world' changes and the Church begins to decline, even to die. The world becomes the death of the Church, so to speak. The Picture of Dorian Gray now takes on a hideous aspect, as the Church looks into the mirror of the world and sees its own mortality.

It is more than apparent that fascist tendencies have long been powerful, at least in American society. The logic of my argument in this book is that they will continue to be so, at least for the future sometimes referred to as 'foreseeable'. Certainly in recent years there have been overt signs of the crudest form of fascist activity: a brutal attack simultaneously on symbols of the central government and on defenceless citizens. Even so, I was as surprised as anyone by the bombing of the Alfred P. Murrah office building in Oklahoma City on 19 April 1995. That tragedy occurred after this book was largely written. My first reaction was to agree with the pundits who wrote about the bombing of the federal office building; they concentrated not only on the danger posed by 'terrorists' but on the danger of repressive over-reactions by the political centre. In the interest of arguing for the maintenance of civil liberties alongside additional precautions for national security, such responses tended to identify the danger with a few groups that were typically extreme in their antipathies. That was clearly a mistake.

It was the ordinary citizen, I will suggest, who understood the danger well enough to dread it. Many who were interviewed by the press found it eerie to have enemies among the familiar. Writing from Kinbard, Illinois on 13 May 1995, Dirk Johnson of *The New York Times* was describing 'this middle-class Chicago suburb':

> Down at the ice cream stand on Main Street, customers relax on sun-dappled benches.
>
> And over at the bowling alley, a right-wing militia meets twice a month.
>
> 'You think that all these groups are living out on the middle of nowhere,' said Matt Tabbert, a 35-year-old special education teacher here. 'And then you find out they're meeting

> twice a month over at Lombard Lanes. And you say, "Now wait a minute, this is scary!"'
>
> His wife, Vickie, a 36-year-old school administrator, put in: 'You wonder if you know who these people are, if they're working with you, living in your neighborhood. It's really kind of creepy, thinking that they're part of the mainstream.'[31]

In speaking to 'about 100 people' in various parts of the country, the reporter Mr Johnson claims to have found 'a sense of deep anxiety among most of them over the militias', which were seen as 'shadowy groups' rather than as a clearly defined source of danger. Not only did their shadowy quality make it hard to distinguish them from the mainstream, but Johnson also found quite a few in the mainstream who were willing to say that they shared some of the fear and resentment of the central government expressed by the militias themselves. They lived in the same towns, shared the same civil liberties, and belonged to the same organizations as many of those who found the militias deplorable.

> Nick Boorman, 34, an engineer on a plane bound for Seattle, said he had always dismissed the 'macho talk' he heard on job sites as nothing more than mouthy bravado.
>
> 'But now you can see what can really happen,' he said, 'and you wonder just a little bit, "Could this guy really be involved in something dangerous?" It scares you.'[32]

Of course, there are neo-Nazis and former members of the Ku Klux Klan who are now involved in the militia movements. It is their presence which makes it easy to dismiss the militias themselves as populated only by the radical and deranged. On the other hand, there are many members of these militias who are distinguishable from many other citizens only by their willingness on occasion to don military fatigues. As Peter Applebome put it in a perceptive piece for *The New York Times*,

> to a degree unusual in the recent history of the radical right, the obsessions of these extremists are overlapping with ele-

> ments of the nation's mainstream political culture . . . members of the radical right see a historic juncture in which their agenda – grounded in a hatred for the Federal Government and vehement opposition to taxes and gun control, with racial and anti-Semitic rhetoric as an important but less conspicuous thread – has the potential to resonate with a large part of the American public.[33]

In looking at these strange figures in military fatigues, many Americans are therefore looking at a shadow of themselves. The militia-man in a butch haircut who caused untold grief in Oklahoma City was seething with some of their own rage at a government which is often not only uncaring but corrupt and intrusive. Much of that anger is fed not only by taxation and by political graft but by the extension of environmental controls in ways that conflict with the interests of property owners. It is therefore not surprising to find that one of the suspects in the Oklahoma bombing had been a member of the Michigan Property Owners' Association.[34]

The point is simply that the rage for a restoration of an idealized social order from the past, before aliens and African-Americans and federal agents and judges and bureaucrats invaded their local communities, is now part of the mainstream rather than of the fringe or periphery in American society. Francis X. Clines, writing in *The New York Times*, noted that while there are some who would number the militias among the sects and cults within the nation, the militias actually get their information on how to make bombs from various networks available on the Internet.[35] The views of Timothy McVeigh, one of the men accused of exploding the bomb in Oklahoma City, were first publicized in the Lockport, NY *Union-Sun and Journal*, a local newspaper in upstate New York, over two years before the disastrous explosion. In what the editor of that newspaper characterized as 'a very eerie and prophetic statement' in view of McVeigh's later role in the bombing in Oklahoma, McVeigh had asked as early as 1992, 'Do we have to shed blood to reform the current system? I hope it doesn't come to that, but it might.'[36]

The Internet, the local bowling lanes, one's next door neighbours, one's buddies in the Army, members of something as benign in name as the 'Michigan Property Owners' Association' and the ordinary writer of letters to the editor of the local newspaper: these are the familiar scenes and faces where one can now expect to meet a covert terrorist. It is therefore missing the point to speak of a 'fringe world of paramilitary groups' or to decry 'a coven of psychopaths'.[37]

Attempts to isolate the danger posed by terrorism may be motivated, at least in part, by a legitimate desire to counter a political tendency to over-react to the violence by curtailing civil liberties for the sake of surveillance. Such attempts to bracket and relativize the danger posed by such groups, however, miss the danger that they present to the fabric of trust without which civil liberties are endangered regardless of the law and the Constitution. More than civil liberties are at stake, when dread of the familiar becomes pervasive. When the ordinary becomes 'eerie', it is no longer possible to contain the sense of an evil presence by calling it 'psychopathic' or by placing it on an hypothetical 'fringe'. Madness becomes hard to distinguish from the commonplace, and the fringe becomes mainstream.

If fascist states of mind are no longer found solely on the periphery of the larger society, or contained within the rituals of religious communities and institutions, it is because the political centre itself has had a pervasive influence on communities and groups that are sacred at least to their members. If a political centre is powerful but distant, I would argue, its occasional presence in a given locale has an increased potential to be disruptive to everyday life and transforming of individual identity. That latter transformation may indeed be benign, as when individuals feel dignified by their contact with a visiting president or by some high official passing through their district. That same contact, however, may be experienced as malign if it is accompanied in any way by a threat to the individual's way of life, social supports, or particular interests. When the political centre is experienced as disruptive and invasive, individuals may mount symbolic or political resistance to that intrusion. The radical right, as we have seen, experiences the political centre as a threat to the local community's control over children and property. Governmental prohibitions of prayer in the public schools threaten the community's control over the next generation; so does a 'secular humanist' curriculum. The Internal Revenue Service and various environmental regulations – for example, those affecting the use of forest or wetlands – are additional sources of conflict between centre and periphery. With intrusions like these, it is understandable that many individuals feel embattled: deeply threatened not only in their way of life but in their inner selves.

It is just such a sense of mortal combat that appears in the defensive communiqués from the National Rifle Association. A board member of the NRA, one Harry Thomas, is reported to have placed this message to the United States Attorney General on its own electronic bulletin board:

> And Miss Reno, I say to you: If you send your jackbooted, baby-burning bushwackers to confiscate my guns, pack them a lunch – it will be a damned long day ... The Branch Davidians were amateurs. I am a professional.[38]

Slightly more lyrical are the sentiments of a song called 'Head Like a Hole', performed by the Nine Inch Nails. Reportedly a favourite of the man who delivered and detonated the bomb in Oklahoma City, Mr McVeigh, the song includes the following ultimatum: 'I'd rather die than give you control. Bow down before the one you serve. You're going to get what you deserve. You know who you are.'[39]

This murderous reaction to the power of the political centre is not confined to individuals whom it is easy to dismiss as psychopathic. On the contrary, among the antipathies that are chronic on American campuses there may also be a similar aversion to the political centre on both the left and the right. When couched in the rhetoric of the right, such hostility may sound like the following invective from a history professor on the faculty of the University of Alabama. That professor, a Mr Michael Hill, is reported to have told a 'right-wing' gathering that

> In remembering Randy Weaver in Idaho and the Branch Davidians in Waco, we must understand one thing above all else. Our enemies are willing to kill us. It is open season on

> anyone who has the audacity to question the dictates of an all-powerful federal government or the illicit rights bestowed on a compliant and deadly underclass that now fulfills a role similar to that of Hitler's brown-shirted street thugs in the 1930s.[40]

When militias or the National Rifle Association speak of the federal government as being full of Nazis, it is easy to detect a shared delusion: a social form of madness that is patently paranoiac. Belief in such conspiracies, however, is not confined to the militias; ordinary citizens have the same sense of being embattled and in danger from their own government. Others have reported hearing of similar conspiracies from individuals who are not associated in any way with militias or associations such as the NRA. The radical right in its rhetoric rounds up not only the usual suspect minorities (liberals, feminists, gays, blacks, Jews and immigrants) but the government itself.

There is a widespread and deeply held dread of the government and all its works. It is one thing for the militias, for instance, to fear the incursions of the FBI, the IRS or the Federal Bureau of Alcohol, Tobacco, and Fire Arms. Dread, I believe, is the proper word for the apprehension of many that they are already hostages to a secret government and its agencies. For instance, *The New York Times* reports that some members of right-wing militias

> contend that the United Nations plans to conquer the United States, using a secret strike force made up of the National Guard and foreign troops and hiring Los Angeles street gangs to confiscate the guns of private citizens. Some think that United States currency is imprinted with secret bar codes so that Government officials in vans equipped with microwave scanners can drive by their homes and count their money. Others fear that the United States is run by a secret organization.[41]

So far from being the fantasies of a few paranoid militia-men, these are thoughts which one might hear in a wide range of relatively normal contexts. One is called World Wide Christian

Radio, which airs the views of paramilitary leaders like Mark Koernke, and another, operating from Costa Rica under liberal management, is called Radio for Peace International.[42] Transcripts of Koernke's broadcasts, furthermore, can be found on the Internet.

Belief that a 'new world order' is about to invade the privacy of ordinary citizens, subvert their government and take their guns is not the preserve, however, of short-wave radio and local militias. Perhaps the most well-known purveyor of such universal dread is Pat Robertson, President of the Christian Coalition. Through his Christian Broadcasting Network, indeed, one can trace the claims of Koernke and others regarding the danger of imminent subversion by foreign and domestic agencies to a publication by Robertson in 1991 appropriately entitled *The New World Order*.[43]

I mention that the militias and the radical Christian right are not the only ones to have a palpable dread of invisible forces polluting the social order or to long for the restoration of a social system of the imagined past. Haunted though they are, it is clear from what we have already said that there is indeed something haunting about social life. Individuals leave indelible impressions of themselves in the minds of others, and others occupy psychic space within our own hearts and minds: so much so that it is not always clear whose projects or feelings, theirs or our own, we are entertaining at any given moment.

The more individuals are exposed to others, whether in everyday, face-to-face settings or through the mass media, on the street or over the Internet, in person or through intermediaries such as teachers or government agents, the more they will live in a world that is at least beset by invisible presences. The more complex is social life, the more pervasive is the sense that it is haunted by others. The popularity of angels or other avatars of New Age religiosity is to be understood on these grounds. Speaking more clinically, as a psychoanalyst, Bollas points out that he is

> inhabited ... by inner structures that can be felt whenever their name is evoked; and in turn, I am also filled with the ghosts of others who have affected me ...

> This suggests, among other things, that as we encounter the object world we are substantially metamorphosed by the structure of objects; internally transformed by objects that leave their traces within us, whether it be the effect of a musical structure, a novel, or a person. In play the subject releases the idiom of himself to the field of objects, where he is then transformed by the structure of that experience, and will bear the history of that encounter in the unconscious.[44]

Let me hasten to add at this point that we are not merely the product of these spiritual encounters: not merely the place where the ghosts of others roam in our unconscious. The house of the mind may indeed be haunted. Nonetheless it is a mind that is experiencing itself in this way, and it is necessary to account for the fact that there is someone there who can experience herself or himself as being the host to a variety of spiritual presences. That mind is not merely an 'idiom', to use Bollas's metaphor: the idiom being 'the peculiar manner each individual possesses of shaping the contents of life'.[45] There is a self whose mind is responsible for selecting and imagining certain people and experiences as characters and events in one's internal novel, so to speak. There is someone at home in this haunted house who is capable of experiencing these other presences within one's character. Indeed, Bollas would no doubt agree that the capacity to experience the self as being the novelist whose selfhood encompasses these various, internal characters is at the core of self-awareness.

Bollas speaks of 'intense ghosts who do not populate the machine, but inhabit the human mind'.[46] What, then, is this mind, if it is not the one who surveys the contents, so to speak, of one's psyche? Now, it is very difficult for a mind to survey itself, but the experience of being the surveyor of one's own mental house is essential to the awareness of one's own being. Bollas goes on to say that 'the inner senses we have when we think of our inner objects seem more a part of us than anything else'.[47]

I am suggesting that one way, perhaps in the last analysis the only way, to avoid a fascist state of mind is to become capable of being the host, as it were, to these internal presences without anxiety or panic. To be aware of others within our own psychic space, and to be aware that we in turn are real presences in the mental life of others, can induce serious anxiety if the core of the self is not relatively solid.

If the life of the psyche is social, so also is social life fundamentally psychological. That is, social life places each of us in the position of being a character in each other's novel. How we imagine others, furthermore, and how they imagine us has continuing effects on the contents of our internal, mental space. Not only what blacks and whites, men and women, people and politicians, strangers and neighbours say about each other, but also their sheer presence as objects of our own imaginations, create in each person's mind a house full of spirits. We are haunted not only by what we do to others in our minds but by what they do to us, since we do become aware of our roles as characters in their novels. To paraphrase Allen Baldwin: If others are not who we think they are, then we are not who we think we are. If blacks and whites, or men and women, demonize each other, then each of us knows that there is a presence within us that has been defined by someone's fantasies about who we are. Psychoanalysts are trained, of course, to become consciously aware of how one becomes a host to others' spirits, but everyone else is also more or less aware of being used in this fashion. Bollas says it very well:

> Being a character, then, means bringing along with one's articulating idiom those inner presences – or spirits – that we all contain, now and then transferring them to a receptive place in the other, who may knowing or unknowingly be inhabited by them ... As we collide with other subjectivities, we exchange different syntheses, and leave the other with his or her inner senses of our self, just as we carry the spirit of the other's idiom within our unconscious.[48]

To be haunted by the presence of others, not only in our lives but in our psyches, intensifies social dread. The states of mind that Freud saw among his patients he could also find in everyday life among quite ordinary people. Certainly many of his patients were beset by the images that they harboured of others: internalized fathers and mothers or siblings whose presence in the psyche was deeply troubling. Some of these internal presences were felt to be malignant; certainly they were the object of very mixed feelings on the part of the patients who were host to these images.

In a modern society, where not only everyday life but the mass media vastly expand the range of imaginative association, individuals may become preoccupied with the internal presences of many different individuals or scenes. Not only family members and close associates but the specialized co-workers, the homeless on the street, distant consumers, and the victims of terror and famine in other countries, take up psychic space in the mind.

Under these conditions, I would argue, dread becomes more pervasive and less intense: conducive less to hysteria than to depression and anxiety. Hysteria is an intense relation of a person to an object in which the self is literally entranced; for the moment the internalized presence of the other within the psyche displaces the individual's own sense of self. The host becomes lost in the internal presences of others. In modern societies individuals are confronted with a barrage of images of others, both in person, on the street, at work, and through the mass media. The home is increasingly invaded, and as a psychological space it, too, becomes host to a variety of presences through telemarketing and television over which it is becoming increasingly difficult to exert control. Many of the images of the 'other' are less appealing and more threatening; so also are the defences of anger and disgust that accompany this over-exposure to these internalized presences. Under these conditions of psychological overload it becomes increasingly necessary and difficult for the individual to have the experience of a self in the process of hosting these images of others. Self-regard, which comes from being aware that one is in fact providing space for the psychological presence of others, becomes ever more vital for the experience of one's own being: more vital, and also more difficult to achieve.

Social life, even a carefully chosen and controlled group of friends, is too complex to be fully understood and experienced. Individuals therefore seek to reduce that complexity by retreating into a few close relationships, and it is why they often imagine their present, complex though it is, in terms of the relatively primitive relationships of the family. Just as in dreams one tries to come to terms with the mixture of people and objects, of feelings and memories, that constitute our everyday life, so we come to terms with everyday life in ways that are very much like our dreams.

As Bollas goes on to observe, moreover, it is not only the individual's imagination of social life that reflects the strange associations, over-simplification, fantasies and distortions of the dream. There is 'a madness always latent in groups'.[49] In this connection Bollas goes on to remark that

> psychoanalytic studies of the group process have taught us what we already knew as children: not only that groups are not fair but that they often operate according to psychotic principles. It can be a form of madness to live in a group. Or the group as a reliable presence is a delusion.[50]

These are strong words. To live in a group that is psychotic enough to split off its negative feelings from its positive ones, and to attribute to outsiders its own greed and hostility, is indeed to share a psychotic state of mind. That mental state can produce dread of those outsiders who represent what the group does not want to know about itself.

The Fascist State of Mind

There is something very ordinary about the fascistic state of mind that Bollas and others have observed. Indeed, most individuals have the same psychological processes within them as do the neurotic or psychotic. There is an element of narcissism in everyone which makes them reluctant to depend on others, and yet most also have a sense of obligation or mutality that deprives them of some of the satisfactions that they might otherwise wish to enjoy. Some garden-variety masochism is therefore simply the price that one pays, as Freud put it, for 'civilization'. Children are trained in some societies, from an early age, to 'postpone gratification', that is, to conform their internal demands to the timing and schedules of the school or the family. Most individuals develop a minimal amount of the asceticism necessary for social life. They are less governed by their own impulses than by the disciplines imposed by the ordered spheres of social life: by the family itself, the school, the community, the workplace, and by fiscal or academic calendars, and so on. In a society where the ascetic social character is highly valued, individuals will experience strong social pressures to subordinate the timetable of their own needs to the regularities imposed by the larger society. If one attempts to follow a timetable that reflects one's own internal sense of timeliness, one may be criticized, censured and disciplined.

How is the individual to cope with this psychological and social complexity? On the one hand, the life of groups and communities is delusional. I would say that with the collapse of the boundaries between communities and organizations, with the permeability of national boundaries to outside influences, with the collapse of the isolation of traditional communities, and with the expansion of federal and other national bureaucracies into local areas, the complexity of social life is drastically increased. That complexity, moreover, is partly spiritual, as communities enter into imaginary relationships with other communities far removed in space and perhaps also in time from each other. Furthermore, with the exposure of the individual to more complex social networks, and the openness of the individual to a variety of media that communicate information and images from a wide range of potent and graphic sources, the mind is increasingly host to the presence and suggestions of individuals who are and will remain strange to one another and therefore alien, however much they take up residence, as it were, in the individual psyche. What is experienced as simply too much, as a social or psychological overload, is emotionally akin to abuse: a kinship which may explain some of the paranoid fantasies of groups such as the militias.

One way to respond to this increased social and psychological complexity, of course, is through drastic over-simplification. Such a reduction of complexity may take any of the forms discussed in this book: the imposition of a rigid uniformity on the young; strenuous efforts to separate the living from the dead; mobilization to resist enemies perceived to be at the gate, like the Russian tanks imagined by militias to be marshalled along the border of the United States with Mexico. The over-simplification may take still other forms: an attempt to purify the community or the nation of the influence of unwanted groups, such as secular humanists, or of the presence of various sorts of alien people, products and ideas. Certainly one of the agendas of the radical right has been to restrict the flow of outside influences, whether through the media or through local institutions, into the local community, the school and the home.

On the level of the individual such over-simplification may take a variety of forms, one of which is what Bollas has called a fascistic state of mind which is intolerant of internal sources of weakness and of passions or anxiety that require satisfaction. This self is delusional and destructive, as Bollas has pointed out, because it believes that it can create and sustain the self by eliminating – literally killing – the unwanted aspects of the psyche. Like the comic book heroes who come to the relief of the city beleaguered by some demonic enemy, the fascistic self comes in the nick of time but with terrible destructiveness to the more vulnerable and therefore unwanted aspects of the self. Impervious to its own pain and vulnerability, the fascistic self rises again and again from what would seem to have been its own ashes.

With such extraordinary internal sources of help, however, the psyche does not need enemies. The rest of humanity becomes emblematic of the vulnerability or greed that has been extruded from self-consciousness. As Bollas points out, the self moves toward a fascistic form of organization which is intolerant of its own humanity:

> In object relations terms, humanity is presumably represented or representable by the presence of different capacities of the self (such as empathy, forgiveness, and reparation) which had been squeezed out of the self.
>
> Kleinian psychoanalysts frequently refer in their literature to the 'killing off' of those parts of the self, thereby emphasizing the fact of murder as an ordinary feature of psychic life. Rosenfeld, for example, describes an aggressive aspect of the narcissistic self state achieved by 'killing their loving dependent self and identifying themselves almost entirely with the

> destructive narcissistic parts of the self which provides them with a sense of superiority and self admiration'.[51]

No wonder that David Bollas describes such an idealized image of the self as a fascist state of mind.[52] This totalitarian organization of the psyche tolerates no contradictions within the self, tolerates no internal messiness, condemns the affectionate and dependent aspects of the self to destruction, and displaces all these unwanted aspects of the self on to others. It is they, these 'others', who are therefore the source of pollution and constitute a continuing danger to the self that must constantly guard its own purity. Bollas sums up:

> The moral void created by the simplifying violence of an ideology that brooks no opposition is also an essential consequence of this stage in the evolution of the Fascist state of mind ... On the verge of its own moral vacuum, the mind splits off this dead core self and projects it into a victim henceforth identified with the moral void ... Mental contents are now regarded as contaminates, and the Fascist mind idealizes the process of purging itself of what it has contained. The cleansing of the self suggests the possible birth of a new, forever empty self to be born with no contact with others, with no past (which is severed), and with a future entirely of its own creation.[53]

This new-born self is no stranger to most Americans. Among citizens of the United States, for instance, there are millions who claim to have been born again. While it is not possible to generalize from such a figure to the characters of the individuals themselves, Bollas and Strozier clearly imply that the more fundamentalistic of these twice-born individuals do indeed fit the outline given above of a self that seeks to be purified of all contradictions and impurities. The ideology of the twice born also emphasizes the need to cleanse the community of those who do not belong in such a purified moral order: the weak and the dependent, for instance, and those whose affections are not under strict control. As I have noted, many fundamentalists tolerate no opposition from the many and various sources of social pollution which they discern in American society. In psychoanalytic terms, their form of the sacred is an idol that can destroy the self: a set of binding symbols and beliefs that displace whatever parts of the self do not fit within its tight constraints.

Certainly Christian discipleship has repeatedly been described in Kierkegaardian terms as a certain purity of the mind or will which transcends uncertainty, mixed motives or internal contradiction. Anyone familiar with the Christian scriptures will immediately recognize the religious aspects of this state of mind: one which Bollas himself ascribes to 'delusional narcissism'.[54] Christianity has no monopoly or patent on such delusions, however. As Bollas goes on to point out, science and even psychoanalysis itself can be used as a basis for delusions about the ability to purge the self of contradiction.[55] The individual thus cleansed from anything that might contaminate the psyche is in a position to generate the self, as it were, from nothing: a form of creativity which, at least in the Old Testament, is ascribed to God alone.

If individuals are to resist the appeal of fascist social movements in the future, they will have to be able to resist these grandiose and narcissist temptations to create a self that is immune to longing, dependency, suffering and death. It is not only a society, seeking to stand the test of time, that becomes host to fascist tendencies. These tendencies, after all, resonate with and seek to mimic the individual's own longing to transcend the passage of time and to stare unharmed and unpanicked into the face of death. The face of death, moreover, can be encountered in the course of everyday life; we have just discussed, for instance, the rivalry between generations for transcendence over the passage of time. It is a rivalry that is rooted, as Bollas has observed, in the Oedipus complex, as one generation looks ahead to the fulfilment of its projects and finds that it is in mortal danger. A sense of guilt then adds insult to the injury of the prospect of death. One lives in the world of Kafka's 'Trial': faced with a prosecution and certain conviction for offences that we have not committed, the sentence for which is death. It is a trial that is then re-enacted as the older generation finds its own projects discarded and sentenced to death by the younger.

There is something grandiose and deluded about the human mind when it seeks immunity from the prosecution of everyday life. That 'prosecution', as Bollas has reminded us, can make the individual seek a sanctuary from which he or she can cling to the certainties and simplicities of the initial family and of the individual's earliest character. The inevitable, however slow, disintegration of that character under the impact of complexity fills the individual with sufficient dread of the community that he or she takes refuge in various asylums, such as churches or other groups, or such as other imaginary worlds of the individual's own construction. From these sanctuaries the individual can 'play' with social reality and with the slow decomposition of the child's initial certainties. In this regression the individual finds partial protection from the fact that he or she has started out, like Oedipus, on a road that inevitably leads to destruction.[56]

Such delusions, however, are not only personal; they may be widely shared by communities and institutions who project their own turmoil and doubt on to outsiders. Bollas describes the 'false self' that characterizes such an institution, and the individual's own false self that requires such a context in order to preserve his or her delusions:

> Imagine an institution of a hundred people. Like so many places, it may be strife-ridden; there are unpleasant rivalries, vicious gossips, and powerful people jockeying for positions of authority. Imagine that its shared fantasy is that it is an admirable place, a cut above comparable institutions. Perhaps I should term this a shared false self that conceals the true states of mind, as the place, let's say, believes it could not survive the truth about itself. But in such a place, though everyone knows how awful some of the dynamics are, each also believes that part of the price of continued admission is to collude with a collective false self. Although privately, to one's closest colleagues and spouses, one could say how it really feels to be part of the place, in the public domain one reckons it is best to say that it is 'inspiring' or 'stimulating' to be there. We could say that a violent innocence is present in that each appears innocent of the more disturbing truths that are a part of the place. And those who are exceptionally gifted at false-self technique will contribute to the structure of innocence that climatizes the institution.[57]

For Bollas, this false self is intrinsic to the fascist state of mind, and it is fostered in institutions which have a false self of their own. These institutions claim to be sacred; that is, like the fascist state of mind, sacred institutions claim a certain immunity to misfortune and humiliation and entertain delusions of their own grandeur and internal purity. Like the fascist state of mind, sacred groups and communities divide the world into two halves: those who share one's fate, and those who do not.

Fascist tendencies are most likely to flourish wherever vestiges of a traditional community, bound together by ties of race and kinship, persist in a society largely dominated by large-scale organizations, by an industrial class system, and by a complex division of labour. Under these conditions the traditional community itself becomes threatened; its members all the more readily dread and demonize the larger society. Conversely, the larger society has its own remnants of communal attachment, often represented by the dominant religious community and its institutions. Under these conditions it is all the more inevitable for the traditional communities of racial and ethnic minorities to be the objects of considerable dread and of attempts to demonize them. When two incompatible types of social system interpenetrate each other, the suppressed aspects of the one will not only be projected upon the other and perceived there in exaggerated form; the 'other' will be perceived as a danger in the midst of the community itself.

We are now in a better position to understand why there was such chronic suspicion among the people of Springfield, Massachusetts. In the study of that community by Demerath and Williams, you will remember, the authors could find little if any support for the widespread public fear that the Catholic Church was exercising improper influence on politics through the Catholic mayor and city hall. I am suggesting that the fear of such influence was produced by the interpenetration of the two communities: the one based on the requirements of a secular society ruled by law; the other based on loyalties to traditional communities based on kinships, ethnicity, language, and religion.

There are various ways that two such systems can interpenetrate each other. In the case of Springfield, of course, no one is suggesting that the Catholic Church had become subject to Protestant influence, or that the Catholic community was losing members to the Protestants; conversely no one documented Catholic inroads on the Protestant community and its institutions. On the other hand, there were increasing opportunities for Protestants and Catholics to have exchanges with one another: in the school system, in work, in politics, as well as in less formal contexts such as the neighbourhood. They inhabited the same cultural spaces and increasingly joined forces on specific social issues for limited periods of time. A sense that the Catholic community was becoming increasingly influential in the social space formerly occupied exclusively by Protestants could well stimulate a dread of that community as Protestants and Catholics entered more closely into one another's imagination and experience.

A similar process, I would argue, is responsible for the dread which many Americans have felt at the presence not only of minorities in their communities but of agencies of the federal government. In the last few years there has indeed been an increase of bombings and threats directed at federal buildings, but there has also been an increase in attacks on synagogues or on churches and institutions of the African-American community.[58] It is as if the failure of the churches to 'Americanize' minorities has led to a last-ditch stand in various areas of the United States against the forces which seem most invasive of white ethnic communities. Those forces are sometimes the Jewish and African communities, and thus the targets have often been their churches and synagogues. It is the federal government and its policies, however, which have seemed to pose the most extraordinary threat to certain white communities. The following news report from *The New York Times* is therefore a sign of this trend and, perhaps, of further violence to come:

> Two members of the Minnesota Patriots Council were convicted in March of Federal conspiracy charges that they had planned to use a lethal biological poison called ricin to kill Federal employees and law enforcement agents. A Missouri state trooper was shot in his home by a sniper after a September 1994 raid at the compound of a paramilitary

> group called Citizens for Christ that turned up a large quantity of dynamite, electric blasting caps, machine guns and ammunition.[59]

It is important to understand that the reaction of these embattled communities is not merely to minorities, troubling as their presence may be to certain white ethnic Christian groups. As I have suggested, social dread is heightened when one social system interpenetrates another so that its sense of its own integrity is impugned. With the collapse of boundaries against the outside 'world', imagined to be alien and 'other', the sacralized community feels its own purity, even its life, to be endangered. Communal defences take on the proportions one would expect of a final day of accounting: a rural Armageddon fought with advanced biological and assault weapons. Claiming the support of vast numbers of soldiers in the Armed Forces, the radical right-wing groups boast of unlimited access to advanced weaponry. As one group, The National Association for the Advancement of White People put it,

> Americans had better get used to Trade Center-like bombing and Okie City . . . They're only the tip of the iceberg. People are fighting back against government.[60]

If the crime experienced by groups on the defence is that they live in dread of an outside world that is no longer external to their communities, the punishment is, fittingly enough, that that world should also live in dread. It has become the policy of right-wing groups to keep the larger society in a permanent state of dread. Keith Schneider reports that a training manual which was distributed by one Western militia urges its members to kill ordinary citizens who might give information on paramilitary groups to the government.[61] The same manual also exhorts the destruction of property and business owned by those who are 'not Americans', along with sabotage of sensitive targets in the nation's economy, e.g. transportation and communications networks. A report in *The New York Times* goes on to detail plans in the manual for disrupting law enforcement with false information:

> The aim of the disinformation campaign, the manual says, is to create an 'air of nervousness, discredit, insecurity, uncertainty and concern on the part of the government'.[62]

The failure of the churches to create a moral community in which minorities and white Protestant Americans could live with each other on equal terms is only partly responsible for the latest wave of political atrocities in the United States. I am suggesting, moreover, that the same religious divide between the 'Church' and the 'world' is indeed responsible for a cultural climate which is hospitable to varieties of fascist social movements, including those which use the term Christian. Among the latter are not only the extremist militias like the 'Citizens for Christ' but Robertson's Christian Coalition, whose rhetoric is widely used by paramilitary groups to legitimate their hostility to the government and to various minorities. One might call this process the contagion of social dread, to indicate that its roots are deeply planted in the cultural soil of the United States and not only on what is sometimes still, quite mistakenly, called 'the fringe'.

The point, as I have argued throughout this book, is simply that the traditional division between the sacred and the secular, expressed in various other distinctions such as that between 'the Church' and 'the world', provides a cultural matrix in which social dread can take root and flourish. Once seen as 'the world', those outside the sacred community, whatever that is, can be portrayed as needy and hungry, as greedy and insatiable, or even as polluting and destructive. Indeed, the mainline Protestant tradition has turned this distinction into a variety of symbolic and social boundaries at the expense of the relatively poor or the resident alien. It is therefore not surprising, to say the least, to see a similar distinction used by the radical right to distinguish 'Americans' and 'Christians' from a host of dangerous influences in their midst, from synagogues to federal agencies. The clearly fascist tendencies of these movements have flourished in part because they are growing in a cultural matrix which continues to be receptive and nourishing.

NOTES

INTRODUCTION

1. Paul Boyer, *When Time Shall Be No More: Prophecy Belief in Modern American Culture*, Cambridge, Mass. and London, The Belknap Press of Harvard University Press, 1992, pp. 181ff.
2. ibid., p. 224.
3. ibid.
4. Otto Rank, *The Double: A Psychoanalytic Study*, Chapel Hill, NC, University of North Carolina Press, 1971.
5. Zeev Sternhell, *Neither Left Nor Right: Fascist Ideology in France*, Berkeley, University of California Press, 1986.
6. ibid., p. 271.
7. ibid., p. 250.
8. ibid., p. 252.
9. Niklas Luhmann, *The Differentiation of Society*, New York, Columbia University Press, 1982, p. 56; emphasis in original.
10. Charles B. Strozier, *Apocalypse: On the Psychology of Fundamentalism in America*, Boston, Beacon Press, 1994.
11. Susan D. Rose, *Keeping Them Out of the Hands of Satan: Evangelical Schooling in America*, New York and London, Routledge, 1990.
12. Strozier, *Apocalypse*, p. 137.
13. ibid., p. 142.
14. ibid., pp. 136–7.
15. Donald Capps, 'Erikson's Theory of Religious Ritual: The Case of the Excommunication of Ann Hibbens', *Journal for the Scientific Study of Religion* 18, pp. 337–49.
16. Edward Shils, *Center and Periphery: Essays in Macrosociology*, Chicago, IL., University of Chicago Press, 1975.
17. For a discussion of the propriety of using such a term in sociological discourse, see Richard K. Fenn and Donald Capps, eds., *On Losing the Soul: Essays in the Social Psychology of Religion*, Albany, NY, State University of New York Press, 1995.
18. Christopher Lasch, *The Culture of Narcissism*, New York, Norton, 1978.
19. Daniel L. O'Keefe, *Stolen Lightning: The Social Theory of Magic*, New York, Vintage Books, 1983, p. 299.

20. John Demos, *Entertaining Satan: Witchcraft and the Culture of Early New England*, New York, Oxford University Press, 1982, pp. 99ff.
21. ibid., p. 129.
22. ibid., pp. 99ff.
23. Ervin Staub, *The Roots of Evil: The Origins of Genocide and Other Group Violence*, Cambridge, Cambridge University Press, 1992.
24. Walter Burkert, *Homo Necans: The Anthropology of Ancient Greek Sacrificial Ritual and Myth*, trans. Peter Bing, Berkeley, University of California Press, 1983.
25. O'Keefe, *Stolen Lightning*, p. 15.
26. ibid., p. l.
27. ibid., p. 14.
28. ibid., p. 10.
29. Richard K. Fenn, *The Death of Herod*, Cambridge, Cambridge University Press, 1992.
30. Josephus, *The Jewish War*, Book II, ch. 7, l. 223ff.
31. ibid., Book I, ch. 7.
32. Josephus, *Antiquities of the Jews*, XX, 164–7; Loeb Classical Library, vol. IX, 1965, p. 479.
33. Peter Gay, *Freud for Historians*, New York and Oxford, Oxford University Press, 1986, p. 123.

CHAPTER 1

1. Ervin Staub, *The Roots of Evil: The Origins of Genocide and Other Group Violence*, Cambridge, Cambridge University Press, 1992, p. 117.
2. Norman Cohn, *The Pursuit of the Millenium*, revised and expanded edition, New York, Oxford University Press, 1970, pp. 61–2 (emphasis added).
3. ibid., pp. 56ff.
4. Staub, *Roots of Evil*, pp. 121–2 (emphasis added).
5. From 'Durch Domestikation verursachte Storungen arteigenen Verhaltens', *Zeitschrift fur angewandte Psychologie und Charakterkunde* (*Journal of Applied Psychology and the Science of Character*), 59, 66.71; quoted in Staub, *Roots of Evil*, p. 123.
6. Leo Wine, in a radio programme; quoted in Staub, *Roots of Evil*, p. 62.
7. Staub, *Roots of Evil*, p. 115.
8. ibid., p. 85.
9. Maurice Bloch, *From Prey into Hunter: The Politics of Religious Experience*, Cambridge, Cambridge University Press, 1992, p. 27 (emphasis added).
10. ibid., pp. 8ff.
11. ibid., p. 245.

12. Ernesto De Martino, *Primitive Magic: The Psychic Powers of Shamans and Sorcerers*, Dorset, Prism Press, 1988.
13. Bloch, *Prey into Hunter*, p. 14.
14. Jean-Pierre Vernant, *Mortals and Immortals: Collected Essays*, ed. Froma I. Zeitlin, Princeton, NJ, Princeton University Press, 1991, p. 231.
15. ibid., p. 232.
16. ibid., p. 231.
17. Readers familiar with the work of Otto Rank will recognize in this passage a strong resemblance to his theory of the Double. The mask is a Double: a representation of the self is purported to stand the test of time. That Double is also a primitive image of the soul and a safeguard against the utter loss of one's own sense of being in control as a real presence in the world. The double, however, disguised first as an ideal of the self and then as a rival, finally emerges as a rather terrifying image of the self as mortal. Abel, for instance, is in Rank's view the image of that very mortality, and as an abhorrent reminder of the self that is headed for death, Abel is dispatched by Cain.
18. Vernant, *Mortals and Immortals*, p. 138.
19. Sternhell, *Neither Left Nor Right: Fascist Ideology in France*, Berkeley, University of California Press, 1986, p. 261.
20. David I. Kertzer, *Ritual, Politics, and Power*, New Haven and London, Yale University Press, 1988, p. 129.
21. Vernant, *Mortals and Immortals*, p. 252.
22. ibid., p. 256.
23. ibid., p. 251.
24. ibid., p. 256.
25. Nikolas Rose, *Governing the Soul: The Shaping of the Private Self*, London and New York, Routledge, 1989.
26. Victor Turner, *Process, Performance, and Pilgrimage: A Study in Comparative Symbology*, New Delhi, Concept, 1979.
27. Cohn, *Pursuit of the Millenium*, pp. 71ff.
28. ibid., p. 71.
29. ibid., pp. 72–3.
30. ibid., p. 75.
31. ibid., p. 77.
32. ibid., p. 67.
33. ibid., p. 125.
34. ibid., p. 112.

CHAPTER 2

1. James S. Preus, *Explaining Religion: Criticism and Theory from Bodin to Freud*, New Haven, Yale University Press, 1987, p. 122.
2. Charles B. Strozier, *Apocalypse: On the Psychology of Fundamentalism in America*, Boston, Beacon Press, 1994.
3. ibid., p. 116.
4. Preus, *Explaining Religion*, p. 125.
5. Paul Boyer, *When Time Shall Be No More: Prophecy Belief in Modern American Culture*, Cambridge, MA and London, The Belknap Press of Harvard University Press, 1992, p. 128.
6. cf. Preus, *Explaining Religion*, pp. 123ff.
7. ibid., p. 176.
8. ibid.
9. Arthur Vidich and Stanford Lyman, *American Sociology: Worldly Rejections of Religion and Their Directions*, New Haven, Yale University Press, 1985.
10. ibid., pp. 255–6.
11. ibid., p. 269.
12. ibid., p. 191.
13. John Wilson, in a telling criticism of Robert Bellah's thesis on the civil religion, made this point some time ago; see John F. Wilson, *Public Religion in American Culture*, Philadelphia, PA, Temple University Press, 1979.
14. Vidich and Lyman, *American Sociology*, p. 191.
15. ibid., p. 272.
16. Nikolas Rose, *Governing the Soul: The Shaping of the Private Self*, London and New York, Routledge, 1989.
17. ibid., p. 130.
18. ibid., p. 136.
19. ibid., p. 155.
20. ibid., pp. 130–1 (emphasis added).
21. ibid., p. 141.
22. ibid., pp. 154–5.
23. ibid., p. 156.
24. Zeev Sternhell, *Neither Left Nor Right: Fascist Ideology in France*, Berkeley, University of California Press, 1986, p. 236.
25. ibid., p. 233.
26. Theodor Reik, *Masochism in Modern Man*, tr. Margaret H. Bieigel and Gertrud M. Kurth, New York, Grove Press, 1957.
27. Maulnier, 'Introduction' to Moeller's *Le Troisième Reich*, p. 13; quoted in Sternhell, *Neither Left Nor Right*, p. 234.
28. Norman Cohn, *The Pursuit of the Millenium*, revised and expanded edition, New York, Oxford University Press, 1970, p. 148.

29. ibid., p. 149.
30. As I have noted, it does not add conceptual clarity to call rituals contrived by a rebellious populace by some other name, e.g. rites of degradation, rebellion, protest or revolution. The sponsor of the ritual does not change the transformative function of the ritual itself but only its auspices.
31. What are often called rites of transition belong to this category of rituals.
32. Olivia Harris, 'The Dead and the Devils among the Bolivian Laymi', in Maurice Bloch and Jonathan Parry, eds., *Death and the Regeneration of Life*, Cambridge, Cambridge University Press, 1982, pp. 46–73.
33. ibid., p. 56.
34. ibid., pp. 49ff.
35. ibid., pp. 47–8.
36. ibid., p. 48.
37. ibid., p. 52.
38. ibid., p. 56.
39. ibid., p. 55.
40. Charles B. Strozier, *Apocalypse*, Boston, Beacon Press, 1994, p. 109.
41. Harris, 'The Dead and the Devils', p. 51.
42. Jonathan Parry, 'Sacrificial Death and the Necrophagous Ascetic', in Maurice Bloch and Jonathan Parry, eds., *Death and the Regeneration of Life*, Cambridge, Cambridge University Press, 1982.
43. ibid., p. 74.
44. ibid., p. 75.
45. There are other contradictions that suggest that some funeral rites have not been wholly effective in creating the transformation of the deceased into a member of the ancestral community. On the one hand, the corpse is regarded as a source of impurity from the moment of physiological death and must be approached only by those sufficiently purified. On the other hand, the corpse is the vehicle for a spiritual offering to the gods and is thus regarded as worthy to be sacrificed. This contradiction, I would suggest, is merely a by-product of the compromise with reality that I have already mentioned.
46. Parry, 'Sacrificial Death', p. 80.
47. ibid., p. 79.
48. ibid., p. 77.
49. ibid., pp. 81ff.
50. Joseph G. Jorgensen, 'Religious Solutions and Native American Struggles: Ghost Dance, Sun Dance, and Beyond', in Bruce Lincoln, ed., *Religion, Rebellion, and Revolution*, 1985, p. 104.
51. Parry, 'Sacrificial Death', p. 77.
52. ibid., p. 92.

53. ibid., p. 93.
54. Strozier, *Apocalypse*, p. 113.
55. ibid., p. 113.
56. Harris, 'The Dead and the Devils', pp. 48–9.
57. ibid., p. 49.
58. David I. Kertzer *Ritual, Politics, and Power*, New Haven and London, Yale University Press, 1988, p. 111.
59. ibid., pp. 109–10.
60. Cohn, *Pursuit of the Millenium*, pp. 85ff.
61. Edwin S. Gaustad, *The Great Awakening in New England*, New York, Harper & Brothers, 1957, pp. 103ff.
62. ibid.
63. ibid.
64. Sacvan Bercovitch, *The American Jeremiad*, Madison, WI, University of Wisconsin Press, 1978.
65. ibid.
66. ibid., p. 81.
67. ibid., p. 149.
68. Strozier, *Apocalypse*, p. 78.
69. ibid., pp. 86ff.
70. ibid., p. 85.
71. ibid., p. 87.
72. ibid., p. 91.
73. Residues of the Puritan suspicion of the individual appear in Lyman Giddings, who continued the sociological jeremiad against selfishness in the American spirit and wished to transform individuality into civic virtue. Note his use of circuitous prose to hedge individual freedom with social constraints; consider this passage, for instance:

    > Only through the rationalistic habit of mind can men come to understand how important it is, on the one hand, to assert the rightful supremacy of moral authority, and, on the other hand, to deny the rightfulness of any external authority other than a common or social consciousness of the reality and rightfulness of the moral authority in each individual. (From *Democracy and Empire: With Studies on Their Psychological, Economic, and Moral Foundations*, Freeport, NY, Books for Libraries Press; quoted in Vidich and Lyman, *American Sociology*, p. 107; emphasis added.)

74. Vidich and Lyman, *American Sociology*, p. 108.
75. Strozier, *Apocalypse*, p. 182.
76. ibid., p. 187.
77. ibid., pp. 188–9.
78. Susan Rose, *Keeping Them Out of the Hands of Satan: Evangelical Schooling in America*, New York and London, Routledge, 1990, p. 17.

79. ibid., p. 186.
80. Sternhell, *Neither Left Nor Right*, p. 250.
81. Nikolas Rose, *Governing the Soul.*
82. Strozier, *Apocalypse*, p. 166.

CHAPTER 3

1. Paul Boyer, *When Time Shall Be No More: Prophecy Belief in Modern American Culture*, Cambridge, MA and London, The Belknap Press of Harvard University Press, 1992, p. 144.
2. ibid., p. 141.
3. ibid., p. 26.
4. ibid., pp. 140ff.
5. ibid., p. 143.
6. Norman Cohn, *The Pursuit of the Millennium*, revised and expanded edition, New York, Oxford University Press, 1970.
7. ibid., p. 134.
8. Jean-Pierre Vernant, *Mortals and Immortals: Collected Essays*, ed. Froma I. Zeitlin, Princeton, NJ, Princeton University Press, 1991, pp. 250ff.
9. ibid., pp. 253–4.
10. ibid., p. 254.
11. ibid., pp. 253–4.
12. ibid., p. 255.
13. Ervin Staub, *The Roots of Evil: The Origins of Genocide and Other Group Violence*, Cambridge, Cambridge University Press, 1992, pp. 104ff.
14. ibid., p. 109.
15. ibid., p. 164.
16. ibid., p. 144.
17. Charles B. Strozier, *Apocalypse: On the Psychology of Fundamentalism in America*, Boston, Beacon Press, 1994, p. 131.
18. ibid., p. 131.
19. ibid., pp. 130ff.
20. Christiano Grotanelli, 'Archaic Forms of Rebellion and Their Religious Background', in Bruce Lincoln, ed., *Religion, Rebellion, and Revolution*, 1985, pp. 25–6.
21. David I. Kertzer, *Ritual, Politics, and Power*, New Haven and London, Yale University Press, 1988, p. 155.
22. ibid., pp. 154–5.
23. ibid., pp. 156–7.
24. Maurice Bloch and Jonathan Parry, eds., *Death and the Regeneration of Life*, Cambridge, Cambridge University Press, 1982.
25. Clarke Garrett, 'Popular Religion in the American and French

Revolutions', in Bruce Lincoln, ed., *Religion, Rebellion, and Revolution*, 1985, pp. 69–88.

26. In this argument I remain indebted to the insights of Maurice Bloch, 'Death, Women and Power', in Maurice Bloch and Jonathan Parry, eds., *Death and the Regeneration of Life*, Cambridge, Cambridge University Press, 1982.
27. Eugen Weber, 'Amerloques', a review of Richard Kuisel, *Seducing the French: The Dilemma of Americanization*, University of California Press, 1993; in *The London Review of Books*, 10 March 1994, p. 22.
28. ibid., p. 22.
29. Edwin S. Gaustad, *Dissent in American Religion*, Chicago, University of Chicago Press, 1973, p. 3.
30. Kertzer, *Ritual, Politics, and Power*, pp. 161ff.
31. ibid., p. 163.
32. Garrett, 'Popular Religion', pp. 74–5.
33. ibid., pp. 80ff.
34. ibid., pp. 74.
35. ibid.
36. ibid.
37. Vittorio Lanternari, 'Revolution and/or Integration in African Socio-Religious Movements', in Bruce Lincoln, ed., *Religion, Rebellion, and Revolution*, 1985, p. 136.
38. David Martin, *Tongues of Fire: The Explosion of Protestantism in Latin America*, with a foreword by Peter Berger; Oxford, and Cambridge, MA, Basil Blackwell, 1993.
39. Lanternari 'Revolution and/or Integration', pp. 129–56.
40. ibid., pp. 133–6.
41. ibid., p. 136.
42. ibid., pp. 136ff.
43. ibid., p. 137.
44. ibid., p. 139.
45. Walter Burkert, René Girard, and Jonathan Z. Smith, *Violent Origins*, ed., Robert G.Hamerton-Kelly, with an introduction by Burton Mack and commentary by Renato Rosaldo; Stanford, CA, Stanford University Press, 1987, p. 168.
46. Quoted in Staub, *Roots of Evil*, p. 112.
47. Burkert, Girard and Smith, *Violent Origins*, p. 171 (emphasis added).
48. ibid., p. 173.

CHAPTER 4

1. David I. Kertzer, *Ritual, Politics, and Power*, New Haven and London, Yale University Press, 1988, p. 132.

2. Norman Cohn, *The Pursuit of the Millenium*, revised and expanded edition, New York, Oxford University Press, 1970.
3. ibid., p. 83.
4. ibid., p. 85.
5. ibid., p. 87.
6. Eviatar Zerubavel, *Hidden Rhythms: Schedules and Calendars in Social Life*, Berkeley, Los Angeles, London, University of California Press, 1985, pp. 70ff.
7. Cohn, *Pursuit of the Millenium*, p. 87.
8. ibid.
9. Arthur Maxwell, quoted in Paul Boyer, *When Time Shall Be No More: Prophecy Belief in Modern American Culture*, Cambridge, MA and London, The Belknap Press of Harvard University Press, 1992, pp. 93, 109.
10. ibid., p. 110.
11. ibid., p. 139.
12. Ervin Staub, *The Roots of Evil: The Origins of Genocide and Other Group Violence*, Cambridge, Cambridge University Press, 1992, p. 84.
13. Nikolas Rose, *Governing the Soul: The Shaping of the Private Self*, London and New York, Routledge, 1989.
14. ibid., pp. 117–18 (emphasis added).
15. ibid., p. 108.
16. Charles B. Strozier, *Apocalypse: On the Psychology of Fundamentalism in America*, Boston, Beacon Press, 1994, p. 144.
17. ibid., p. 117.
18. ibid., p. 107.
19. ibid., p. 163.
20. Lionel Caplan, 'The Popular Culture of Evil in Urban South India', in David Parkin, ed., *The Anthropology of Evil*, 1986, pp. 123–4.
21. ibid., p. 123.
22. ibid.
23. Cohn, *Pursuit of the Millenium*, p. 90.
24. ibid., pp. 94ff.
25. ibid., p. 95.
26. Andrew Strathern, 'Witchcraft, Greed, Cannibalism, and Death: Some Related Themes from the New Guinea Highlands', in Maurice Bloch and Jonathan Parry, eds., *Death and the Regeneration of Life*, Cambridge, Cambridge University Press, 1982.
27. ibid., pp. 114–17.
28. ibid., p. 117.
29. Zeev Sternhell, *Neither Left Nor Right: Fascist Ideology in France*, Berkeley, University of California Press, 1986.
30. ibid., p. 221.
31. N. Rose, *Governing the Soul*.

32. Sternhell, *Neither Left Nor Right*, pp. 221–2.
33. Strathern, 'Witchcraft, Greed, Cannibalism, and Death', pp. 116–17.
34. ibid., p. 117.
35. cf. ibid., p. 113.
36. ibid., pp. 112–13.
37. Maurice Bloch, *From Prey into Hunter: The Politics of Religious Experience*, Cambridge, Cambridge University Press, 1992.
38. Caplan, 'Popular Culture of Evil', pp. 112, 114.
39. ibid., p. 15.
40. Strathern, 'Witchcraft, Greed, Cannibalism, and Death', p. 122.
41. Vittorio Lanternari, 'Revolution and/or Integration in African Socio-Religious Movements', in Bruce Lincoln, ed., *Religion, Rebellion and Revolution*, 1985, pp. 147–55.
42. Nikkie R. Keddie, 'Shi'ism and Revolution', in Bruce Lincoln, ed., *Religion, Rebellion, and Revolution*, 1985, p. 172.
43. ibid., pp. 172–3.
44. cf. Lanternari, 'Revolution and/or Integration', p. 154.
45. Frank Graziano, *Divine Violence: Spectacle, Psychosexuality, and Radical Christianity in the Argentine 'Dirty War'*, Boulder, San Francisco, and Oxford, Westview Press, 1992.
46. ibid., p. 64.
47. ibid., p. 68.
48. ibid.
49. Daniel L. O'Keefe, *Stolen Lightning: The Social Theory of Magic*, New York, Vintage Books, 1982, p. 321.
50. Graziano, *Divine Violence*, p. 77.
51. ibid., pp. 71–3.
52. ibid., pp. 73–4.
53. ibid., pp. 75–6.
54. ibid., p. 77.
55. ibid., p. 75 (emphasis added).
56. Cf. Adam Philips, 'The Shock of the Old', *London Review of Books*, 16.3, 10 February 1994, p. 14, reviewing Christopher Bollas, *Being a Character: Psychoanalysis and Self-Experience*, Routledge, 1993.
57. Lanternari, 'Revolution and/or Integration', p. 140.
58. ibid., p. 141.

CHAPTER 5

1. Years ago Reik argued precisely that point: that dreams of eventual glory often require payment in advance for the imaginary satisfaction of revenge and triumph. Reik's point was that sadistic fantasies are

enjoyed at a cost; those who entertain them will find ways of suffering in order to assuage their guilt over future triumphs at the expense of others.

2. Paul Boyer, *When Time Shall Be No More: Prophecy Belief in Modern American Culture*, Cambridge, MA, and London, The Belknap Press of Harvard University Press, 1992, pp. 209–10.
3. ibid., p. 70.
4. ibid., pp. 69, 72.
5. ibid., p. 73.
6. ibid., pp. 108–9.
7. ibid., pp. 115ff.
8. ibid., p. 126.
9. ibid., p. 135.
10. Arthur Maxwell, in *History's Crowded Climax*, quoted in Boyer, *When Time Shall Be No More*, p. 110.
11. Boyer, *When Time Shall Be No More*, pp. 131–2.
12. ibid., p. 72.
13. ibid., p. 121.
14. Vittorio Lanternari, 'Revolution and/or Integration in African Socio-Religious Movements', in Bruce Lincoln, ed., *Religion, Rebellion, and Revolution*, 1985, pp. 135ff.
15. David I. Kertzer, *Ritual, Politics, and Power*, New Haven and London, Yale University Press, 1988, p. 161.
16. ibid., pp. 161–2.
17. Zeev Sternhell, *Neither Left Nor Right: Fascist Ideology in France*, Berkeley, University of California Press, 1986, p. 250.
18. Eviatar Zerubavel, *Hidden Rhythms: Schedules and Calendars in Social Life*, Berkeley, Los Angeles, London, University of California Press, 1985, p. 92.
19. ibid., p. 85.
20. ibid., p. 87.
21. ibid., pp. 86–8.
22. Norman Cohn, *The Pursuit of the Millenium*, revised and expanded edition, New York, Oxford University Press, 1970, pp. 50ff.
23. ibid., pp. 46ff.
24. ibid., p. 49.
25. ibid., p. 50.
26. In this discussion I am drawing indirectly on the work of Otto Rank in *The Double: A Psychoanalytic Study*, Chapel Hill, NC, University of North Carolina Press, 1971. Note the development of the centre as a 'double' for the periphery, and of the periphery as a 'double' for the centre. The double is an image of the self in terms of the other: a primitive self-object, to use more contemporary psychoanalytic notions. As an image of the self, therefore, the double represents first an ideal,

but the ideal, because it is an other, soon becomes a rival. The purpose of the double is to provide an external guarantee of the psyche: a way of assuring the self that it will not perish or be cut off. Because the double is an antidote to death, however, it is also a reminder of death. The fear of extinction that is suppressed in the image of the double eventually emerges, and the double becomes a sign of the death of the self.

27. Sternhell, *Neither Right Nor Left*, p. 250.
28. ibid., p. 250.
29. Boyer, *When Time Shall Be No More*, p. 53.
30. *The Book of a Hundred Chapters*, quoted in Cohn, *Pursuit of the Millenium*, p.117.
31. Scott Lash, *Sociology of Postmodernism*, London and New York, Routledge, 1989, p. 159; quoting Walter Benjamin, 'A Small History of Photography', in *One Way Street and Other Writing*, London, New Left Books, 1979; and 'The Work of Art in the Age of Mechanical Reproduction', in *Illuminations*, London, Fontana, 1975.
32. N. J. Demerath and Rhys Williams, *A Bridging of Faiths: Religion and Politics in a New England City*, Princeton, NJ, Princeton University Press, 1992.
33. ibid., p. 262.
34. ibid., p. 259.
35. ibid., pp. 260–1.
36. ibid., p. 259.
37. ibid., pp. 258, 261–2.
38. ibid., p. 257.
39. ibid., p. 255.
40. *Wall Street Journal*, 18.2.92, p. A1.
41. ibid.
42. Demerath and Williams, *A Bridging of Faiths*, pp. 255ff.
43. James Clifford and George E. Marcus, eds., *Writing Culture: The Poetics and Politics of Ethnography*, Berkeley,University of California Press, 1986.
44. Demerath and Williams, *A Bridging of Faiths*, p. 271.
45. Lash, *Sociology of Postmodernism*.
46. Scott Lash, 'Towards a Sociological Account', in *Sociology of Postmodernism*, 1989, pp. 33ff.
47. ibid., pp. 37, 40.
48. James Fernandez, 'Setting the Record Straight on "Children of the Rainbow"', *Wall Street Journal*, 10.12.92, p. A19.
49. Cf. Lash on Bourdieu, in *Sociology of Postmodernism*, p. 244.
50. Demerath and Williams, *A Bridging of Faiths*, p. 201.
51. ibid., p. 191.
52. ibid., p. 208.

53. ibid., pp. 190, 204–5.
54. ibid., p. 191.
55. ibid., p. 222.
56. Steven Hart, *What Doth the Lord Require? How American Christians Think about Economic Justice*, New York, Oxford University Press, 1992.
57. See, for a related concept (disembedding), Anthony Giddens, *The Consequences of Modernity*, Stanford, CA, Stanford University Press, 1990.
58. Hart, *What Doth the Lord Require?*
59. *Wall Street Journal*, 2.3.92, p. A1.
60. ibid., 11.10.89, p. A1.
61. ibid., 2.12.91, p. A12.
62. ibid., 21.12.89, p. C1.
63. ibid., 19.11.90, p. A1.
64. Demerath and Williams, *A Bridging of Faiths*, p. 279.
65. ibid., p. 168.
66. *Wall Street Journal*, 15.4.91, p. A14.
67. D. Rabinowitz, ibid., 16.12.91, p. A13.
68. S. Tsurumi, ibid., 5.12.91, p. A14.

CHAPTER 6

1. Daniel L. O'Keefe, *Stolen Lightning: The Social Theory of Magic*, New York, Vintage Books, 1983, p. 268.
2. Ervin Staub, *The Roots of Evil: The Origins of Genocide and Other Group Violence*, Cambridge, Cambridge University Press, 1992, p. 110.
3. ibid., p. 111.
4. ibid., p. 82.
5. Nikolas Rose, *Governing the Soul: The Shaping of the Private Self*, London and New York, Routledge, 1989, pp. 19–20.
6. ibid., p. 21.
7. ibid., p. 32.
8. Norman Cohn, *The Pursuit of the Millenium*, revised and expanded edition, New York, Oxford University Press, 1970, p. 153.
9. ibid., p. 173.
10. ibid., p. 177.
11. ibid., p. 286.
12. ibid., p. 134.
13. ibid., pp. 150, 152.
14. Charles B. Strozier, *Apocalypse: On the Psychology of Fundamentalism in America*, Boston, Beacon Press, 1994, p. 117.
15. Christopher Hill, 'Popular Religion and the English Revolution', in Bruce Lincoln, ed., *Religion, Rebellion, and Revolution*, 1985, p. 53.

16. ibid., pp. 54–5.
17. ibid., p. 58.
18. ibid., p. 51.
19. Maurice Bloch and Jonathan Parry, eds., *Death and the Regeneration of Life*, Cambridge, Cambridge University Press, 1982, p. 18.
20. Hill, 'Popular Religion and the English Revolution', p. 51.
21. ibid., pp. 50–2.
22. ibid., p. 58.
23. ibid., p. 48.
24. Strozier, *Apocalypse*, pp. 164–5.
25. ibid., p. 165.
26. Bloch and Parry, *Death and the Regeneration of Life*, p. 17.
27. Joseph G. Jorgensen, 'Religious Solutions and Native American Struggles: Ghost Dance, Sun Dance, and Beyond', in Bruce Lincoln, ed., *Religion, Rebellion, and Revolution*, 1985, p. 107.
28. John C. Sommerville, *The Secularization of Early Modern England: From Religious Culture to Religious Faith*, New York and Oxford, Oxford University Press, 1992, pp. 33ff.
29. Hill, 'Popular Religion and the English Revolution', pp. 60ff.
30. ibid., pp. 63–4.
31. Strozier, *Apocalypse*, p. 117.

CHAPTER 7

1. Christopher Bollas, *Being a Character: Psychoanalysis and Self-Experience*, New York, Hill and Wang, 1992, p. 262.
2. ibid., p. 263.
3. ibid., p. 258.
4. Emile Durkheim, *The Division of Labor in Society*, Glencoe, IL, The Free Press, 1933, p. 100.
5. ibid., p. 101.
6. Benedict Anderson, *Imagined Communities: Reflections on the Origin and the Spread of Nationalism*, London, Verso, 1983.
7. James W. Lewis, *The Protestant Experience in Gary, Indiana, 1906–1975: At Home in the City*, Knoxville, University of Tennessee Press, 1992, pp. 160ff.
8. ibid., p. 160.
9. ibid., p. 162.
10. ibid., p. 163.
11. ibid., p. 164.
12. ibid., pp. 164–9.
13. Michael Lienesch, *Redeeming America: Piety and Politics in the New Chris-*

tian Right, Chapel Hill, NC, University of North Carolina Press, 1993, pp. 128–9.
14. ibid.
15. ibid., p. 134.
16. ibid., p. 134; quoting George Grant, *Bringing In the Sheaves: Transforming Poverty into Productivity*, rev. and exp. edn., Brentwood, Tenn., Wolgemuth and Hyatt, 1988, pp. 77, 162.
17. Bollas, *Being a Character*, pp. 245–6.
18. Margaret Lamberts Bendroth, *Fundamentalism and Gender, 1875 to the Present*, New Haven and London, Yale University Press, 1993, p. 42.
19. ibid., p. 43.
20. ibid.
21. cf. ibid., p. 45 on the 'moral disability' and 'humiliation' of women.
22. Lewis, *Protestant Experience*, p. 54; quoting Raymond A. Mohl and Neil Betten, 'Paternalism and Pluralism: Immigrants and Social Welfare in Gary, Indiana, 1906-1940', *American Studies* 15 (Spring 1974), pp. 5–30. Cf. p. 15.
23. ibid., pp. 58ff.
24. ibid., pp. 96–7.
25. ibid., pp. 96–7.
26. ibid., pp. 129, 131.
27. ibid., p. 132.
28. ibid., p. 136.
29. ibid., p. 142.
30. ibid., p. 141.
31. Dirk Johnson, *The New York Times*, 14.5.95, p. A20.
32. ibid.
33. *The New York Times*, 23.4.95, p. A33.
34. John H. Cushman, *The New York Times*, 5.4.95, p. A22.
35. *The New York Times*, 28.4.95, p. A25.
36. James Barron, *The New York Times*, 27.4.95, p. A20.
37. Linda Greenhouse, *The New York Times*, 23.4.95, section 4, p.1; Bob Herbert, *The New York Times*, 22.4.95, p. A23.
38. *The New York Times*, 28.4.95, p. A25.
39. *The New York Times*, 30.4.95, p. A26.
40. *The Wall Street Journal*, 28.4.95, p. A1.
41. *The New York Times*, 23.4.95, p. A32.
42. David Stout, *The New York Times*, 30.4.95, p. A28.
43. Frank Rich, *The New York Times*, 27.4.95, p. A25.
44. Bollas, *Being a Character*, p. 59.
45. ibid., p. 71.
46. ibid., p. 59.
47. ibid., p. 61.
48. ibid., pp. 62, 65.

49. ibid., p. 242.
50. ibid., p. 243.
51. ibid., p. 198; quoting Herbert Rosenfeld, *Impasse and Interpretation*, London, Tavistock, 1987.
52. ibid., pp. 193ff.
53. ibid., p. 203.
54. ibid., p. 203.
55. ibid., pp. 204–5.
56. ibid., p. 239.
57. ibid., p. 184.
58. *The New York Times*, 30.4.95, p. A27.
59. ibid.
60. ibid.
61. *The New York Times*, 29.4.95, p. A10.
62. ibid.

REFERENCES

Anderson, Benedict, 1983. *Imagined Communities: Reflections on the Origin and Spread of Nationalism*. London, Verso.

Bendroth, Margaret Lamberts, 1993. *Fundamentalism and Gender, 1875 to the Present*. New Haven and London, Yale University Press.

Bercovitch, Sacvan, 1978. *The American Jeremiad*. Madison, WI, University of Wisconsin Press.

Bettini, Maurizio, 1991. *Anthropology and Roman Culture*, tr. John van Sickle. Baltimore and London, Johns Hopkins University Press.

Bloch, Maurice, 1992. *From Prey into Hunter: The Politics of Religious Experience*. Cambridge, Cambridge University Press.

Bloch, Maurice and Parry, Jonathan, eds., 1982. *Death and the Regeneration of Life*. Cambridge, Cambridge University Press.

Bollas, Christopher, 1992. *Being a Character: Psychoanalysis and Self-Experience*. New York, Hill and Wang.

Boyer, Paul, 1992. *When Time Shall Be No More: Prophecy Belief in Modern American Culture*. Cambridge, MA and London, The Belknap Press of Harvard University Press.

Bremmer, Jan, 1983. *The Early Greek Concept of the Soul*. Princeton, NJ., Princeton University Press.

Burkert, Walter, Girard, René, and Smith, Jonathan Z., 1987. *Violent Origins*, ed. Robert G. Hamerton-Kelly, with an Introduction by Burton Mack and commentary by Renato Rosaldo. Stanford, CA, Stanford University Press.

Caplan, Lionel, 1986. 'The Popular Culture of Evil in Urban South India', in David Parkin, ed., *The Anthropology of Evil*, pp. 110–27.

Capps, Donald, 1979. 'Erikson's Theory of Religious Ritual: The Case of the Excommunication of Ann Hibbens', *Journal for the Scientific Study of Religion* 18, pp. 337–49.

Clifford, James, and Marcus, George E., eds., 1986. *Writing Culture: The Poetics and Politics of Ethnography*. Berkeley, University of California Press.

Cohn, Norman, 1970. *The Pursuit of the Millenium*, revised and expanded edition. New York, Oxford University Press.

De Martino, Ernesto, 1988. *Primitive Magic: The Psychic Powers of Shamans and Sorcerers*. Dorset, Prism Press.

Demerath, N. J. and Williams, Rhys, 1992. *A Bridging of Faiths: Religion and Politics in a New England City*. Princeton, NJ, Princeton University Press.

Demos, John, 1982. *Entertaining Satan: Witchcraft and the Culture of Early New England*. New York, Oxford University Press.

Durkheim, Emile, 1933. *The Division of Labor in Society*. Glencoe, IL, The Free Press.

Fenn, Richard K., 1992. *The Death of Herod*. Cambridge, Cambridge University Press.

Fenn, Richard K. and Capps, Donald, eds., 1995. *On Losing the Soul: Essays in the Social Psychology of Religion*. Albany, NY, State University of New York Press.

Fernandez, James, 1992. 'Setting the Record Straight on "Children of the Rainbow"', *The Wall Street Journal*, 10.12.92, p. A19.

Garrett, Clarke, 1985. 'Popular Religion in the American and French Revolutions', in Bruce Lincoln, ed., *Religion, Rebellion, and Revolution*, pp. 69–88.

Gaustad, Edwin S., 1957. *The Great Awakening in New England*. New York, Harper & Brothers.

— 1973. *Dissent in American Religion*. Chicago, University of Chicago Press.

Gay, Peter, 1986. *Freud for Historians*. New York and Oxford, Oxford University Press.

Giddens, Anthony, 1990. *The Consequences of Modernity*. Stanford, CA, Stanford University Press.

Graziano, Frank, 1992. *Divine Violence: Spectacle, Psychosexuality, and Radical Christianity in the Argentine 'Dirty War'*. Boulder, CO, San Francisco and Oxford, Westview Press.

Grotanelli, Christiano, 1985. 'Archaic Forms of Rebellion and Their Religious Background', in Bruce Lincoln, ed., *Religion, Rebellion, and Revolution*, pp. 15–45.

Harris, Olivia, 1982. 'The Dead and the Devils among the Bolivian Laymi', in Maurice Bloch and Jonathan Parry, eds., *Death and the Regeneration of Life*, pp. 46–73.

Hart, Steven, 1992. *What Doth the Lord Require? How American Christians Think about Economic Justice*. New York, Oxford University Press.

Hill, Christopher, 1985. 'Popular Religion and the English Revolution', in Bruce Lincoln, ed., *Religion, Rebellion, and Revolution*, pp. 46–68.

Hunter, James Davison, 1991. *Culture Wars: The Struggle to Define America*. New York, Basic Books.

Jorgensen, Joseph G., 1985. 'Religious Solutions and Native American Struggles: Ghost Dance, Sun Dance, and Beyond', in Bruce Lincoln, ed., *Religion, Rebellion, and Revolution*, pp. 97–128.

Keddie, Nikkie R., 1985. 'Shi'ism and Revolution', in Bruce Lincoln, ed., *Religion, Rebellion, and Revolution*, pp. 157–82.

Kertzer, David I., 1988. *Ritual, Politics, and Power*. New Haven and London, Yale University Press.

Lanternari, Vittorio, 1985. 'Revolution and/or Integration in African Socio-Religious Movements', in Bruce Lincoln, ed., *Religion, Rebellion, and Revolution*, pp. 129–56.

Lasch, Christopher, 1978. *The Culture of Narcissism*. New York, Norton.

Lash, Scott, 1989. *Sociology of Postmodernism*. London and New York, Routledge.

— 'Towards a Sociological Account', in *Sociology of Postmodernism*, pp. 33ff.

Lewis, James W., 1992. *The Protestant Experience in Gary, Indiana, 1906–1975: At Home in the City*. Knoxville, University of Tennessee Press.

Lienesch, Michael, 1993. *Redeeming America: Piety and Politics in the New Christian Right*. Chapel Hill, NC, University of North Carolina Press.

Lincoln, Bruce, ed., 1985. *Religion, Rebellion, and Revolution: An Interdisciplinary and Cross-Cultural Collection of Essays*. New York, St Martin's Press.

Luhmann, Niklas, 1982. *The Differentiation of Society*. New York, Columbia University Press.

Martin, David, 1993. *Tongues of Fire: The Explosion of Protestantism in Latin America*, with a Foreword by Peter Berger. Oxford, and Cambridge, MA, Blackwell.

Middleton, John, 1982. 'Lugbara Death', in Maurice Bloch and Jonathan Parry, eds., *Death and the Regeneration of Life*, pp. 134–54.

O'Keefe, Daniel L., 1983. *Stolen Lightning: The Social Theory of Magic*. New York, Vintage Books.

Parkin, David, ed., 1986. *The Anthropology of Evil*. Oxford, Blackwell.

Parry, Jonathan, 1982. 'Sacrificial Death and the Necrophagous Ascetic', in Maurice Bloch and Jonathan Parry, eds., *Death and the Regeneration of Life*.

Philips, Adam, 1994. 'The Shock of the Old', *London Review of Books*, vol. XVI, no. 3, 10 February 1994, p. 14, reviewing Christopher Bollas, *Being a Character: Psychoanalysis and Self-Experience*, Routledge, 1993.

Preus, James S., 1987. *Explaining Religion: Criticism and Theory from Bodin to Freud*. New Haven, Yale University Press.

Rank, Otto, 1971. *The Double: A Psychoanalytic Study*. Chapel Hill, NC, University of North Carolina Press.

Reik, Theodor, 1957. *Masochism in Modern Man*, tr. Margaret H. Beigel and Gertrud M. Kurth. New York, Grove Press.

Rose, Nikolas, 1989. *Governing the Soul: The Shaping of the Private Self*. London and New York, Routledge.

Rose, Susan D., 1990. *Keeping Them Out of the Hands of Satan: Evangelical Schooling in America*. New York and London, Routledge.

Shils, Edward, 1975. *Center and Periphery: Essays in Macrosociology*. Chicago, IL, University of Chicago Press.

Sommerville, C. John, 1992. *The Secularization of Early Modern England: From Religious Culture to Religious Faith*. New York and Oxford, Oxford University Press.

Staub, Ervin, 1992. *The Roots of Evil: The Origins of Genocide and Other Group Violence*. Cambridge, Cambridge University Press.

Sternhell, Zeev, 1986. *Neither Left Nor Right: Fascist Ideology in France*. Berkeley, University of California Press.

Strathern, Andrew, 1982.'Witchcraft, Greed, Cannibalism, and Death: Some Related Themes From the New Guinea Highlands', in Maurice Bloch and Jonathan Parry, eds., *Death and the Regeneration of Life*.

Strozier, Charles B., 1994. *Apocalypse: On the Psychology of Fundamentalism in America*. Boston, Beacon Press.

Turner, Victor, 1979. *Process, Performance, and Pilgrimage: A Study in Comparative Symbology*. New Delhi, Concept.

Vernant, Jean-Pierre, 1991. *Mortals and Immortals: Collected Essays*, ed. Froma I. Zeitlin. Princeton, NJ, Princeton University Press.

Vidich, Arthur and Lyman, Stanford, 1985. *American Sociology: Worldly Rejections of Religion and their Directions*. New Haven, Yale University Press.

Webber, Alan, 1991. 'Essay on the Ethos of Business Leaders', *The Wall Street Journal*, 15.4.91, p. A14.

Weber, Eugen, 1994. 'Amerloques', a review of Richard Kuisel, 1993, *Seducing the French: The Dilemma of Americanisation*, University of California Press; *The London Review of Books*, 10 March 1994.

Wilson, John F., 1979. *Public Religion in American Culture*. Philadelphia, PA, Temple University Press.

Zerubavel, Eviatar, 1985. *Hidden Rhythms: Schedules and Calendars in Social Life*. Berkeley, Los Angeles, London, University of California Press.

INDEX